Mastering
the Ultimate
High Ground

Next Steps in the Military Uses of Space

Benjamin S. Lambeth

Prepared for the
United States Air Force

RAND
Project AIR FORCE

The research reported here was sponsored by the United States Air Force under Contract F49642-01-C-0003. Further information may be obtained from the Strategic Planning Division, Directorate of Plans, Hq USAF.

Library of Congress Cataloging-in-Publication Data

Lambeth, Benjamin S.
    Mastering the ultimate high ground : next steps in the military uses of space / Benjamin S. Lambeth.
        p. cm.
    "MR-1649."
    Includes bibliographical references.
    ISBN 0-8330-3330-1 (pbk.)
    1. Astronautics, Military—United States. 2. United States. Air Force. 3. United States—Military policy. I. Rand Corporation. II.Title.

UG1523.L35 2003
358'.8'0973—dc21

                                                                2002155704

Original cover photo by Eric Simonsen.

RAND is a nonprofit institution that helps improve policy and decisionmaking through research and analysis. RAND® is a registered trademark. RAND's publications do not necessarily reflect the opinions or policies of its research sponsors.

Cover design by Pete Soriano.

Published 2003 by RAND
1700 Main Street, P.O. Box 2138, Santa Monica, CA 90407-2138
1200 South Hayes Street, Arlington, VA 22202-5050
201 North Craig Street, Suite 202, Pittsburgh, PA 15213-1516
RAND URL: http://www.rand.org/
To order RAND documents or to obtain additional information, contact Distribution Services: Telephone: (310) 451-7002; Fax: (310) 451-6915; Email: order@rand.org

This study assesses the military space challenges facing the Air Force and the nation in light of the watershed findings and recommendations of the congressionally mandated Space Commission that were released in January 2001. It seeks to capture the best thinking among those both in and out of uniform who have paid especially close attention to military space matters in recent years. After a review of the main milestones in the Air Force's ever-growing involvement in space since its creation as an independent service in 1947, the study examines the circumstances that occasioned the commission's creation by Congress in 1999, as well as some conceptual and organizational roadblocks both within and outside the Air Force that have long impeded a more rapid growth of U.S. military space capability. It concludes by exploring the most urgent space-related concerns now in need of Air Force attention. Although the study offers a number of suggestions for shifts in emphasis in U.S. military space policy, it is primarily analytical rather than prescriptive. As such, it aims more to promote a better understanding of the issues than to advocate specific policy recommendations.

The research documented herein represents one set of findings of a broader Project AIR FORCE effort entitled "Thinking Strategically About Space," which was carried out under the joint sponsorship of the Director of Space Operations and Integration (AF/XOS), Headquarters United States Air Force, and the Director of Requirements, Headquarters Air Force Space Command (AFSPC/DR). It was conducted in Project AIR FORCE's Strategy and Doctrine Program. The study should interest Air Force officers and other members of the national security community concerned with air and space doctrine, organizational and investment issues related to the national military space effort, the overall weight of effort that should be directed to space mission support, and the appropriate trade-offs between space and other mission needs in all mediums across service lines. Research in support of the study was completed in November 2002.

Project AIR FORCE

Project AIR FORCE (PAF), a division of RAND, is the U.S. Air Force's federally funded research and development center for studies and analyses. PAF provides the Air Force with independent analyses of policy alternatives affecting the deployment, employment, combat readiness, and support of current and future aerospace forces. Research is performed in four programs: Aerospace Force Development; Manpower, Readiness, and Training; Resource Management; and Strategy and Doctrine.

Additional information about PAF is available on our web site at http://rand.org/paf.

CONTENTS

Mounting concerns in some quarters toward the end of the 1990s that the Air Force was failing to exercise proper stewardship of the nation's military space effort led to the establishment by Congress in 1999 of a Space Commission to assess the adequacy of existing arrangements for military space. In its final report, released in January 2001, the commission concluded unanimously that the creation of a separate space service was not warranted—at least yet. It also determined, however, that the nation is not developing the military space cadre it requires and that military space is underfunded for its growing importance to the nation's security. It further found that the other services are not paying their fair share for the space product they consume and that the nation's on-orbit assets are becoming increasingly vulnerable to a potential "space Pearl Harbor."

As first steps toward addressing these concerns, the commission recommended that the Air Force be designated the executive agent for space within the Department of Defense (DoD), that a separate DoD budget category for space be created to ensure greater transparency of space spending by all services, and that a serious effort be pursued in the realm of space control to ensure protection of the nation's increasingly vital space capabilities. The Secretary of Defense promptly accepted these recommendations, assigned executive-agent authority for all DoD space programs to the Air Force, and directed the creation of a new Major Force Program (MFP) budget category that would allow for unprecedented accountability in the way the nation's defense dollars are spent on space.

Thanks to these and related moves, the Air Force entered the 21st century with much of the preceding debate over military space essentially resolved by leadership decree. Against that background, this study offers a framework for understanding the most pressing military space needs and challenges now facing the Air Force and the nation. The study begins by reviewing the highlights of the Air Force's effort since the end of World War II to become accepted as the nation's military space custodian. In the process, it shows how space has been anything but an Air Force birthright. On the contrary, the Air Force had to fight hard at every step of the way, often in the face of heavy resistance from the other services and the civilian leadership, to earn its now dominant role in the U.S. military space program. The history of that fight is well worth recalling by today's Air Force planners for the cautionary note it offers against presuming that space is somehow a natural Air Force inheritance.

The study next explores the often deep differences of opinion that, until recently, had fundamentally divided the Air Force over the important question of whether air and space should be treated as a unitary extension of the vertical dimension or as two separate and distinct operating mediums and mission areas. Starting in 1958, a portrayal of air and space as a seamless continuum from the earth's surface to infinity was advanced by the service's leadership in an effort to define an expanded "aerospace" operating arena for future Air Force assets. Once it became clear, however, that space had much to offer not only to the nation's top leadership in connection with nuclear deterrence but also to theater commanders in support of conventional operations, many of the Air Force's most senior leaders at the major command level came to realize that space deserved to be treated as separate from the realm of aerodynamic operations. Such thinking eventually led to the creation of Air Force Space Command. Yet the single-medium outlook persisted in many Air Force circles. It received renewed emphasis by the Air Force leadership in 1996 and for a time thereafter. A key chapter in this study points out some of the opportunity costs that were incurred over time by that outlook and considers the greater benefits that should accrue to the Air Force by treating air and space as separate and distinct mediums and mission areas.

The most consequential opportunity cost of the Air Force's single-medium outlook is that the service has lately found itself in the discomfiting position of having to make increasingly hard choices between competing air and space systems in its resource allocations. This predicament has forced it, ever more so in recent years, to short-change its air responsibilities as a necessary condition for retaining its increasingly costly stewardship of space. As long as the Air Force had so little invested in space by way of hard resource commitments, it could easily nurture a vision that proclaimed both air and space as a single medium and mission area. Once it began buying into space-based equities in a serious way, however, it soon learned that a downside of having staked out a mission claim on both air *and* space was that it now had to pay for both its air and its space obligations out of its relatively constant percentage of annual defense funding. The Air Force now faces the challenge of working out an arrangement that will underwrite the nation's military space needs yet not at the unacceptable expense of the service's mandated air responsibilities. The recently established DoD budget category for space should help provide some relief toward that end by allowing senior officials to examine military space spending across the board, with a view toward better sizing the military space budget and scrubbing excessive service requirements that may be desirable in principle but that do not emanate from any compelling operational need.

With the Space Commission's recommendations now promulgated and accepted by DoD, the Air Force's charter to proceed with next steps is clear. To make good on that charter, the service will need to accept and honor both the important physical and mission-area differences between air and space and the need for continued operational integration along with a clear organizational differentiation of the two mediums. Through such a bifurcated approach, space can be effectively harnessed to serve the needs of all warfighting components in the joint arena. At the same time, it can be approached, as it richly deserves to be, as its own domain within the Air Force in the areas of program and infrastructure management, funding, cadre-building, and career development.

As for strategy and mission-development implications, a number of space-related concerns, both institutional and operational, are explored in detail in this study. Two are of special importance to U.S. national security:

Acquiring a credible space control capability. Although the space control mission has been consistently endorsed as a legitimate U.S. military activity by every high-level guidance document since the first national space policy was enunciated in 1958, such declarations have hitherto paid only lip service to the goal of ensuring freedom of U.S. operations in space. They also have been belied by a sustained record of U.S. inaction when it comes to actual hard spending on space-control mission development. Yet the United States is now more heavily invested in space than ever before, and the importance of space control as a real-world mission area has finally begun to be taken seriously at the highest echelons of the U.S. government. In light of the well-documented potential for the early emergence of hostile threats, this deep and growing national dependence on space-based capabilities warrants the Air Force's working ever more intently toward acquiring effective space control measures. For this important effort to enjoy the greatest likelihood of successfully transiting the shoals of domestic politics, the Air Force should cleanly separate it from the more contentious and, at least for now, premature goal of force application through weaponization aimed at attacking terrestrial targets from space.

Exercising due caution in migrating intelligence, surveillance, and reconnaissance (ISR) capabilities to space. Just because an ISR mission *can* be performed from space does not necessarily mean that it *should* be. However much some may deem such migration to be an absolute must for ensuring the Air Force's future in space, not every investment area need entail a crash effort like the Manhattan Project, which developed the first American atomic bomb. Any transfer of operational functions from the atmosphere to space should be preceded by a determination that the function in question can be performed more cost-effectively from space than from the air. Moreover, the survivability of follow-on ISR systems migrated to space must be ensured beforehand by appropriate space control measures. Otherwise, in transferring our asymmetric technological advantages to space, we may also risk creating for ourselves new asymmetric vulnerabilities. This means that attention to potential system vulnerabilities must be paramount in any ISR mission migration planning. Should the nation move to migrate critical capabilities to space before first ensuring that a credible enforcement regime is in place to hold any possible threat systems at risk, we may simply compound our existing vulnerabilities—all the more so if those moves supplant rather than merely supplement existing air-breathing capabilities. This constitutes yet another reason why seeking the essential foundations of a credible space control capability should represent the next U.S. military space mission development priority.

All things considered, the assignment of executive-agent status to the Air Force for military space by the Secretary of Defense in May 2001 was not only appropriate but arguably a generation late in coming. Now that the Air Force has been granted this authority, it should have every incentive to vindicate its designation as the nation's military space steward by proactively starting to fulfill its newly assigned role. Fortunately in this respect, the Office of the Secretary of Defense (OSD) recently moved to develop and promulgate initial guidelines for the definition and implementation of space executive-agent authority throughout DoD. In late February 2002, it circulated a detailed draft directive on executive-agent implementation for review and comment by the senior working-level principals throughout the military space community. That directive's intent was to clarify the lines of authority, specific responsibilities, and coordination requirements between the executive agent for space and all concerned DoD components.

Although that draft directive (included herein as an appendix for further reference) as of late November 2002 remained caught up in the intra-DoD coordination process and had not yet been formally implemented, it nonetheless represents a significant step forward that should be warmly welcomed by the Air Force, considering that it gives the service, at least in principle, all the needed tools and all appropriate authority to act on its recent empowerment as DoD's executive agent for military space. About the only major areas of concern left unspecified in the implementation directive—and they are important ones—entail the role, responsibilities, and authority of Air Force Space Command within the executive-agent context and the degree to which the new MFP for space (called a "virtual" MFP in the directive) will provide the executive agent real clout by way of an identifying and controlling mechanism for managing cross-service military space programs. Those considerations aside, the Space Commission and DoD accomplished much useful and pioneering work toward putting the American military space effort on the improved institutional and fiscal footing it properly deserves. At the same time, however, the unfinished business alluded to above attests that both the Air Force and DoD need to do additional work to fully define and implement the Air Force's newly acquired status as DoD's executive agent for military space.

The Air Force faces five basic challenges with respect to space:

- Continuing the operational integration of space with the three terrestrial warfighting mediums while ensuring the organizational differentiation of space from Air Force air.

- Effectively wielding its newly granted military space executive-agent status.

- Realizing a DoD-wide budget category for space that imparts transparency to how much money and manpower are going into space each year and for what.

- Showing real progress toward fielding a meaningful space control capability while decoupling that progress from any perceived taint of force-application involvement.

- Making further progress toward developing and nurturing a cadre of skilled space professionals within the Air Force ready and able to meet the nation's military space needs in the coming decade and beyond.

Mastery of these challenges should not only ensure the Air Force a satisfactory near-term future for itself and the nation in space. It also should help enable it, over time, to shore up its end-strength and the intensity of its day-to-day training (both eroded since Desert Storm) to fulfill its no less important mission responsibilities in the *air* arena.

ACKNOWLEDGMENTS

While preparing to undertake this study, I benefited from early exploratory conversations with General Ralph E. Eberhart, then–commander in chief, U.S. Space Command, and commander, Air Force Space Command; Lieutenant General Roger DeKok, vice commander, Air Force Space Command; Major General Gary Dylewski, director of operations, Air Force Space Command; Gene McCall, chief scientist, Air Force Space Command; Colonel William Beck, Air Force Space Command chair, Air University; Colonel Robert Ryals and Lieutenant Colonel Rick Walker, USAF Space Warfare Center; and Lieutenant Colonel Conrad Widman, commander, 527th Space Aggressor Squadron. I also benefited from a special opportunity, at General Eberhart's invitation, to attend the two-day Senior Leaders' Course offered by the USAF Space Warfare School, Schriever AFB, Colorado, on March 27–28, 2001. These inputs helped immensely toward broadening my education into the essential elements of U.S. military space policy and in shaping the structure and content of this study, and I am more than routinely grateful for them. I am also grateful for the feedback, in some cases quite detailed and specific, which I received on an earlier draft from Generals Lew Allen, Joseph Ashy, Bill Creech, Howell Estes III, Robert Herres, and Charles Horner, USAF (Ret.); Lieutenant General Charles Heflebower, USAF (Ret.); the Honorable Peter Teets, Under Secretary of the Air Force; General John Jumper, Air Force chief of staff; General Lance Lord, commander, Air Force Space Command; General Donald Cook, commander, Air Education and Training Command; Lieutenant General William Looney III, commander, USAF Electronic Systems Center; Major General Michael Hamel, commander, 14th Air Force; Major General David MacGhee, commander, Air Force Doctrine Center; Brigadier General Douglas Fraser, commander, USAF Space Warfare Center; George Bradley and Rick Sturdevant, Office of History, Air Force Space Command; Lieutenant Colonel Peter Hays, National Defense University; Barry Watts, Center for Strategic and Budgetary Assessments; and my RAND colleagues Ted Harshberger and Karl Mueller. Finally, I am pleased to acknowledge Colin Gray, University of Reading, United Kingdom, and Lieutenant Colonel Forrest Morgan, School of Advanced Airpower Studies at Air University, for their informed and constructive technical reviews of the manuscript and my editor, Miriam Polon, for her usual fine touch with words. Not all of the above individuals would necessarily agree with every point contained in this study, but all contributed materially to making it a better product. It goes without saying that all responsibility for any errors of fact or interpretation that may remain in the assessment that follows is mine alone.

I wish to dedicate this work to the memory of George K. Tanham, a distinguished member of the RAND family from 1955 until his passing as this study was nearing publication in March 2003. George led Project AIR FORCE (then called Project RAND) from 1970 to 1975 and served as vice president in charge of RAND's Washington Office from 1970 to 1982. Throughout my own many years with RAND going back to 1975, he was an abiding source of valued insight and counsel, as well as a good colleague, a kindred spirit, and a special friend of rare warmth.

AAF   Army Air Force

ABM   Antiballistic Missile

ABMA   Army Ballistic Missile Agency

ADC   Aerospace Defense Command

AFM   Air Force Manual

AFMC   Air Force Materiel Command

AFSC   Air Force Systems Command

AFSPC   Air Force Space Command

AGF   Army Ground Forces

AITF   Aerospace Integration Task Force

AOC   Air Operations Center

AOR   Area of Responsibility

ASAT   Antisatellite

AWACS   Airborne Warning and Control System

C3   Command, Control and Communications

C3I   C3 and Intelligence

C4   C3 and Computers

CAOC   Combined Air Operations Center

CINC	Commander in Chief
CINCNORAD	CINC North American Aerospace Defense Command
CINCSPACE	CINC U.S. Space Command
CSOC	Consolidated Space Operations Center
DAL	Developing Aerospace Leaders
DARPA	Defense Advanced Research Projects Agency
DCA	Defense Communications Agency
DCI	Director of Central Intelligence
DCINC	Deputy CINC
DoD	Department of Defense
DSB	Defense Science Board
DSP	Defense Support Program
EELV	Evolved Expendable Launch Vehicle
EMP	Electromagnetic Pulse
FY	Fiscal Year
GBU	Guided Bomb Unit
GEO	Geostationary Earth Orbit
GMTI	Ground Moving Target Indicator
GPS	Global Positioning System
ICBM	Intercontinental Ballistic Missile
IRBM	Intermediate-Range Ballistic Missile
ISR	Intelligence, Surveillance and Reconnaissance
JDAM	Joint Direct Attack Munition
JFACC	Joint Force Air Component Commander
JFASCC	Joint Force Air and Space Component Commander

JFC	Joint Force Commander
JFSCC	Joint Force Space Component Commander
JROC	Joint Requirements Oversight Council
LEO	Low Earth Orbit
MAJCOM	Major Command
MFP	Major Force Program
MILSATCOM	Military Satellite Communications
MIRACL	Mid-Infrared Advanced Chemical Laser
MOL	Manned Orbiting Laboratory
MSTI	Miniature Sensor Technology Integration
NACA	National Advisory Committee on Aeronautics
NAF	Numbered Air Force
NASA	National Aeronautics and Space Administration
NORAD	North American Aerospace Defense Command
NRO	National Reconnaissance Office
NSC	National Security Council
OSD	Office of the Secretary of Defense
POM	Program Objectives Memorandum
QDR	Quadrennial Defense Review
R&D	Research and Development
ROC	Requirement for Operational Capability
SAB	Scientific Advisory Board
SAC	Strategic Air Command
SAMOS	Satellite and Missile Observation System
SAR	Synthetic Aperture Radar
SBIRS	Space-Based Infrared System

SBR	Space-Based Radar
SMC	Space and Missile Systems Center
SOC	Space Operations Center
STARS	Surveillance Target Attack Radar System
STO	Space Tasking Order
SWC	Space Warfare Center
TAC	Tactical Air Command
TOA	Total Obligational Authority
TWA	Trans World Airlines
UAV	Unmanned Aerial Vehicle
USAF	United States Air Force
USSOCOM	U.S. Special Operations Command
USSPACECOM	U.S. Space Command
USSTRATCOM	U.S. Strategic Command

Chapter One

INTRODUCTION

On January 11, 2001, the long-awaited report of the Commission to Assess United States National Security Space Management and Organization (more commonly known as the Space Commission) was released. It crisply defined an American "whither military space" issue that had been percolating with mounting intensity for several years.[1] Mandated by the fiscal year (FY) 2000 National Defense Authorization Act, largely at the behest of Senator Bob Smith (R-New Hampshire), then-chairman of the Senate Armed Services Committee's Subcommittee on Strategic Forces, the commission was directed to consider possible near-term, medium-term, and longer-term changes in the organization and conduct of U.S. national military space policy. In particular, it was asked to assess the adequacy of existing military space arrangements and the desirability of establishing a separate and independent U.S. space service.

The very creation of the Space Commission in the first place was an implied criticism of the Air Force's recent handling of the nation's military space effort, since that commission's inspiration largely emanated from a sense of growing concern in some congressional and other quarters—justified or not—that the Air Force was not fully living up to its responsibilities of military space stewardship. Naturally in light of that, the Air Force became the prime focus of the commission's inquiry. Although the Air Force's widely touted *Global Engagement* vision statement, promulgated in the wake of its Corona

---

[1] *Report of the Commission to Assess United States National Security Space Management and Organization*, Washington, D.C., January 11, 2001, hereinafter referred to as *Space Commission Report.*

1

leadership conference in 1996, had flatly declared that the service saw itself transitioning from an "air force" to an "air and space force" on an evolutionary path toward becoming a "space and air force," both friends and critics nonetheless expressed concern over the extent to which that service's leaders were genuinely committed to moving the Air Force into space and, indeed, whether the Air Force was even the appropriate service to inherit the mantle of military space exploitation to begin with.[2]

Echoing the concerns of many military space advocates both in and out of uniform, a former commander in chief of U.S. Space Command, retired Air Force General Charles A. Horner, lent an unusually credible voice to these doubts when he observed in 1997 that, with respect to space, "the Air Force is kind of where the Army was in 1920" regarding the nation's embryonic air power—namely, "in a state of denial." Along with others who have since wondered whether the Air Force's claim to being on an evolutionary path toward becoming a full-fledged space force was meant to be taken seriously or merely reflected a clever stratagem to buy off any would-be space separatists who might otherwise seek a divorce from the Air Force to form a separate space service, Horner added that "it almost becomes, at its most cynical, a roles and missions grab on the part of the Air Force to do this air and space to space thing."[3]

Seemingly energized by such expert questioning of the Air Force's depth of commitment to space, Senator Smith fired a clear shot across the Air Force's bow at a conference on air and space power in 1998, in effect challenging the Air Force leadership to prove its commitment by sinking more of its resource share into space or else give up its claim to space and clear the way for the establishment of a separate space service. While freely acknowledging everything the Air Force had done, especially since Operation Desert Storm, to develop a space infrastructure and to bring that infrastructure's contributions to commanders and combatants at all levels, he nonetheless complained that even the most leading-edge space activities had been fo-

---

[2]General Ronald R. Fogleman and the Honorable Sheila E. Widnall, *Global Engagement: A Vision for the 21st Century Air Force,* Washington, D.C.: Department of the Air Force, November 1996, p. 8.

[3]Quoted in Brendan Sobie, "Former SPACECOM Chief Advocates Creation of Separate Space Force," *Inside Missile Defense,* November 19, 1997, p. 24.

cused "primarily on figuring out how to use space systems to put information into the cockpit in order to more accurately drop *bombs* from *aircraft*." Senator Smith added that "this is not space warfare; it is using space to support air warfare." Charging that the Air Force seemed to regard space as little more than an information medium to be integrated into existing air, land, and sea forces rather than as a new arena for being developed as a mission area in its own right, the senator went on to observe that he did not see the Air Force "building the material, cultural, and organizational foundations of a service dedicated to space power." As evidence, he cited its "paltry" investments in such areas as space-based missile defense and a space-plane, its failure to advance more space officers into the most senior general-officer ranks, and its alleged slowness to nurture a cadre of younger officers dedicated exclusively to space warfare.[4]

Warming further to his theme, Smith then pointed out that "the notion that the Air Force should have primary responsibility for space is not sacred," offering as a case in point a challenge issued the previous year by Marine Corps commandant General Charles Krulak, who had declared that "between 2015 and 2025, we have an opportunity to put a fleet on another sea. And that sea is space. Now the Air Force [is] saying, 'Hey, that's mine!' And I'm saying, 'You're not taking it.'" While conceding that any interservice competition that might develop along these lines could easily result in an undesirable Balkanization of space power, the senator nonetheless put the Air Force on notice that if it "cannot or will not embrace space power," Congress would have no choice but to step into the breach and establish a new service.[5]

To be sure, the Air Force has taken numerous salutary steps in recent years to demonstrate that it deems these issues important, that its most senior leaders respect them as such, and that the institution is more than prepared to invest the needed time and energy toward en-

---

[4]Senator Bob Smith, "The Challenge of Space Power," speech to an annual conference on air and space power held by the Fletcher School of Law and Diplomacy and the Institute for Foreign Policy Analysis, Cambridge, Massachusetts, November 18, 1998, emphasis in the original.

[5]Ibid.

suring a seemly development of effective space-related capabilities.[6] Yet at the same time, some of the planning and vision-oriented activities that have galvanized such strong emotional reactions on various sides *within* the Air Force have largely failed to resonate within the broader American defense community. A case in point has been the intensely parochial and, to many observers, obscure and inward-looking back-and-forthing that has gone on inside the Air Force since 1996 over whether air and space should be understood as two separate and distinct operating mediums or as a single and seamless "aerospace" continuum. Indeed, some aspects of recent internal Air Force debate over space have had a downright negative effect outside the Air Force—perhaps best shown by Congress's establishment of the Space Commission, chaired by Donald H. Rumsfeld, who subsequently was selected by President George W. Bush to be Secretary of Defense. That commission's ensuing report not only crystallized the issues but also laid down a clear challenge, both for the defense community in general and for the Air Force in particular, either to grapple with them more effectively or else face a need for change—perhaps significant change—in the nation's existing management arrangements for military space.

The Space Commission's recommendations brought much-needed closure, at least for the interim, to a number of the issues mentioned above. To begin with, the commissioners concluded unanimously that the Air Force was doing well enough at managing the nation's military space effort that there was no immediate need to establish an independent U.S. space service. Not only that, they recommended that the Air Force be formally designated the Defense Department's executive agent for military space, thereby satisfying an Air Force desire that had gone unrequited since the service's earliest involvement in space during the 1950s. They also recommended that a separate and distinct Major Force Program (MFP) budget category for

---

[6]To cite but one example, U.S. Space Command's 1998 *Long Range Plan: Implementing the USSPACECOM Vision for 2020,* developed at the behest of that command's commander in chief at the time, USAF General Howell M. Estes III, represented what one group of Air Force space scholars called "the most comprehensive vision for U.S. military space ever produced." (Peter L. Hays, James M. Smith, Alan R. Van Tassel, and Guy M. Walsh, "Spacepower for a New Millennium: Examining Current U.S. Capabilities and Policies, in Peter L. Hays et al., eds., *Spacepower for a New Millennium: Space and U.S. National Security,* New York: McGraw Hill, 2000, p. 1.)

space be created to render transparent all space spending activity by all services, thus allowing the executive agent for space a clearer picture of both underfunded needs and unintended duplicative activity. Both recommendations were accepted by Secretary Rumsfeld and are now being implemented by the Department of Defense (DoD) and the Air Force.

Yet at the same time, the commissioners rejected the long-standing insistence of some in the Air Force that air and space represented a single "aerospace" continuum and concluded that space was a separate and distinct mission area warranting separate and dedicated organizational and funding support. (Shortly after assuming office, the current Air Force chief of staff, General John P. Jumper, co-opted that view out of his own conviction as the Air Force's corporate position.) They further highlighted the growing vulnerability of the nation's on-orbit assets to a potential "space Pearl Harbor" and implored DoD and the Air Force to pursue more serious efforts to develop a credible space control capability to ensure that the nation's increasingly indispensable space equities are properly protected against hostile threats. Finally, the commissioners found that the nation's military space effort was substantially underfunded for its growing importance to the nation's security. They concluded that if the Air Force fails over the next five to ten years to make the most of what they had recommended by way of increased executive authority to address identified needs, the Department of Defense would have little choice but to move with dispatch toward establishing a separate Space Corps or space service to take over the responsibility for the nation's military space effort on a full-time basis.

Thanks in large part to these developments, the Air Force entered the 21st century with much of the long-simmering debate over military space essentially resolved by leadership decree. As a result, it found itself presented with a clear set of institutional and mission-development challenges in need of attention. Those challenges include organizing more effectively for the proper nurturing of a duly competent and supported military space establishment, making the most of the executive-agent and MFP dispensations which the Space Commission so generously recommended for it, and registering significant headway toward developing and fielding a credible space control capability. To be sure, meeting these and related challenges successfully will require considerable and continuing DoD and congressional support. Yet the initiative clearly lies with the Air Force itself to set the direction and pace for the nation's military exploitation of space.

Without pretending in any way to have all the answers to the Air Force's and the nation's military space challenges, this study aims to illuminate those challenges by first exploring the roots of the developments outlined above and then thinking systematically about the organizational, contextual, and mission-need considerations that will require effective action as the Air Force embarks on its newly mandated space mission. The study begins by reviewing the major benchmarks of the Air Force's uphill struggle since the end of World War II to become accepted as the nation's military space custodian—often in the face of intense resistance both from the other services and from the civilian leadership. It then explores the differences in outlook which, until recently, had the Air Force speaking with more than one voice on the pivotally important matter of whether air and space should be treated as a single and seamless continuum or as two separate and distinct operating mediums and mission areas. Following that, it outlines the highlights of the Space Commission's recommendations, describes how senior civilian defense officials and the Air Force leadership have elected to act on them, and considers various implications for the near-term organization and management of space by the Air Force and the broader defense community.[7] It also looks at the growing need for more serious investment in space control and argues for carefully decoupling this mission need from the more contentious and premature push for

---

[7]One late-breaking development not addressed in this study is the recent merger of U.S. Space Command with U.S. Strategic Command (USSTRATCOM), first announced by Secretary Rumsfeld on June 28, 2002 and formally consummated at Offutt AFB, Nebraska the following October 1. That reorganization move, which surfaced as one of a number of responses to the terrorist attacks of September 11, 2001, followed close on the heels of the establishment of a new U.S. Northern Command to bolster the U.S. military contribution to homeland security. It was justified as one of several Bush administration initiatives to "transform" the U.S. military to better meet the challenges of the 21st century. The merger, which brought an end to U.S. Space Command's 17-year existence as the DoD's unified military space entity, took place as this study was nearing completion and must accordingly remain a topic for others to explore in the detail it deserves. For a brief overview of the merger and the expanded mission portfolio of the reconstituted USSTRATCOM, see William B. Scott, "'New' Strategic Command Could Assume Broadened Duties," *Aviation Week and Space Technology*, October 14, 2002, p. 63.

"space weaponization" aimed at attacking terrestrial targets from space. The study concludes with a synopsis of the most pressing military space policy demands on which the Air Force and the nation should now act.

Chapter Two

THE AIR FORCE'S STRUGGLE FOR SPACE

The idea that space is a natural extension of the third dimension has endured for so long in Air Force folklore that this mission area has been accepted by most airmen as an Air Force birthright almost from the start. Yet nothing could be farther from the truth. On the contrary, even a cursory overview of Air Force involvement in space since the end of World War II makes it clear that that involvement has been one of constant and relentless struggle with the other services, with competing civilian entities, and with the ruling political establishment for control of the nation's military space effort.

Indeed, until 1958, when Air Force chief of staff General Thomas D. White first introduced the term "aerospace" into the defense lexicon to portray air and space as a single continuum (see Chapter Three), the Air Force lacked not only a unifying theme for systematic planning with respect to space but also much interest in space as a domain of future operations warranting significant capital investment. Faced with parsimonious funding in the wake of the nation's postwar demobilization and preoccupied with the overarching need to build a nuclear deterrent force composed of modern jet bombers, the Air Force opted instead to concentrate its research and development (R&D) and procurement efforts almost entirely on the development and fielding of new aircraft. Its primary interest in space during those formative years was entirely bureaucratic, centered on a determination to defend the service's "exclusive rights" to space against perceived encroachments by the Army and Navy.

Indeed, rather than being in any way preplanned, the Air Force's initial approach to space was, in the words of air power historian Walter

Boyne, "both curious and coincidental," in that the need to develop the intercontinental ballistic missile (ICBM) thrust the Air Force into space-related activity almost willy-nilly, before it had either the resources or the inclination to develop any seriously considered concepts for the military exploitation of space.[1] In the years that followed the Air Force's eventual commitment to the practical business of developing satellites for reconnaissance and ballistic missiles for nuclear retaliation, Air Force involvement in space came to reflect a dual-track effort, neither track of which had much to do with any far-reaching "vision" of space as representing the organization's ultimate destiny. The first track, pragmatic in the extreme, sought to convince the nation's civilian and military leaders that the Air Force should be formally designated the "executive agent" for all U.S. military space activity. The second, once Air Force space programs had become sufficiently developed by the early 1980s to have practical relevance to the warfighting community, aimed at removing those programs from the control of the service's R&D and acquisition sector and reconstituting them in a new organizational arrangement in direct support of Air Force operators. Throughout it all, the Air Force had to fight mightily every step of the way to earn its dominant role in the U.S. military space effort. The history of that fight is well worth recalling by today's Air Force planners for the cautionary note it offers against presuming that space has in any way been a natural Air Force inheritance.

EARLY INTERSERVICE CONFLICTS

Ironically, the first manifestation of service interest in military space exploitation after World War II came not from forward-looking Army Air Force (AAF) planners, as one might have expected, but from the Navy. In early 1946, a group of U.S. naval officers who had been conducting a satellite feasibility study sought to carve out a leading role for the Navy in pursuing military satellite development. The Army

---

[1] Walter J. Boyne, *Beyond the Wild Blue: A History of the U.S. Air Force, 1947–1997*, New York: St. Martin's Press, 1997, p. 267. To be sure, on March 16, 1955, the Air Force did initiate procurement of the WS-117L satellite system, the precursor to the Corona film-recovery reconnaissance satellite and the SAMOS electro-optical reconnaissance and MIDAS infrared launch-detection satellites—even before the Atlas ICBM was given the highest national development priority later in September of that year.

also positioned itself ahead of its AAF component during the initial postwar years in seeking a niche for itself in space exploitation. Through its Operation Paperclip, it had brought some 130 German rocket scientists to White Sands, New Mexico, along with nearly 100 V-2 rockets and reams of technical data from the German missile development and launch facility at Peenemunde. Not long thereafter, Army spokesmen began characterizing their rockets as a natural extension of artillery and therefore a legitimate Army preserve.

In the face of these perceived encroachments by the Army and Navy on what they considered to be the AAF's rightful domain, AAF leaders moved with dispatch to challenge the space pretensions of the other services, even though the AAF itself at the time had no comparable satellite or missile plans of its own. Not only did the AAF's deputy chief of staff for research and development, then-Major General Curtis LeMay, decline the Navy's request for AAF participation in its satellite initiative, he insisted that satellite development should be an AAF preserve, on the ground that satellites represented an extension of strategic air power. Rather than sign up with the Navy and thus relinquish the initiative, LeMay instead turned to the AAF's newly established Project RAND to tap the latter's then unmatched scientific and engineering talent for a crash inquiry into the prospects of successfully orbiting an earth satellite. Within three weeks, that initiative led to the renowned RAND study of a "world-circling spaceship," which eventually became widely recognized as the world's first comprehensive satellite feasibility assessment. Armed with the RAND report, LeMay and other AAF principals argued strenuously for AAF primacy in satellite R&D and sought control over any future U.S. military effort to develop a satellite by claiming that their thinking was "as advanced as anyone's" and that any such satellite was "a matter of strategic aviation, their natural responsibility."[2]

As for the Army's missile ambitions, LeMay similarly argued in a September 1946 memorandum to the AAF's chief of staff, General Carl Spaatz, that the AAF must protect its increasingly acknowledged "strategic role," adding that the future of the AAF plainly lay "in the field of guided missiles." LeMay further cautioned that any Army

---

[2]Walter A. McDougall, *The Heavens and the Earth: A Political History of the Space Age,* Baltimore, Maryland: The Johns Hopkins University Press, 1997, p. 102.

success in gaining an inside track in developing missiles would encourage its leadership to seek control not only of the close air support mission, an AAF preserve, but of the AAF's long-range bombers as well.[3] For its part, the Navy elected to shelve its satellite initiative, at least for the time being, after LeMay declined its request for AAF support. At the same time, in response to what it judged to be an unambiguous AAF effort to annex space as a military mission area, the Navy joined hands with the Army in arguing that each service should retain the right to develop missiles in support of its service-specific needs.

After the Air Force gained its independence from the Army in 1947, its leading generals pressed ever harder to be assigned control of any future U.S. satellite and missile development. In September of the following year, DoD engineered a temporary truce between the two services. The newly independent Air Force was persuaded to relinquish the AAF's previous responsibility for conducting missile R&D on behalf of the Army in return for an arrangement—in effect a payback for that concession—whereby the Air Force was given approval to develop both surface-to-surface pilotless aircraft and "strategic," or intercontinental-range, missiles and the Army received authority only to develop "tactical," or battlefield-use, missiles. Yet the Air Force was unwilling to take the next step of actually pursuing the development of missiles and satellites for strategic use.[4] On the contrary, whatever interest AAF airmen may have had in satellites, rockets, and space launch capabilities in the immediate aftermath of World War II was soon displaced by the new service's greater commitment to a force development strategy focused on long-range bombers and air-breathing missiles.

In effect, the Air Force wanted the bonus without the onus. It showed far greater interest in securing what it saw as its rightful prerogatives in the space mission area than in actually getting a funded commitment to develop strategic missiles. Instead, it followed the recommendations of its newly established Scientific Advisory Board and hewed all but exclusively to the development of intra-atmospheric

---

[3] David N. Spires, *Beyond Horizons: A Half-Century of Air Force Space Leadership*, Washington, D.C.: U.S. Government Printing Office, 1997, pp. 18–19.

[4] Ibid., p. 13.

aircraft and jet propulsion systems that promised greater near-term combat potential than space systems.

Yet even as it declined to support satellite development with hard funding, the Air Force vigorously campaigned for "exclusive rights in space," as attested by the declaration of its chief of staff, General Hoyt Vandenberg, in January 1948 that as the service dealing with air weapons, "especially strategic," the Air Force had "logical responsibility" for satellites.[5] "Paradoxically," as space historian David Spires noted, "as the Air Force's commitment to develop an ICBM diminished, its determination to be designated sole authority responsible for long-range missiles increased. . . . The Air Force remained ever vigilant in protecting its authority over satellite and missile development. If it neglected its space programs, it nevertheless kept a wary eye on Army and Navy efforts to weaken the Air Force's claim to exclusive rights to these programs."[6]

A pivotal decision two years later in March 1950 gave the Air Force formal responsibility for developing both long-range strategic missiles and shorter-range theater missiles. Thanks in large measure to that decision, by the end of the Truman administration the Air Force had successfully outmaneuvered the Army in the latter's effort to extend its Redstone battlefield missile's range beyond 200 miles. Henceforth, the development of land-based "strategic" missiles would be an exclusive Air Force preserve.[7] Moreover, a succession of RAND studies that followed the initial satellite report had identified for the Air Force a new mission of space-based strategic reconnaissance. All the same, the remainder of the Truman years saw both satellite and ballistic missile development succumb to doubts about their military worth and to an economic downturn that persisted until the end of the 1940s and beyond. Faced with the hard choice of focusing either on manned aircraft or on satellites and missiles, the Air Force, not surprisingly, elected to concentrate on improving its existing forces rather than investing in a less certain future capability.

---

[5] Ibid., p. 26.

[6] Ibid., pp. 19, 49.

[7] As the subsequent design and development of the Polaris submarine-launched ballistic missile began to unfold several years later, it was clear from the outset that that would be a Navy program.

MORE FRUSTRATIONS FOR AIR FORCE AMBITIONS

In a policy approach characterized by Spires as "far more sophisti-
cated, secretive, and complex . . . than many at the time appreciated," the Eisenhower administration professed a determination to
forestall the militarization of space as long as possible and instead to
stress peaceful applications.[8] This approach, however, was a clever
ploy, its altruistic declarations masking the administration's real underlying intent to develop secret satellite reconnaissance systems. In
keeping with that stratagem, National Security Council (NSC) Directive 5520, issued in May 1955, proved to be pivotal in setting the subsequent direction and tone of national space policy. It affirmed that
the ongoing civilian International Geophysical Year satellite launch
effort must not be permitted to hamper the high-priority ICBM and
intermediate-range ballistic missile (IRBM) development efforts that
were under way by that time. It also decreed, however, that a civilian
scientific satellite *had* to precede a military one into space in order to
establish the legitimate right of unmolested overflight in space. With
a view toward ensuring the success of this stratagem, the Eisenhower
administration adamantly opposed any discussion by the services of
military space operations that might possibly prompt a public debate
over the legitimacy of military space flight.

By that time, the Air Force had become heavily committed to the development of reconnaissance satellites and ballistic missiles. Yet
without an agreed and accepted space "mission," it still found itself
beset by powerful Army and Navy efforts to dominate the nation's
military space programs. The Naval Research Laboratory, having ini-
tiated a satellite development effort as early as 1945, was managing
the official U.S. Vanguard civilian satellite program. Concurrently,
the Army Ballistic Missile Agency (ABMA) in Huntsville, Alabama,
was insisting that the Army possessed the greatest wherewithal for
pursuing military space applications and that space was merely "the
high ground," the taking of which was a traditional Army mission.

Indeed, during the early 1950s both the Army and Navy could claim
more practical experience with space launch activities than could the
Air Force. The Army's V-2 and related launch experiments shortly af-

---

[8]Spires, p. 30.

ter World War II were but precursors to the subsequent Redstone, Juno, and Jupiter rockets developed by Wernher von Braun and his team after 1950, when the latter moved from White Sands to Huntsville to establish the Redstone Arsenal. It also was the Army that succeeded in putting the first man-made object in space, when its WAC Corporal rocket attained a ballistic apogee of some 250 miles in early 1949.

In the wake of the successful launching of Sputnik in October 1957, Deputy Secretary of Defense Donald Quarles had no trouble supporting the Air Force's advanced reconnaissance program for developing satellites, which was not only consistent with but integral to the administration's determination to develop a satellite reconnaissance capability. Yet he bridled at the Air Force's parallel efforts to carve out an offensive space role for itself and insisted that the Air Force cease thinking of satellites as weapon platforms with offensive applications, on the reasonable premise that any talk of weapons in space would threaten to undermine the nation's continuing stress on legitimate passage for reconnaissance satellites, a more important concern. Later comments by Air Force generals calling for missile bases on the moon and militarizing the planets raised both Pentagon and congressional hackles and did little to engender civilian support for the Air Force's nascent space ambitions.

On January 31, 1958, the Army's Explorer 1 finally became the first U.S. satellite to achieve orbit. That and the Navy's eventual success in launching Vanguard gave those services both an operational and a bureaucratic advantage in the space arena, with the Navy claiming legitimate rights of ownership of all military space missions involving weather, navigation, and fleet communications.[9] Soon thereafter, congressional hearings gave all three services an opportunity to state their case, along with the Defense Department, the National Advisory Committee on Aeronautics (NACA), and the Atomic Energy Commission. Each proponent sought to persuade the Eisenhower admin-

---

[9]McDougall, p. 166.

istration and Congress "of its own special capability in space by calling loudly for recognition of its skills and resources."[10]

By the end of 1958, the Air Force had decided to launch a full-court press for control of the American military space effort. As Spires explained, the Air Staff's directorate of plans candidly itemized the Air Force's weaknesses in space organization, operations, and R&D and suggested that "rather than formally requesting operating responsibility for space roles and missions, the Air Force should demonstrate successful stewardship, rely on available hardware, and establish 'squatters rights.'" The director of plans added that the Air Force "must assume the role of opportunity, aggressively taking advantage of each situation as it arises to assure that the Air Force is always predominate [sic] in any action that has a space connotation."[11]

On November 7, 1959, the Air Force's office of legislative liaison voiced concern over apparent congressional preferences for Army space initiatives. Taking its cue from General White's recently enunciated "aerospace" formula, that office called for an Air Force strategy emphasizing that the upper atmosphere and space were extensions of the Air Force's traditional operating arena and thus represented a natural extension of Air Force responsibility. It further encouraged Air Force spokesmen to "emphasize and re-emphasize the logic of this evolution until no doubt exists in the minds of Congress or the public that the Air Force mission lies in space, as the mission of the Army is on the ground and the mission of the Navy is on the seas."[12]

At the same time, however, the Air Force failed to indicate any immediate military space applications that would require it to fund basic research for space. Instead, it spoke expansively of sending pilots up in "aerospace planes" to "orbital bases." That prompted the budget-conscious Eisenhower administration to put the Air Force on an

---

[10]Enid Curtis Bok Schoettle, "The Establishment of NASA," in Sanford Lakoff, ed., *Knowledge and Power: Essays on Science and Government*, New York: Free Press, 1966, p. 187.

[11]Spires, p. 68.

[12]Memorandum by Colonel V. L. Adduci, assistant director, legislative liaison to the Assistant Deputy Chief of Staff for Plans and Programs, November 7, 1957, quoted in Spires, p. 54.

ever shorter leash.[13] Such efforts to propound grandiose schemes for eventual space force application soon led the Air Force into political trouble when a "directorate of astronautics" was established within the Air Staff without any prior Air Force consultation with senior civilian officials. That move drove several senior civilian defense principals to charge the Air Force with seeking to "grab the limelight and establish a position" in the ongoing interservice jousting for bureaucratic dominance over military space. Secretary of Defense Neil McElroy personally bridled at the Air Force's use of the term "astronautics" and at its having made an end run around the civilian leadership to pursue public support for its space ambitions. By direction of the Office of the Secretary of Defense, the use of the term "astronautics" by the Air Force was formally proscribed and the new Air Staff office was redesignated the Directorate of Advanced Technology.[14]

Thus chastened, the Air Force backed away from its effort to lay the groundwork for force employment applications in space and instead adopted a strategy more consistent with administration programs and goals and aimed principally at getting the Air Force formally designated the executive agent for all U.S. military space activities. Toward that end, General Bernard Schriever played a pivotal role by arguing that the Air Force's near-monopoly in managing and operating the nation's military space systems by that time had naturally come to warrant its acquiring greater responsibility for military space in future years. That effort, however, scarcely deterred the other services from continuing to jockey for a larger share of the action with respect to military space. The Army, in particular, clung tenaciously to its residual space programs in the face of the Air Force's accelerated push for controlling the nation's military space effort. That push eventually drove Army General John B. Medaris, the commander of ABMA, to complain to Congress that the Air Force had evinced a long record of noncooperation with Army space launch programs.[15]

---

[13]McDougall, p. 200.

[14]Bruno W. Augenstein, *Evolution of the U.S. Military Space Program, 1945–1960: Some Key Events in Study, Planning, and Program Management*, Santa Monica, Calif.: RAND, P-6814, September 1982, p. 11.

[15]For example, in early 1959, the Army revealed its Man Very High proposal, which envisaged firing a man riding in a Jupiter reentry vehicle on a ballistic trajectory 150 miles downrange. This proposal was ridiculed by Dr. Hugh Dryden, the director of

The Army and Navy also countered the Air Force's push for dominance in the space arena by calling for the establishment of a joint military command that would operate and manage all U.S. military space systems. The lead role in that effort was played by the chief of naval operations, Admiral Arleigh Burke, who argued in April 1959 for the creation of a joint military space agency based on what he called "the very indivisibility of space." The Army's chief, General Maxwell Taylor, agreed with Burke, insisting that the possibilities held out by space transcended the interests of any single service. The Air Force chief, General White, however, opposed that idea, insisting that it violated the time-honored practices of treating space systems on a functional basis and of integrating weapon systems within unified commands. Since space systems merely enabled a more effective execution of existing missions, White countered, they rightfully belonged within the appropriate unified or specified command.[16]

In adjudicating these opposing arguments, Defense Secretary McElroy made three decisions in 1959 that substantially bolstered the Air Force's bureaucratic position with respect to space. First, he rejected Admiral Burke's proposal for the establishment of a joint military space command. Second, he disapproved the proposed creation of a Defense Astronautical Agency and instead picked the Air Force to be the assigned military supporter of the newly created National Aeronautics and Space Administration (NASA).[17] Finally, he gave the Air Force responsibility for the development, production, and launching of military space boosters and for military space payload integration, thereby stripping the Army and Navy of any significant space responsibilities and leaving only the Air Force and NASA as significant players in space systems development. Congress ratified that decision on June 1, 1960.[18]

NACA, as having "about the same technical value as the circus stunt of shooting a young lady from a cannon" (Spires, p. 75). The Office of the Secretary of Defense rejected it forthwith. Once NASA got the civilian space portfolio, however, it did exactly that with Project Mercury.

[16]Spires, p. 76.

[17]NASA, an evolutionary development of the previous NACA, was established by the National Space Act of 1958 to manage the nation's civilian space effort.

[18]As consolation prizes, the Navy was granted control of the Transit navigation satellite and the Army received four communications satellites. (Transit's purpose was to help U.S. Navy ballistic-missile submarine crews determine their position before launching.)

Ultimately, the Air Force emerged from the post-Sputnik interservice struggle over space with the lion's share of oversight authority in that domain. Spires called the rejection of the Navy's proposal for a joint military space agency and Secretary McElroy's designation of the Air Force as the nation's military space booster service "a landmark decision on the Air Force's road to space."[19] Historian Walter McDougall likewise observed that it "solidified the USAF hold on military spaceflight."[20] Not long after these decisions were made, Congress increased the Air Force's space funding by a factor of almost 120, from $2.2 million to $249.7 million. Shortly thereafter, General Medaris retired from the Army in bureaucratic defeat and his Huntsville facility was transferred to NASA. In Spires' assessment, "if the Air Force had not achieved the complete victory sought by its leaders, it nonetheless seemed well on its way to gaining management responsibility for all service requirements as the Defense Department's executive agent for space."[21]

SUBSEQUENT AIR FORCE GAINS

Throughout much of the 1950s, the Air Force did not sufficiently appreciate the important nuances of the Eisenhower administration's strategy to legitimize space reconnaissance. Air Force leaders instead regarded that strategy merely as a politically imposed stranglehold whose principal effect was to inhibit a more energetic military exploitation of space. By the early 1960s, however, the Air Force's pursuit of institutional dominance over military space had finally begun to show signs of real progress—once its leadership acknowledged, for the first time, the usefulness of space in enabling and supporting traditional military functions. In one of the first clear manifestations of that progress, the Defense Department moved in May 1960 to integrate the strategic communications systems of the three services under the newly established Defense Communications Agency (DCA). As a result, neither the Army nor any other service would exercise exclusive control over the military satellite communications system (MILSATCOM). Instead, the Air Force was granted the

---

[19]Spires, p. 78.

[20]McDougall, p. 198.

[21]Spires, p. 80.

spacecraft development and launch charter for MILSATCOM. The Army received only the ground communications portion and DCA assumed responsibility for coordinating Air Force and Army activities to ensure commonality and consistency.[22]

The advent of the Kennedy administration in January 1961 marked another important milestone for the Air Force. A report issued that same month by presidential science adviser Jerome Wiesner faulted the nation's "fractionated military space program" and maintained that the Air Force was the logical choice to become the sole agency for managing that program's diverse systems and activities, considering that it was already providing 90 percent of the space-related resources and support for the other services and defense agencies in any case. Two months later, President Kennedy approved a Pentagon directive assigning the Air Force responsibility for the overwhelming majority of the nation's military space effort, making it the lead space service and, as such, the de facto executive agent for military space. In that directive, Secretary of Defense Robert McNamara formally designated the Air Force as the military service for space R&D, mandating that any exceptions to that rule had to be authorized by him personally. That directive largely foreclosed the interservice tugging and hauling over space that had predominated throughout so much of the Eisenhower era. Later, in 1963, in a punctuation of his earlier directive, McNamara transferred the Pacific Missile Range from the Navy to the Air Force and also assigned the global satellite tracking system to the Air Force.

In the meantime, the highly classified Corona satellite reconnaissance program was finally vindicated when a film capsule containing overhead imagery of the Soviet Union was returned from low earth orbit after 14 failed attempts. Despite efforts from some quarters to assign the Corona program, the U-2, and the Satellite and Missile Observation System (SAMOS) to a civilian defense agency, the Air Force's Office of Missile and Satellite Systems was redesignated the secret National Reconnaissance Office (NRO), headed by the Under Secretary of the Air Force. Thanks to that move, the Air Force was able to retain nominal ownership of the Corona program, although that program's assignment to the civilian Air Force secretariat and its

---

[22]Ibid., pp. 138–139.

direct subordination to the Director of Central Intelligence with respect to tasking effectively cut the uniformed Air Force out of Corona's day-to-day operations and management.[23]

What continually got the Air Force into hot water in its campaign to gain civilian endorsement of its space ambitions during the Eisenhower and Kennedy years were those instances when it reached beyond its pursuit of executive-agent status with respect to the management and operation of the nation's military space effort and pursued more ambitious goals having to do with force application—goals which ran directly counter to the "peaceful uses" proclivities of those administrations. The Air Force also encountered an unresponsive and occasionally even hostile civilian audience whenever it sought to claim exclusive corporate ownership of a seamless vertical dimension that included both air and space. As just one illustration in point, the deputy director of war plans on the Air Staff in 1960 issued a paper advocating an aggressive Air Force effort to seize control of all new U.S. military space programs. That paper's issuance was accompanied by a major public-relations push to promote Air Force interests to congressmen, business leaders, opinion makers, and other civilian elites. It triggered a major protest by the media against what was portrayed as a transparent Air Force political effort to force a change in national policy with respect to the peaceful uses of space. Seemingly undaunted, however, the first commander of the newly established Air Force Systems Command (AFSC), General Schriever, complained pointedly in congressional testimony in July 1961 that the nation had been "inhibited in the space business through the 'space for peace' slogan."[24]

In much the same spirit, the Air Force continued to press hard for a more combat-oriented military space program, to include the development and testing of antiballistic missile and space-based antisatellite systems. It also continued to develop future space plans in an Air Force Objectives Series paper that would be complemented by a requirement for operational capability (ROC) statement to identify

---

[23]The Air Force's loss of control of Corona and SAMOS led it to establish the Aerospace Corporation to ensure that it would, in the future, possess the on-call engineering skills needed to meet future space challenges. (Spires, p. 85.)

[24]Ibid., p. 101.

specific fielded capabilities needed to achieve Air Force objectives. In direct connection with that approach, the Air Staff's chief of R&D argued forcefully in 1962 that the best way to ensure the peaceful use of space was through the pursuit of what he called "space superiority," to include an offensive capability to inspect satellites by rendezvousing with noncooperative targets.[25]

Such clamoring by the Air Force for offensive capabilities in space severely tried the patience of McNamara and his senior subordinates, to say nothing of their disposition to lend the Air Force a receptive ear. In response to the Air Force's advocacy of such programs, the director of defense research and engineering, John Rubel, responded tersely that the Defense Department's space spending was already as high as it would be permitted to go, given the "uncertainties" of the nation's military space effort, and that any new Air Force space program proposals would receive more than the usual exacting scrutiny for what they promised to contribute to traditional military mission fulfillment. More to the point, Rubel added that many such recently submitted proposals by the Air Force had not met the high technical standards of his office but instead, as Spires noted, merely "served abstract doctrines about the military space role." Rubel went out of his way to disparage the Air Force's "aerospace" formula, finding no use in vague theories suggesting that space would be the next battleground or that "control" of space, whatever that meant, promised control of the earth.[26] Similarly, McNamara saw the Air Force as fixating excessively on alternative hardware means for getting into and out of orbit rather than on the more strategically important question of what the Air Force really wanted to do in space and why. He was plainly dissatisfied with the Air Force's answers to the latter question, particularly with respect to offering persuasive military functions for its proposed Dyna-Soar and, later, for Manned Orbiting Laboratory (MOL) astronauts to perform while in space.

In the end, the Dyna-Soar and MOL programs were both terminated in close succession and, with them, the Air Force's near-term hope of making manned spaceflight the main focus of its space plans. Im-

---

[25]Ibid., pp. 104–105.
[26]Ibid., p. 115.

plicitly referring to those cancellations, the Secretary of the Air Force at the time, Robert Seamans, observed that the costs of putting airmen into space were prohibitively high for the payoff offered and that the Air Force would be better served by concentrating on modernizing its fighters and bombers rather than getting diverted by space technology ventures that promised little, if any, combat leverage of significant note.[27] Moreover, as evidence that the Air Force was divided regarding its R&D and procurement priorities, Spires observed that for many of the service's leaders, space represented "abstract goals and assets that drained scarce operational funding from terrestrial needs." As if to reinforce that more traditional school of thought, the retirement of General Schriever in 1966 had the effect of depriving the Air Force of its most vocal and influential space advocate and of accelerating a shift in Air Force emphasis, already set in motion by the emerging exigencies of Vietnam, from ambitious force-application schemes to a more low-key and incremental approach to military space.

In the early 1970s, the interservice competition that had loomed so large during the Eisenhower years surfaced anew as the Navy again challenged the Air Force's exclusive claim to military space, arguing that the 1961 Pentagon directive against a joint military space command had been superseded by new military requirements. Worse yet for Air Force fortunes, Secretary of Defense Melvin Laird declared in 1970, against express Air Force preferences, that the acquisition of military space systems would henceforth be undertaken in the same manner as all other defense procurement programs and in accordance with the same guidelines. Laird further decreed that the three services would compete on an equal footing for future space programs in such areas as communications, navigation, surveillance, and weather.

Rightly assessing any outright attempt by the Air Force to get Laird's directive reversed as a recipe for failure, Secretary of the Air Force John McLucas instead cleverly highlighted that directive's potential for fostering interservice rivalry and, using that argument, convinced Laird to amend it to require all military space developments to be coordinated with the Air Force before being funded and set in mo-

---

[27]Ibid., p. 133.

tion. That tactic had the effect of undoing the most potentially harmful implications of Laird's ruling for Air Force interests. On September 1, 1970, Defense Department Directive 5160.22 stipulated that "the Air Force will have the responsibility of development, production, and deployment of space systems for warning and surveillance of enemy nuclear capabilities, and all launch vehicles, including launch and orbital support operations."[28] Despite that good news, however, the Nixon administration's consuming preoccupation with Vietnam had led to a growing parsimony when it came to funding new R&D initiatives, especially with respect to space. The handwriting on the wall indicated that if the Air Force wished to secure for itself a predominant role in military space once and for all, it would have to begin thinking less about pursuing new systems and programs per se and more about acquiring and refining the technical expertise, management skills, and organizational wherewithal not only to make such systems and programs work most effectively but also to justify the Air Force's claim to overseeing them.

THE CONSOLIDATION OF AIR FORCE SPACE ACTIVITIES

For the first 10–15 years of American military space involvement, those who created U.S. space systems devoted themselves almost exclusively to supporting the nation's highest-level security needs and imperatives (such as intelligence, C3, and missile launch warning). The mission of nuclear deterrence predominated. Their early interests were focused mainly on gaining a position of strategic advantage for the United States through the deployment of advanced space capabilities. For that reason, their training and career development were not in the art of operational flying but rather, for the most part, in applied science, engineering, and systems management. As the Air Force's most senior space officer, then–Lieutenant General Thomas S. Moorman, Jr., observed in 1992 of that formative era, ". . . because the new medium [of space] had uncertain operational applications, the research and development community took the lead in acquiring and operating our space systems."[29] That

---

[28]Boyne, *Beyond the Wild Blue*, p. 268.

[29]Lieutenant General Thomas S. Moorman, Jr., USAF, "Space: A New Strategic Frontier," *Airpower Journal*, Spring 1992, p. 14.

made for an almost preordained divide between the air and space components of the Air Force—a divide that became ever more apparent as military space systems increasingly emerged from the black world of secrecy into the light of day.

Indeed, one could go further yet by observing that, in fact, there were *three* schisms in the Air Force with respect to space during the early formative years of the service's space involvement: (1) the separation between blue Air Force flight operations and black space noted immediately above; (2) the separation between Air Force Systems Command's R&D and acquisition establishment and the Aerospace Defense Command (later Air Force Space Command) space combat operations community; and (3) the entire Air Force space community's near-exclusive focus on supporting strategic nuclear deterrence and warfare, which produced yet a third divide separating Air Force space concerns from the conventional warfare orientation that eventually came to dominate the rest of the Air Force.

That reality was to change dramatically, however, as it became increasingly clear by the mid-1970s that the nation's fielded military space assets offered great potential not only for the most senior civilian leadership with respect to nuclear crisis management, but also for the uniformed conventional warfighting community. Indeed, the first glimmer of an effort to bring space more closely into the organizational fold of the mainstream Air Force had occurred fully a decade earlier, when then-Colonel Robert T. Marsh suggested that a space directorate be established within the Air Staff. In what Boyne called "a non-turf-conscious manner that was typical of his leadership," Marsh further suggested the need for a separate space directorate within AFSC.[30] Marsh briefed these suggestions in 1965 to the Air Force's chief of staff, General John P. McConnell, who quickly approved them.[31]

For the most part, however, the Air Force's space activities remained more a focus of R&D and acquisition activity than a day-to-day concern of Air Force operators. As a result, the Air Force showed little

---

[30]Boyne, *Beyond the Wild Blue*, p. 270.

[31]Later, as the four-star commander of AFSC, Marsh, in another non-turf-conscious move, was among the first to advocate the creation of a separate Air Force Space Command.

interest in seriously committing itself to taking on space operations as a core institutional goal. Because of that neglect at the higher command levels, the service's most devoted space professionals were left to find allies primarily within the middle ranks of the officer corps rather than among the senior Air Force leadership.[32]

In 1977, however, chief of staff General David C. Jones issued a watershed letter on Air Force space policy that portrayed the development of space weapons and operational concepts as among the Air Force's uppermost responsibilities.[33] Later during Jones' tenure as chief, the Air Staff's directorate of plans and operations issued a study of future Air Force space objectives that repeated General White's 1958 "aerospace" mantra that space was but a continuation of the third dimension. That study further maintained that the Air Force deserved to manage all U.S. military space activities because it possessed both a rich history of working in space and a near-monopoly on space technology expertise. The latter rationale came close to offering the most compelling argument yet for the Air Force's long-standing pursuit of stewardship over the nation's military space effort. The prominent use of the term "aerospace," however, bore witness to a continued belief in some senior quarters that air and space should, in the Air Force's best interest, be treated as a single medium and mission area.

In yet another indication that space was no longer solely a concern of the Air Force's R&D and acquisition communities, the 1979 Air Force Manual 1-1 on basic doctrine identified space operations, for the first time, as one of the nine basic Air Force operational missions. The following year, the Air Force Scientific Advisory Board (SAB) conducted a summer study that concluded that although the Air Force had successfully performed military space operations throughout the preceding 15 years, it remained "inadequately organized for operational exploitation of space and [had] placed insufficient emphasis on inclusion of space systems in an integrated force

---

[32]Spires, p. 175.

[33]Walter J. Boyne, "A Great Tradition in the Making: The United States Air Force," *Aviation Week and Space Technology*, April 16, 1997, p. 126.

study."[34] In a determined step toward correcting that assessed shortcoming, the Air Staff in 1981 established a directorate for space operations under the then-serving deputy chief of staff for plans and operations, Lieutenant General Jerome O'Malley, who previously had emerged as a forceful advocate of making space operations a normal Air Force activity. That move was intended, at least in part, to honor the SAB's finding that space technology did not adequately support operational commanders, that the Air Force's operational space goals were not clearly defined, that space systems were not well integrated into the larger force structure, and that Air Force space objectives were both poorly understood and financially unattainable.

Even before these developments occurred, the initial groundwork had been laid by a group of like-minded operators on the Air Staff and elsewhere in senior Air Force circles for the creation of a separate Air Force Space Command (AFSPC). One of those officers, then–Major General John T. Chain, Jr., worked for O'Malley as director of operations on the Air Staff. In 1981, Chain called for getting the operational Air Force "more involved in space" and for developing and nurturing "more space-qualified blue-suiters," calling that "one of the most important issues facing the Air Force." He stressed that those in key operational positions needed to become more knowledgeable about space issues and to weigh in more heavily in shaping the Air Force's space strategy.[35] In October 1982, the first Air Force manual on space doctrine, AFM 1-6, resolved clearly, at least for the time being, the question of whether space was a distinct Air Force mission or merely a place by calling space "the ultimate high ground," as chief of staff General Charles Gabriel put it. Space was portrayed in that manual as a medium whose exploitation served *all* Air Force operational missions.

Of crucial importance to this process of giving space its full due within the Air Force, those in the most senior leadership positions who had been most determined to develop a separate space com-

---

[34]Quoted in Brigadier General Earl S. Van Inwegen, USAF (Ret.), "The Air Force Develops an Operational Organization for Space," in Cargill Hall and Jacob Neufeld, eds., *The U.S. Air Force in Space: 1945 to the 21st Century*, Washington, D.C.: USAF History and Museums Program, 1995.

[35]Major General John T. Chain, Jr., USAF, AF/XOO, remarks at the Air University Air Power Symposium, Maxwell AFB, Alabama, February 23, 1981, pp. 11–14.

mand as an entity in its own right clearly understood air and space to be separate and distinct operating mediums and recognized that the Air Force's increasingly routinized space and space-related operational functions warranted an organizational home of their own. For example, the commander of Tactical Air Command (TAC) at the time, General W. L. Creech, freely attested that the Air Force's embryonic F-15-launched antisatellite (ASAT) demonstrator weapon entailed a space-specific mission application that did not properly belong in TAC, even though the ASAT was carried by a TAC-operated fighter. Creech was more than willing to have TAC unburdened of that capability, since he had for years been involved in the Air Force's quest to give space operations a proper institutional home.[36]

Indeed, General Creech and by then General Robert T. Marsh, the commander of AFSC, were working with their fellow four-star Air Force major-command (MAJCOM) commanders to inculcate the idea that the time had come to have a dedicated operational command for space and that it should be a separate Air Force command standing on its own, in lieu of continuing to have the operational space mission assigned to an existing MAJCOM—or spread among several of them. As Creech later recalled, General Marsh's total lack of concern for "turf protection" of the space authority then vested in AFSC played a key role in convincing the other four-star MAJCOM commanders of the idea's worth. Creech helped Marsh round up the other MAJCOM commanders and get them behind the idea. All readily came on board, including the commander in chief of Strategic Air Command (SAC) after some initial reservations within SAC over the possible infringement of a new Air Force Space Command on SAC's recently acquired prerogatives with respect to space systems and warning.[37]

To be sure, one of the reasons for General Marsh's lack of concern for turf protection was almost certainly that AFSC lost almost no turf in the initial transaction. The three major installations, 20 smaller sites, and almost 4000 personnel that became the eventual nucleus of AFSPC in 1982 were not carved out of AFSC's R&D and acquisition community. Rather, they represented the missile warning and space

---

[36]Telephone conversation with General W. L. Creech, USAF (Ret.), November 23, 2001.
[37]Ibid.

surveillance networks that the Aerospace Defense Command (ADC) operated until its demise in December 1979. At that time, the warning and attack assessment functions were turned over to SAC until AFSPC's creation nearly three years later.

With all of the MAJCOM commanders thus solidly united on the point that a separate Air Force Space Command was urgently needed, Air Force chief of staff General Lew Allen encountered not just unanimous consent but powerful encouragement when it came time for him to introduce the subject at a scheduled meeting of all the Air Force four-stars. In the end, that initiative from the major field commanders, along with O'Malley's and Chain's urgings from within the Air Staff, carried the day. General Allen, after some initial hesitation, elected to approve the creation of a new and independent MAJCOM for space in one of his last official acts as Air Force chief of staff.

In an important step toward that end, construction of a Consolidated Space Operations Center (CSOC) was begun in FY 1982 at Falcon Air Force Station near Colorado Springs, Colorado, to provide a centralized facility for operating all Air Force satellites on orbit. (At the time, however, those satellites made up only a small number of the nation's total on-orbit military resources, and AFSC's control center in Sunnyvale, California, continued operating most of the rest.) On September 1, 1982, just two months after Allen's retirement, AFSPC itself was moved to Colorado Springs. Its first commander, General James V. Hartinger, was assigned the responsibility of managing and operating all Air Force on-orbit space assets, including controlling operational spacecraft and managing DoD-sponsored shuttle flights. Hartinger had served previously in a number of operational command positions, including as commander of both 9th and 12th Air Forces in TAC. Accordingly, he had the credentials to be a credible commander of the new AFSPC, where he was expected to exercise operationally related cognizance over the separate space medium and mission area. It further bears noting that although this seminal phase of Air Force space history indeed saw an eventual transfer of operational responsibility for Air Force space systems from AFSC to AFSPC, AFSPC itself was largely *not* a child of AFSC's R&D and acquisition community. Rather, it inherited the space combat operations community that previously had resided in ADC.[38]

Several years later, in his post-retirement oral history interview, General Allen recalled that although the Air Force had been responsible for a long time for an extremely active space program that was working well, "there were many within the Air Force, and some without, who felt strongly that the Air Force was not organizing itself appropriately for what they foresaw as a much different and increased set of activities in space." [39] In light of that, he added, "the pressure to do something about a Space Command [had] built during all of the four years of [his] term as chief. . . . The advantage [of creating AFSPC] was that one had a [space] commander who would advocate and have access to [Air Force] headquarters and . . . a structure on which one could build as other matters evolved. Those were probably good things."[40]

Once AFSPC was up and running, it was only a matter of time before a unified U.S. Space Command would also be activated, since that joint-service entity was an unavoidable concession by the Air Force to the Navy and Army to secure the blessing of its sister services for the creation of AFSPC.[41] That finally occurred three years later, on September 23, 1985. On this issue, the Air Force was obliged to reverse its former position of staunchly opposing such a joint command that went back to the initial proposal put forward for such a move in 1959 by Admiral Burke. However, the Air Force did not in any way resist the creation of that command. On the contrary, both General Gabriel and Secretary of the Air Force Verne Orr had previously come to espouse the establishment of a unified command for

---

[38]Then–Lieutenant General Creech, at the time the Air Force's assistant vice chief of staff, chaired a closely held study that ultimately led to a recommendation to disestablish ADC. For an authoritative account of this history, see Van Inwegen, "The Air Force Develops an Operational Organization for Space."

[39]General Lew Allen, Jr., USAF (Ret.), U.S. Air Force oral history interview, Maxwell AFB, Alabama, Air Force Historical Research Agency, January 1986, p. 164.

[40]Ibid., pp. 164–165. Allen also later recalled (p. 193) that his deputy for plans and operations, General O'Malley, "was convinced that we should have a Space Command; and furthermore, he was the individual who convinced me that it was better to have me do it before I left than have it done by my successor for various reasons. Therefore, he did take the leadership in making that move out quickly."

[41]Spires, p. 217.

space, declaring that no single military entity had an exclusive claim on or sole authority over the nation's military space systems. Once U.S. Space Command was on the verge of opening for business, General Hartinger proposed that AFSPC become the core component of the new unified command, since that was where the nation's military space activity and expertise were ultimately destined to be most heavily concentrated—even though they were still, at the time, largely lodged in AFSC and the NRO.

On November 19, 1983, AFSPC assumed formal stewardship of the Space Plan, the first such plan endorsed by the Air Staff since the early 1960s. The genesis of that plan lay in the continued organizational tension between AFSPC and AFSC over which command held the principal responsibility for Air Force space activities. Among other things, the Space Plan for the first time defined and articulated the four now-familiar military space mission areas of space support, force enhancement, space control, and force application—mission areas which were by no means universally accepted throughout the Air Force. The increasingly contentious issue of where stewardship for space belonged within the Air Force was finally forced into the open in 1987 when the Secretary of the Air Force released a white paper on space policy and leadership. Among other things, that white paper noted that General Gabriel's statement as chief four years before that the Air Force had assumed responsibility for most military space missions had in fact *not* been vindicated and that the rest of the defense establishment was increasingly coming to believe that the Air Force "only grudgingly supported space activities." The white paper further charged that the Air Force had failed to "exhibit a sense of institutional purpose or responsibility toward space" and had relegated space to a distant fourth priority behind its bomber, fighter, and airlift activities.[42]

Not surprisingly in the wake of this document's release, the other services were quick to take advantage of the Air Force's seemingly lackluster interest in space, and outside challenges to Air Force stewardship of space, as well as hard questions concerning whether the Air Force was properly fulfilling its role as de facto executive agent for military space, began to arise again. In a clear bid to exploit this ap-

---

[42]Ibid., p. 229.

pearance of an emergent Air Force window of vulnerability in the roles and missions arena, the Army and Navy turned to writing their own space "master plans." As Spires put it, "the white paper's authors [had] posed a central question: did the Air Force wish to act as the lead service for space? They declared that the answer should be 'yes' because of the service's space expertise. At the same time, however, the Air Force had neither a mission statement for space nor a current space operations doctrine, and its operational space command could not play a strong advocacy role throughout the corporate Air Force and Defense Department because its leader [at that time] was only a two-star commander."[43] In prescribing a strategy for redressing these deficiencies, the white paper laid out some explicit measures the Air Force needed to undertake—starting with articulating a new declaratory policy reasserting the Air Force's claim to being the "lead" service for space but conceding that this did not imply an "exclusive" Air Force role.

That task was taken up in the single most important Air Force document on space to have appeared up to that time: the report of the Blue Ribbon Panel on Space Roles and Missions, which was commissioned by chief of staff General Larry Welch in 1988 to address the full spectrum of military space concerns. The panel's executive steering group was chaired by the Air Force vice chief of staff and included the AFSPC commander, Lieutenant General Don Kutyna, and the vice commanders of the other major commands. The panel's study group zeroed in on the Air Force's alleged ambivalence toward space, notwithstanding the facts that the institution had been at the forefront of military space activity for some 30 years and already commanded half of the national space budget and three-quarters of the Defense Department's space budget. In the process, it discovered that the Air Force leadership's declared commitment to the institutionalization of space was in no way universally shared among the Air Force rank and file, thanks to persistent confusion about what space actually promised to the warfighter, a multiuser approach to systems that placed space at a disadvantage in the budget process, and the historically closed nature of the space community.[44]

---

[43]Ibid., p. 230.

[44]Ibid., p. 235.

In its final report, the Blue Ribbon Panel called for a principal but not exclusive role for the Air Force as the Defense Department's agent for military space exploitation. It also advocated a deliberate Air Force pursuit of capabilities for performing warfighting functions in and from space. As for the ownership and control of the nation's military space equities, it recommended that AFSPC continue to be the central advocate, operator, and manager for military space support (that is, the launching and operating of satellites) and that the unified U.S. Space Command refine its relationship with its AFSPC component by returning operational control of Air Force space assets to the latter during peacetime, in light of AFSPCs "organize, train, and equip" functions as mandated by Title X of the U.S. Code.

The Blue Ribbon report's findings and recommendations encountered an uphill struggle for acceptance within the Air Force because of a persistent absence of broad corporate Air Force involvement in the space effort; the overwhelming concentration of space expertise within AFSPC and a conspicuous absence of it elsewhere throughout the Air Force, notably in the major commands; and a general lack of sufficiently developed Air Force–wide space awareness and appreciation. The implementation plan for the report's recommendations, issued by the Air Staff in February 1989, stated prominently that "the Air Force is and will be responsible for the global employment of military power above the earth's surface." It directed AFSPC to develop a "space roadmap" to update the Space Plan by integrating all Air Force space activities and tying the latter to warfighter needs, national strategy, and the four specified mission areas of space support, force enhancement, space control, and force application. The plan further anticipated that "space power" would eventually become as important as air power in future warfare and declared that the Air Force must accordingly orient its thinking and activities toward preparing "for the evolution of space power from combat support to the full spectrum of military capabilities." It also called for the development and aggressive pursuit of a "coherent Air Force role in space."[45] An important step in that direction was taken two years later in October 1990, when AFSC finally relinquished to AFSPC its launch centers, ranges, bases, and the Delta II and Atlas E launch missions, with provision for the remaining Atlas II, Titan II, and Titan

---

[45]Ibid., p. 236.

IV missions to be handed over in due course. Ratifying that transfer of ownership, Secretary of the Air Force Donald Rice stated that "the change in assignment of roles and missions further normalizes space operations and pursues our corporate commitment to integrate space power throughout the full spectrum of Air Force operational capabilities."[46]

SOME IMPLICATIONS FOR TODAY'S PLANNERS

The preceding overview of the Air Force's history of involvement with space, cursory as it has necessarily been, offers some instructive insights for those who are currently concerned with charting the institution's next steps with regard to space. The first impression from this history is that the Air Force in its earliest years was far more interested in space as a domain of organizational turf to be defended than as a prospective new medium within which to conduct combat and combat-support activities. Although the Air Force was slow to embrace space as a mission area warranting significant investment for technology development, it lost no time claiming "exclusive rights" to space in the face of perceived threats of encroachment into that domain by the Army and Navy. When it came to hard resource apportionment, however, the Air Force until well into the 1950s focused almost solely on building a modern inventory of jet bombers and fighters. That was, of course, entirely reasonable at the time, considering that advanced aircraft development was what the newly independent Air Force was all about. Indeed, it had been the successful application of strategic bombardment in both the European and Pacific theaters during World War II that had represented the service's principal claim to separation from the Army to begin with. Nevertheless, it remains a fact of Air Force life that the institution became the nation's custodian of military space activity more by organizational and bureaucratic determination than by any natural selection or mission evolution.

Second, so long as the Air Force leadership was content to argue for—and to position itself to earn—custodial status with respect to the nation's military space effort, it was largely successful in captur-

---

[46]Ibid., p. 240.

ing and retaining the civilian leadership's attention and support, even if it had to fight with the Army and Navy along the way. Whenever the Air Force went beyond its bounded goals of acquiring a credible space launch capability to support the nation's growing military satellite requirements and sought to pursue a more aggressive effort to acquire space force-application capabilities, however, it ran directly against the prevailing national stress on "peaceful uses" of space and gained nothing but the disapprobation—and sometimes outright animosity—of the Eisenhower and Kennedy administrations. That experience, one might add, has continued with all subsequent administrations, with the singular exception of President Reagan's, right up to the present. It suggests that the Air Force has been predestined to failure whenever it has called forcefully for the pursuit of space force-application measures, since neither the civilian policy establishment nor, for that matter, American public opinion or even objective need has yet indicated a serious readiness to countenance crossing the "weapons in space" threshold. It also suggests, more importantly, that charges from various quarters that the Air Force has failed to honor its responsibilities of space stewardship by not plumping hard enough for "space warfare" capabilities have been badly misdirected. Any fault here has lain not, at least in the first instance, with the Air Force but rather with America's elected leaders—including many in Congress. Whether or not the Air Force has evinced adequate determination over the years to pursue such mission applications is a subject over which reasonable people can differ. But it has been well beyond the bureaucratic power of the Air Force leadership, as a practical matter, to do much on its own with respect to bringing such applications to fruition.

Third, and perhaps most notable, as the following chapter will explain in further detail, the Air Force entered the 21st century with a five-decade history of space involvement that not only was bereft of a coherent concept of operations with respect to the military uses of space but also left the institution fundamentally divided over the issue of whether air and space should be treated as two separate and distinct mediums or as a single and seamless continuum. Clearly, those Air Force leaders who worked so hard during the 1970s to find a suitable home for Air Force space activity within a separate command tasked with supporting regional warfighters around the world believed that space was, and deserved to be, approached as an arena distinct from the realm of Air Force aerodynamic operations. Yet General White's "aerospace" formula, first enunciated in 1958, that defined—seemingly by fiat—the vertical dimension as indivisible has persisted in many Air Force circles as the preferred intellectual organizing concept for space. As a result, the Air Force in its day-to-day operations has routinely treated air and space as separate mediums because those mediums have involved fundamentally different technologies and skill sets. Yet in its formal doctrine and its sloganeering in the roles and missions arena, at least until recently, the Air Force has tended to speak of "aerospace" not just as a unitary environment, but as one that naturally belongs to the Air Force and to the Air Force alone. An unfortunate consequence of this ambivalence is that, at the same time as the Air Force has achieved great success in acquiring a preeminent military space capability, it has made scant progress toward developing and promulgating an agreed frame of reference for thinking systematically about the military potential of space.

Chapter Three

AIR AND SPACE VERSUS "AEROSPACE"

From the earliest days of its independence from the Army in 1947 until nearly the end of the next decade, the Air Force paid close attention to space as an arena of interservice feuding over rightful prerogatives when it came to missile and satellite development. However, not only did it do little to begin actually pursuing the requisite missile and satellite technologies for exploiting space until well into the 1950s, it did virtually nothing to develop a coherent set of principles for understanding how space related to its evolving air doctrine.[1] Indeed, during that period, the Air Force did not invest in space as an operating environment in any significant way. It merely asserted jurisdictional claims to the development and ownership of any missiles and military satellites that might happen to operate in or transit it. To all intents and purposes, the Air Force's first decade was doctrine-free with respect to space and its potential contributions to joint warfare.

Then, in 1958, came Air Force chief of staff General Thomas D. White's introduction of the term "aerospace," a new construct that depicted air and space as a seamless continuum stretching from the earth's surface to infinity. More important yet to an understanding of the organizational politics of military space, that term further claimed *both* parts of the continuum as the Air Force's due preserve. Although the term's advent was preceded by no evident conceptual

---

[1]The December 1945 report of the AAF's Scientific Advisory Board (headed by Theodore von Karman), entitled *Toward New Horizons,* placed its greatest weight on the postwar AAF's most immediate concern—developing jet-propelled aircraft. It paid only lip service to missiles and satellites.

deliberations or serious debate within the Air Force, it became the service's new mantra almost overnight and was soon inserted into formal Air Force doctrine.

Not everyone in the Air Force during the ensuing years, however, signed up to the notion of air and space as a unitary operating environment. Not only did the rest of the national security community continue to view air and space as separate mediums, even many among the Air Force's most senior leaders demurred on the proposition that air and space represented an indivisible whole, at least when it came to the everyday practicalities of institutionalizing space as a military mission area. As the previous chapter showed in broad outline, those Air Force leaders—from the highest level on downward—who engineered the establishment of Air Force Space Command well appreciated that space was a separate medium warranting separate mission-area development. Nevertheless, throughout the Air Force's history since 1958, "aerospace" has figured prominently in the service's rhetoric. Moreover, the idea behind it underwent a forceful resurgence during the second half of the 1990s, as the Air Force leadership declared that the service had become an "air and space force" on an evolutionary path toward becoming a "space and air force." That refrain appeared at first glance to recognize air and space as separate mediums. In fact, in keeping with the earlier logic of aerospace, it considered them a seamless continuum comprising the Air Force's rightful milieu—but with the added implication that military space operations, once fully developed and proven, would eventually displace air operations as the service's main activity.

As a result, the Air Force entered the 21st century deeply divided over space and heavily caught up in what one space officer called "a heated and ongoing debate between two schools of thought."[2] One school stressed "aerospace" as a single continuum in the vertical dimension. The other regarded space as an operating medium separate and distinct from the earth's atmosphere. For those espousing the single-continuum idea, that approach was seen as the only way to ensure that the Air Force retained an organizational lock on space.

---

[2]Major M. V. Smith, USAF, "Ten Propositions Regarding Spacepower," M.A. thesis, School of Advanced Airpower Studies, Maxwell AFB, Alabama, June 2001, p. 2.

For those on the other side of the debate, the term "aerospace" was considered a guaranteed recipe for space *not* to get the attention it properly deserved and, hence, an approach that threatened to lose space for the Air Force sooner or later.   ·

THE ROOTS OF THE "AEROSPACE" CONSTRUCT

There continues to be disagreement over the precise origin of the "aerospace" idea. A respected chronicler of Air Force doctrine, Robert Frank Futrell, has ascribed the term's provenance to Woodford Hefflin of the Air University's Research Studies Institute, who issued a document on February 23, 1958 called "Interim Glossary, Aero-Space Terms."[3] Another Air Force writer has countered that it was he who introduced the term, in an Air Force News Service release issued on July 8, 1958.[4] Whatever the term's exact derivation, however, it seems clear that the idea behind it had not been given much serious reflection within the Air Staff before General White formally introduced it into official Air Force rhetoric.

In an important precursor statement that anticipated the term by indicating the direction of Air Force leadership thinking, General White declared in testimony to the House Appropriations Subcommittee in 1957 that "missiles are but one step in the evolution from manned high-performance aircraft to true manned spacecraft; and in the force structure of the future . . . we will have all three systems."[5] Later, on November 29, 1957, the Air Force chief observed at the National Press Club that just as air power enabled land and sea operations, so henceforth "whoever has the capability to control space will likewise possess the capability to exert control of the surface of the earth." Continuing, White said, "I want to stress that there

---

[3] Robert Frank Futrell, *Ideas, Concepts, Doctrine: Basic Thinking in the United States Air Force, 1907–1960*, Vol. 1, Maxwell AFB, Alabama: Air University Press, 1989, p. 553.

[4] Frank W. Jennings, "Doctrinal Conflict over the Word Aerospace," *Airpower Journal*, Fall 1990, p. 52. See also Frank W. Jennings, "Genesis of the Aerospace Concept," *Air Power History*, Spring 2002, pp. 46–55.

[5] Futrell, pp. 545–546.

is no division, per se, between air and space. Air and space are an indivisible field of operations."[6]

Finally, the term "aerospace" itself officially surfaced for the first time during the summer of 1958 when General White announced that Americans were now living in "the aerospace age." Succinctly stating the Air Force's newly emergent position on air and space, he said: "Air and space are not two separate media to be divided by a line and to be readily separated into two distinct categories; they are in truth a single indivisible field of operations. Space is the natural and logical extension of air; space power is merely the cumulative result of the evolutionary growth of air power. . . . Air Force goals have changed in degree only; the basics have been constant—greater speed, longer range, and higher altitude."[7]

That declaration, characterized by Walter Boyne as "intuitive" on White's part, seems in hindsight to have been impromptu in its genesis rather than arrived at in any systematic and considered way.[8] One observer has maintained that the single-medium idea had its origins in a vision of air and space as a unitary continuum constituting the natural province of airmen first enunciated in 1945 by Army Air Force (AAF) chief of staff General Henry H. "Hap" Arnold, who was said to have "formally introduced the aerospace concept."[9] Yet although that observer offers a rich and insightful accounting of the Air Force's early struggle for dominance of space as a mission area, his case for General Arnold's "vision" of aerospace as an Air Force birthright is based entirely on presumption, apparently derived from little more than a report by Arnold to Secretary of War Robert Patterson in November 1945. That report made passing reference to the

---

[6]General Thomas D. White, USAF, "At the Dawn of the Space Age," *The Air Power Historian*, January 1958, pp. 15–19.

[7]General Thomas D. White, USAF, "The Inevitable Climb to Space," *Air University Quarterly Review*, Winter 1958–59, pp. 3–4.

[8]Walter J. Boyne, *Beyond the Wild Blue: A History of the U.S. Air Force, 1947–1997*, New York: St. Martin's Press, 1997, p. 267.

[9]Major Stephen M. Rothstein, USAF, *Dead on Arrival? The Development of the Aerospace Concept, 1944–58*, Maxwell AFB, Alabama: Air University Press, November 2000, p. 11.

possibility of delivering high-velocity projectiles from "true space ships, capable of operating outside the earth's atmosphere."[10]

Indeed, quite to the contrary, it is all but beyond dispute that the Air Force's earliest motivations with regard to space had to do with turf protection rather than with any bona fide interest in space operations concept development. Fears of Army pretensions and a staunch determination to stake out a forceful claim to space-related systems by the AAF were first manifested in a January 1946 memorandum from Colonel T. A. Sims of the AAF's new R&D Division to the vice chief of staff, General Ira Eaker: "Many [Army] Ordnance developments encroach on the AAF field. . . . The [issue] is whether we should continue as is for the time being . . . or whether we should attempt to energize our guided missiles program and take over some of the projects started by Ordnance. . . . Admittedly, we do not know the composition of a guided missile launching force . . . [but] just to indicate progressive thinking and the AAF interest in taking a major part in the lightning warfare of the future. If we do not do this, the Artillery may beat us to the punch."[11]

Similarly, the head of AAF R&D, then–Major General Curtis LeMay, wrote to the AAF's chief of staff, General Carl Spaatz, later that September: "At the outset, it was recognized that Ordnance was entering the [space] field early and aggressively to antedate AAF competition. . . . One very serious reason for not giving ground is the stated opinion of Army Ground Forces that AGF should operate its own guided missiles, close support aircraft, and strategic bombardment aircraft, classing all these as extensions of artillery. It is fairly certain that if development of missiles is turned over to Ordnance, operation will be done by Army Ground Forces, and it will be only a short and logical step from this to operation of support and strategic aircraft by AGF. . . . Our best course seems to be to . . . [seek] assign-

---

[10]Ibid., pp. 11–12. No reference to any such "aerospace" vision can be found in a substantial recent treatment of Arnold's career by Dik Alan Daso, *Hap Arnold and the Evolution of American Air Power*, Washington, D.C.: Smithsonian Institution Press, 2000.

[11]Memorandum from Colonel Sims to General Eaker, January 2, 1946, cited in Edmund Beard, *Developing the ICBM: A Study in Bureaucratic Politics*, New York, Columbia University Press, 1976, p. 33.

ment of all guided missiles."[12] By the same token, when the Navy in December 1947 submitted to the Defense Department's Research and Development Board a claim for sole rights to satellite development, the AAF's deputy chief of staff, General Hoyt Vandenberg, countered with a policy statement declaring that "the USAF, as the service dealing primarily with air weapons—especially strategic—has the logical responsibility for the satellite."[13] It was with these bureaucratic rights-of-ownership concerns uppermost in his mind that General White first introduced the term "aerospace" into the Air Force's lexicon in 1958.

Five months after White first broached the "aerospace" idea in a public statement, the assistant vice chief of staff, Major General Jacob E. Smart, sent a letter to the commander of Air University outlining how that idea should be folded into the Air Force's prevailing doctrine. In that letter, Smart recommended that the new Air Force doctrine include the assertion that "the positioning of aerospace power geographically and/or astronautically may have dominating significance in peace or war."[14] In 1959, the Air Force adopted as its official slogan "U.S. Air Force—Aerospace Power for Peace."[15] By the end of that year, the word *aerospace* had entered formal Air Force doctrine and was used not only as an adjective but as a noun. As defined by the edition of Air Force Manual (AFM) 1-2, *United States Air Force Basic Doctrine*, that was promulgated on December 1, 1959, "aerospace is an operationally indivisible medium consisting of the total expanse beyond the earth's surface. The forces of the Air Force comprise a family of operating systems—air systems, ballistic missiles, and space vehicle systems. These are the fundamental aerospace forces of the nation."[16]

---

[12]Major General Curtis E. LeMay, DCAS (Deputy Chief of the Air Staff), R&D, memorandum to General Carl A. Spaatz, September 20, 1946, cited in Beard, pp. 37–39.

[13]Robert L. Perry, *Origins of the USAF Space Program, 1945–1956*, Vol. 4, History of DCAS 1961, Air Force Systems Command Historical Publications Series 62-24-10, Los Angeles, Space Systems Division, AFSC, 1961, p. 30.

[14]Futrell, p. 553.

[15]Jennings, pp. 46–58.

[16]Futrell, pp. 553–554.

In sum, the bulk of evidence suggests that the "aerospace" idea was advanced by the Air Force leadership almost entirely by fiat, with little serious analysis or prior systematic thought given to it. Not only that, it was pressed into Air Force doctrine in complete indifference to the important physical and operational differences which exist between the two mediums (see the next section). As a testament to the failure of senior Air Force leaders to think very far beyond aerospace as a slogan for advancing the service's programmatic interests, even General Bernard Schriever, the acknowledged father of serious Air Force involvement in space, had trouble articulating a persuasive aerospace concept of operations when pressed by a senator in congressional testimony to say whether he thought that "control of space [was] extremely important to the free world." Schriever replied: "Well, I certainly do, although I would not give you exactly why in tangible terms. . . . A year ago, I thought perhaps the future battles would be space battles instead of air battles, and I still feel that way about it."[17] As space historian David Spires observed, "While the so-called indivisibility of 'aerospace' provided a conceptual approach to space that supported the service's quest for military space missions, it did not contribute effectively to a planning process that required consideration of space as a separate medium."[18]

CONCEPTUAL PROBLEMS WITH THE IDEA OF AEROSPACE

It is revealing of the aerospace construct's origins and early intent that, whereas one looks in vain for a body of writing to develop the case for that perspective beyond its value in helping to justify an Air Force claim to space stewardship, there has been a profusion of thoughtful commentary by Air Force space professionals laying out variations on the argument for treating space as a separate medium and mission area. This commentary starts from the premise that the idea of aerospace is not only logically but empirically flawed. As one space weapons officer has compellingly noted, although the aerospace formula has long insisted that there is no clear line of demarcation between air and space, that formula ignores the 60-mile-

---

[17]"The USAF Reports to Congress," *Air University Quarterly Review,* Spring 1958, pp. 50–51.

[18]David N. Spires, *Beyond Horizons: A Half-Century of Air Force Space Leadership,* Washington, D.C.: U.S. Government Printing Office, 1997, p. 82.

high band separating the highest altitude at which air-breathing aircraft can sustain flight and the lowest at which satellites can remain on orbit—and within which *no* systems can sustain other than ballistic flight. This transverse region begins at around 28 miles above the earth's surface, the upper limit of air-breathing engines, and ends at around 93 miles' altitude, the lowest sustainable perigee of an orbiting satellite. It is, in effect, an aerospace no-man's land. Vehicular operations within it are not practical with current and foreseeable technologies, since the energy expenditures required for maneuvering are prohibitively costly due to the laws of physics. The wings on so-called "aerospace" vehicles like the space shuttle and the abortive X-33 (canceled by NASA in March 2001) are only recovery systems analogous to parachutes.[19] By this account, the rule of thumb that "if it's on orbit, it's in space" flatly belies the "aerospace" refrain that air and space are indivisible.

There are also some fundamental differences between air and space vehicles with respect to their freedom of operation.[20] To begin with, aircraft are fully maneuverable. Spacecraft, in contrast, operate at higher altitudes and speeds than do aircraft, and they cannot maneuver except through the costly expenditure of extremely limited onboard fuel provided for occasional orbital repositioning. Similarly, aircraft can mass repeatedly by maneuvering as appropriate within an area of operations. Spacecraft, in contrast, can mass for short periods of time with great effort and expenditure of fuel, but they will disperse almost immediately, and a repeat massing will be unlikely. In addition, air operations can be performed on demand. Spacecraft operations, in contrast, occur as scheduled or when on-orbit assets are available. Finally, the would-be inseparability of air and space is belied by important contrasts in the way international law and political conventions apply to the two. On the first count, aircraft do not enjoy unrestricted overflight rights over sovereign territory, especially over denied areas, whereas spacecraft do. On the second count, aircraft carrying bombs (and even ballistic missile warheads that traverse space en route to their targets) are not considered "space

---

[19]Smith, "Ten Propositions Regarding Spacepower," pp. 34–35.

[20]For amplification of these points, see Lieutenant Colonel Michael R. Mantz, *The New Sword: A Theory of Space Combat Power*, Maxwell AFB, Alabama: Air University Press, May 1995, pp. 79–80.

weaponization," whereas placing offensive space-to-ground muni-tions on orbit would most definitely be so considered.[21]

These and other differences one might list between air and space vehicles are far from inconsequential. On the contrary, they attest that air and space are separate mediums not only with respect to the laws of physics, but also in an important operational and tactical sense with regard to systems employment opportunities and con-straints. For example, air power *can* be global in its reach and ability to impose effects on an opponent, whereas space power, by its very nature, can *only* be global.[22] Because orbiting assets in space are widely separated, however, they cannot offer as much concentrated presence as can air power. On the upside, satellites—especially those in geosynchronous orbit—can be persistent in a way that aircraft cannot. (Even satellites in low earth orbit can offer discontinuous persistence.) The downside of this is that satellite movements are completely predictable and lack the freedom of maneuver enjoyed by aircraft.

Such contrasts between air and space as operating mediums point up the limits of the aerospace construct as a helpful framework for nurturing the sort of unrestricted theory of space power that was fi-nally developed for air power after the latter was fully freed from the inhibiting bonds of land-warfare concepts of operations. An overly restrictive conception throughout much of the cold war cast air power in terms of either intercontinental nuclear attack or theater and battlefield support to land operations. It barely recognized the broad spectrum of conventional air employment options in between, such as those that were finally developed during the 1980s and show-cased for the first time during the 1991 Gulf War—to say nothing of

---

[21]Smith, "Ten Propositions Regarding Spacepower," p. 39.

[22]This contrast in relative breadth of regard offered by the two mediums has been manifest in recent practice in one interesting respect: The one Air Force Space Opera-tions Center (SOC) attached to 14th Air Force at Vandenberg AFB, Calif., maintains a global perspective by its very nature, whereas the numerous Air Operations Centers (AOCs) attached to U.S. regional joint-force headquarters around the world maintain only theater-wide perspectives. This important difference between the two was masked in an artificial and unconstructive way, however, by an exercise in verbal sleight of hand several years ago by which the very different terms "Air Operations Center" and "Space Operations Center" were superseded by "Aerospace Operations Center." (The term now in use is "Air and Space Operations Center.")

the potential for producing strategic outcomes independently of ground actions.[23] By the same token, the hobbled appreciation of what space might offer joint force commanders in principle—which has been occasioned by viewing space through the lens of air power theory—has arguably hindered our pursuit of the potential promise of space for achieving desired objectives independently of air or other terrestrial force applications.

OPPORTUNITY COSTS OF THE AEROSPACE EMPHASIS

As noted at the outset of this chapter, the aerospace idea was first put forward by the Air Force leadership during the late 1950s in an attempt to define an expanded operating arena for future Air Force assets. Yet that leadership did not offer, nor did it even attempt to offer, a convincing basis for explaining and justifying to a skeptical Eisenhower administration what the Air Force's role in space should be and how it should be fulfilled. It is tellingly indicative of the parochial and organizationally self-serving roots of the term aerospace that only the Air Force routinely employs it. Neither any of the other services nor the Office of the Secretary of Defense has ever endorsed the idea, and the term does not resonate in the joint arena. For example, it does not appear in the Defense Department's 1999 directive entitled *Space Policy.* Nor does it figure in any way in the unified U.S. Space Command's expansive *Long-Range Plan* which was promulgated in March 1998. It cannot be found anywhere in the Space Commission's report to Congress issued in January 2001. Consistent with these examples, all other U.S. national security documents similarly treat space as both a medium and a mission area separate and distinct from air. As early as 1958, concurrent with the initial surfacing of General White's idea of a unitary aerospace continuum, the National Security Council formally demurred, proclaiming on June 20, 1958 that the realm above the earth's surface was "divided into two regions: 'air space' and 'outer space.'"[24] That perspective has

---

[23]For more on this topic, see Benjamin S. Lambeth, *The Transformation of American Air Power*, Ithaca, N.Y.: Cornell University Press, 2000, especially pp. 1–11 and 297–321.

[24]NSC 5814, *U.S. Policy on Outer Space*, June 20, 1958, quoted in Rothstein, p. 2. That same NSC document for the first time also declared as national policy that although the U.S. government would take all appropriate measures in space to ensure the

unwaveringly stood as declared U.S. policy throughout the four decades since.[25]

To many observers outside the Air Force, the aerospace construct tends to be understood primarily as a flawed but handy device for enabling that service to justify a roles and missions claim to space as well as to air.[26] To skeptics within the Air Force, it is widely viewed as a doctrinal liability—which has given the service a convenient, if not wholly convincing, basis for articulating that claim, albeit at the cost of limiting the development of a more robust space power theory unburdened by the baggage of familiar air power thinking. On the latter count, a midcareer Air Force space officer wrote as far back as 1985 that the very term "aerospace doctrine . . . inappropriately links our air and space doctrines." In truth, he insisted, space systems have characteristics fundamentally different from those of air-breathing systems, "which cause differences in the principles of war as they apply to possible conflicts in space."[27] He went on to suggest that "the environmental principles of aerospace war do not uniformly apply to space because the air and space environments are different." Given the distinctive characteristics of orbital operations, he declared, there is no doctrinal foundation for the term aerospace.

---

nation's security, it was the government's intent that space "be used only for peaceful purposes."

[25] It bears noting, however, that the term had gained enough popular currency by 1991 that it was defined in Webster's as "the earth's atmosphere together with cosmic space beyond." (*The New Lexicon Webster's Dictionary of the English Language*, New York: Lexicon Publications, Inc., 1991, p. 13.)

[26] Soon after the Air Force introduced the term aerospace, Major General Dwight Beach of the Army's Office of the Deputy Chief of Staff for Military Operations was asked by Congressman John McCormick during testimony before the House Committee on Science and Astronautics what he thought of the term and which service he believed should have overall responsibility for military space activity. The Army general replied disdainfully: "Well, I never heard of that term before. I always heard of 'armospace.'" . . . Congressman McCormick, I don't believe any one service should have overall responsibility. It should be a national effort. . . . The Army has specific requirements in space, and our position is that no single military department should be assigned sole responsibility for military space operations." (House of Representatives, *Missile Development and Space Sciences: Hearings Before the Committee on Science and Astronautics*, 86th Congress, 1st Session, February–March 1959, pp. 76–77.)

[27] Lieutenant Colonel Charles D. Friedenstein, USAF, "The Uniqueness of Space Doctrine," *Air University Review*, November–December 1985, p. 13.

He further charged that existing space doctrine was "highly constrained by . . . the misapplication of air principles to space."[28]

As for outsider perspectives, Colin Gray more recently observed in a similar vein that "aerospace is an unfortunate term because it denies the laws of physics and implies an operational continuum which technology and its dependent tactics thus far flatly deny. . . . A concept such as aerospace that effects a linguistic fusion of physically and operationally distinctive elements needs to be treated with caution. . . . Space is as geophysically, and hence technologically, tactically, and operationally distinctive from the air as it is from the land and the sea."[29] Offering a concrete example of how the Air Force's use of aerospace as a concept of force employment has tended to inhibit the fuller development of a pure theory of space power, two critics recently noted how the Air Force from the very beginning simply substituted the word "aerospace" for "air" in its doctrine manuals and thereby "inappropriately ascribed such [well-known attributes of air power] as speed, range, and flexibility to space forces," when, in fact, the three main distinguishing features of space forces should more properly be thought of as "emplacement, pervasiveness, and timeliness."[30]

Of arguably even greater consequence than impeding the growth of a more forward-looking theory of space power, the aerospace construct has put the Air Force in the discomfiting predicament of having to make trade-offs between competing air and space systems in its resource allocations. Given its limited funds for R&D and procurement, these choices have increasingly forced it to sell *both* mediums and mission needs short. The latter problem can be traced to the early 1970s or thereabouts, when the Air Force first began acquiring a costly array of spaceborne assets aimed at serving the needs of not only nuclear deterrence by providing strategic

---

[28]Ibid., p. 21.

[29]Colin S. Gray, *Explorations in Strategy*, Westport, Connecticut: Praeger Publishers, 1996, pp. 64–65.

[30]Lieutenant Colonel Peter Hays, USAF, and Karl Mueller, "Going Boldly—Where? Aerospace Integration, the Space Commission, and the Air Force's Vision for Space," *Aerospace Power Journal*, Spring 2001, p. 37. The latter characteristics were first proposed by Colonel Kenneth A. Myers and Lieutenant Colonel John G. Tockston, USAF, in "Real Tenets of Military Space Doctrine," *Airpower Journal*, Winter 1988, p. 59.

intelligence, enemy missile launch warning, and attack characterization, but also senior warfighters by better enabling the application of conventional firepower in joint warfare. As long as the Air Force had so little invested in the space portion of aerospace, it could easily indulge itself with a vision that proclaimed both air and space as its rightful domain.[31] Once it began buying into space-based equities in a serious way, however, it quickly learned that a major downside of staking out a mission area that included both air *and* space was that it now had to pay for both its air *and* space programs out of its largely fixed share of annual defense total obligational authority (TOA).

In brief, from a resource-apportionment perspective, the net result of insisting on aerospace as a single medium belonging primarily to the Air Force has been to saddle the service with the burden of funding what are, in fact, *two* mission areas with a share of TOA intended only for one—at least when it comes to needed hardware and investment in infrastructure and personnel. As a serving space officer has well described the Air Force's conundrum in this respect, "today's zero-sum budget environment does not provide enough money for organizations to support both their core competencies and other essential, though ancillary, functions. . . . Indeed, in many cases, the majority of users of space services resides outside the organization paying the bills. . . . Under today's configuration, the Air Force is expected to equally prioritize funding opportunities for its own direct war-fighting capabilities as well as its own and its customers' [space] support needs. These space services represent non-core, non-war-fighting services that carry some of our nation's largest must-pay bills."[32] Former commander in chief of U.S. Space Command (CINCSPACE) General Charles Horner has been even more outspoken on this point since his retirement from the Air Force in 1994. As he has complained time and again, "as long as each

---

[31]That was a time, one may recall, when the term aerospace was not taken seriously in most Air Force circles, since the "space" portion of it remained so underdeveloped in any operationally significant way. People merely giggled when ground power carts to start aircraft jet engines were grandiosely referred to as "Aerospace Ground Equipment."

[32]Lieutenant Colonel Cynthia A. S. McKinley, "The Guardians of Space: Organizing America's Space Assets for the Twenty-First Century," *Aerospace Power Journal*, Spring 2000, pp. 40–41.

service is funded at an artificial rate almost equal to one-third of the defense budget, the Air Force will be hard-pressed to fill its core air responsibilities while expanding its role in space. . . . At some point, the nation must ask itself whether our air and space capabilities should remain artificially limited with the present budgeting methodology, when both functions are becoming of greater importance to our defense strategy."[33]

A RESURGENT AIR FORCE FIXATION ON AEROSPACE

For a time during the 1980s and early 1990s, it appeared that the differentiation between the two mediums of air and space had come to be at least tacitly accepted by the fielded Air Force at senior leadership levels. Although aerospace rhetoric continued to find its way into Air Force vision and policy statements, Air Force Space Command had been activated and had begun to function as a space operations entity parallel to, but apart from, the Air Force's other air-related major commands. To all intents and purposes, at least when it came to the day-to-day organization and management of the Air Force's assets, the two mediums of air and space were each considered to be sui generis. The latter was viewed as supporting and enhancing the former, yet both were treated as operating arenas in and of themselves rather than part of a seamless aerospace continuum.

Then, at a high-level Corona meeting of the Air Force's top leadership in 1996, the chief of staff, General Ronald R. Fogleman, led a novel initiative to characterize the Air Force as a service transitioning from an "air force" to an "air and space force" on an evolutionary path toward becoming a "space and air force."[34] In that bold initiative, space was portrayed not only as the Air Force's rightful domain and destiny, but also as an arena that would eventually displace air as the service's primary realm of operations. In effect, Corona 1996 promised that air operations would eventually be supplanted by space functions and that the service's space

---

[33]General Charles A. Horner, USAF (Ret.), "Air Power: Growing Beyond Desert Storm," *Aviation Week and Space Technology*, April 16, 1997, p. 73.

[34]General Ronald R. Fogleman and the Honorable Sheila E. Widnall, *Global Engagement: A Vision for the 21st Century Air Force*, Washington, D.C.: Department of the Air Force, November 1996, p. 8.

professionals would, in the fullness of time, inherit the Air Force and its most senior leadership positions. It most definitely regarded air and space as a seamless continuum in all but name.

The Corona 1996 line, however, was not universally accepted in senior Air Force circles. One Air Staff three-star general frankly wondered whether the statement about transitioning from "air and space" to "space and air" was sincerely motivated or merely represented a ploy aimed at staking a renewed claim to Air Force rights of military space ownership while also striving to co-opt any would-be space separatists who might otherwise become inclined at some point to abandon the Air Force and press for the establishment of an independent U.S. space force. He added that the statement was most definitely the product of a conscious effort to keep space within the Air Force family at all costs. He further observed that in so doing, it both overpromised and embraced the wrong vision.[35] Other skeptics questioned the extent to which the service was determined to back its rhetorical assurances with the appropriate resource allocations, with one senior space general noting wryly that however much the idea of transitioning to a bona fide "air and space force" may have been accepted by the Air Force leadership in principle, genuine commitment to it had yet to attain what he called "brush-fire proportions."[36]

Indeed, a concern voiced in at least some Air Force quarters was that if the Corona 1996 formula was pursued to its natural conclusion, the Air Force could end up having to mortgage its *air* force-projection responsibilities in order to pay for its declared commitment to developing space as an expanded mission area. Nevertheless, Air Force space professionals seemed understandably inclined to take the promise at face value. The vice chief of staff and most senior serving Air Force space officer at the time, General Thomas S. Moorman, Jr., characterized Corona 1996 as an "incredibly significant" watershed, representing not merely the thinking of "a subset of folks doing a focused study, but rather the consensus of the

---

[35]Interview by the author, Headquarters U.S. Air Force, Washington, D.C., April 30, 1998.

[36]Interview by the author, Headquarters Air Force Space Command, Peterson AFB, Colorado, June 18, 1998.

Air Force leadership."[37] An unfortunate by-product of that reaction was a fear among some Air Force leaders that the service's space professionals may have been set up for what could prove to be unrealistic expectations. As long as the present arrangement for funding Air Force air and space programs remained unaltered, it would become ever harder as a practical matter to provide for the legitimate resource needs of both.

Partly as an outgrowth of that concern, Fogleman's successor as Air Force chief, General Michael E. Ryan, concluded that the Corona 1996 formula was more divisive than unifying for the service's air and space communities. Attempting to apply a corrective, he reaffirmed in late 1997 that the Air Force's destiny was indeed as a "space and air force." Yet he endorsed more resoundingly than ever the single-medium/single-mission outlook in stressing that "air and space are a continuum—forever . . . [and that] requires a clear realization that there is no delineation, break, or boundary in the third dimension. There is space in air and air in space; it's just that the molecules further out are a long way apart. . . . We can have no fire-support coordination line in the vertical dimension."[38]

Early the following year, General Ryan moved to reconsider the wisdom and appropriateness of continuing to use the "air and space" formula put forward at Corona 1996. In a memorandum to the Air Force's top generals, he reported that "at Corona South '98, the senior Air Force leadership committed to the integration of air and space power into an aerospace force." He then directed the creation of an Aerospace Integration Task Force (AITF) composed of the Air Force's "best 'aerospace' thinkers" to work toward building "a single, consolidated plan that will provide continued integration of air and space power and orderly migration to future capabilities which best exploit the seamless aerospace dimension."[39]

The AITF eventually concluded that the Air Force should more assertively play up the "aerospace" theme to underscore the pro-

---

[37]Letter to the author from General Thomas S. Moorman, Jr., USAF, July 8, 1997.

[38]General Michael E. Ryan, USAF, speech to the Air Force Association national symposium, Los Angeles, November 14, 1997.

[39]General Michael E. Ryan, USAF, memorandum on Aerospace Integration Plan Task Force, April 13, 1998, quoted in Rothstein, pp. 2–3.

claimed indivisibility of the two mediums. In short order, the Air Force vision statement released in June 2000 duly spotlighted that theme and called for more fully melding the Air Force's air and space equipment, capabilities, and personnel toward the common goal of improving the effectiveness of "aerospace power" in joint warfare.[40] In a similar vein, a white paper issued by the Air Force a month earlier posited an Air Force view of the "flight domains of air and space as a seamless operational medium." It added: "The environmental differences between air and space do not separate the employment of aerospace power within them. . . . [Our] vision includes a mix of air and space capabilities interacting for maximum effect throughout the aerospace continuum."[41] As but one of many symbolic totems attesting to that change, the name of the Air University's professional quarterly, *Airpower Journal*, was summarily changed to *Aerospace Power Journal* in late 1999.[42]

In a subsequent effort to clarify the reasons for the change, former CINCSPACE General Howell M. Estes III described the Air Force of the late 1990s as standing "at a crossroads much like the one encountered earlier this century between land forces and air power advocates. The result of the Army's inability to make the necessary culture change was decades of delay, higher costs and casualties, and finally a separate service."[43] The implication was that the Air Force would run a comparable risk of losing space to another organizational entity if it failed to embrace space as an inherent part of its own corporate charter. How the Air Force might increase overall funding for

---

[40]General Michael E. Ryan and the Honorable F. Whitten Peters, *Global Vigilance, Reach and Power: America's Air Force Vision 2020*, Washington, D.C.: Department of the Air Force, June 2000.

[41]General Michael E. Ryan and the Honorable F. Whitten Peters, *The Aerospace Force: Defending America in the 21st Century*, Washington, D.C.: Department of the Air Force, May 2000.

[42]Action officers on the Air Staff also became single-minded terminology policemen in their blanket insistence on indiscriminately and uniformly substituting the word "aerospace" for "air" whenever the latter was invoked, even if the intended usage was only in reference to "air" power more narrowly construed. One such case in which the author was involved was *Aerospace Operations in Urban Environments: Exploring New Concepts* by Alan Vick et al., RAND MR-1187-AF, 2000. The title originally submitted was *Air Operations in Urban Environments*.

[43]General Howell M. Estes III, USAF (Ret.), "The Aerospace Force of Today and Tomorrow," in Hays et al., eds., *Spacepower for a New Millennium*, p. 165.

new space systems within its own limited budget, however, was left unexplained. Estes suggested that a proper funding level for military space would give it 20 percent of the Air Force's TOA from FY03 to FY15. Yet he did not indicate what other Air Force programs should be cut in order to free up that additional funding, let alone broach the delicate but increasingly unavoidable question of how to get the other services to help underwrite those Air Force–provided space support and force-enhancement functions of which they were and remain the principal beneficiaries.

On a related but separate issue, Estes saw as "problematic" the use of the "air and space" and "space and air" formulations that had been endorsed at Corona 1996, suggesting that they had led to "community entrenchment and fruitless debates about when the transitions might occur," to say nothing of causing Air Force airmen "to lose sight of our true vision, namely, that airmen must control the *vertical dimension*" [emphasis in the original]. Estes added that those on the "space and air" side were perceived by their air-oriented brethren as space zealots, whereas those on the "air and space" side were seen by Air Force space professionals as back-pedalers. The undesirable result, he said, was a perpetuation of two separate and segregated Air Force communities, those of air and space, "rather than encouraging cooperation between, and integration of, the two." He insisted that the Air Force needed to think in terms of "aerospace solutions . . . rather than air or space solutions."[44] In explaining the intent and results of General Ryan's AITF, he added that the Air Force had "resolved to get back on course by dropping the original *Global Engagement* terminology in favor of the single term aerospace" and to encourage airmen to think in terms of exploiting the vertical dimension, or, as he characterized it using a noun, "the aerospace."

---

[44]Ibid., p. 167. In a telling reflection of the Air Force's conceptual drift with respect to the core issue of whether air and space should be treated as a single medium and mission area or as two separate and distinct operating mediums and mission areas, General Estes only two years earlier, while still on active duty as CINCSPACE, had routinely referred to space as "the fourth medium of military operations" whose time for full and deserved mission development had finally come. Similarly, U.S. Space Command's *Vision for 2020* expressly portrayed space as a separate medium in its declaration that "the goal is to achieve the same level of joint operations between space and other mediums of warfare as land, sea, and air currently enjoy today." See General Howell M. Estes III, USAF, "Posture Statement for Senate Armed Services Committee Hearings," Washington, D.C., March 11–12, 1997.

Ultimately, Estes suggested, Air Combat Command might become Space Combat Command, or else the two would merge to become the Aerospace Combat Command, all with a view toward controlling "the aerospace" and transitioning the Air Force into "the United States Aerospace Force."[45] All of this, observed defense analyst Barry Watts, made it clear that the then-incumbent Air Force leadership had "rejected the possibility of evolutionary progress toward distinct, much less separate, space and air forces."[46]

THE CALL FOR AEROSPACE INTEGRATION

In keeping with this shift in emphasis, "aerospace integration" be-came the new Air Force rallying cry during General Ryan's tenure as chief. The focus was on the seamless melding of the service's atmo-spheric and orbital assets in support of a more effective strategy for pursuing terrestrial goals. As the Air Staff's director of strategic plan-ning, Major General John Barry, later explained, that idea constituted "one of the latest steps" in the process of changing "the way we think about air and space power." To those who maintained that "operations in the air and space differ so fundamentally as to require separate organizations," Barry countered that this argument was "unsound" because it was "based on physics, not military art" and ignored the fact that "military operations in the aerospace contin-uum require a mix of air and space systems."[47] Although Barry admitted that "all military communities [now] use space on a daily basis," he nevertheless took a narrow service perspective rather than an overarching national view of space as an enabling medium. In so doing, he cut almost directly against the grain of the broader notion of "full force integration" that had been so carefully laid out two years earlier in the unified U.S. Space Command's *Long-Range Plan,*

---

[45]Estes, "The Aerospace Force of Today and Tomorrow," p. 174.

[46]Barry D. Watts, *The Military Use of Space: A Diagnostic Assessment,* Washington, D.C.: Center for Strategic and Budgetary Assessments, February 2001, p. 47. Watts was subsequently appointed director of the Office of Program Analysis and Evaluation in the Department of Defense.

[47]Major General John L. Barry and Colonel Daniel L. Herriges, USAF, "Aerospace In-tegration, Not Separation," *Aerospace Power Journal,* Summer 2000, p. 42.

defined as "integrating space forces and space-derived information with their counterparts on land, sea and air."[48]

An Air Force space officer astutely divined the underlying dynamic at work here in commenting that while the Air Force's leaders at Corona 1996 "originally viewed integration as a method by which to guarantee continued Air Force stewardship of space, within months of the meeting, integration was being interpreted as the *necessary and sufficient* condition by which the Air Force could seize the opportunity to call itself an aerospace force."[49] As if to bear that out, General Barry acknowledged that the heavy multiservice dependence on space was an argument used by some in favor of concentrating "all space assets in a dedicated organization." He also conceded that the notion of "aerospace integration" was "opposed by . . . people [who] argue that operations in the air and in space differ so fundamentally as to require separate organizations." He concluded, however, by taking exception to "those who would split air and space today," thereby tacitly confirming that a barely hidden consideration behind this line of reasoning was an underlying Air Force fear that military space might end up in a separate service.[50] As another space-literate skeptic who had given much thought to the issue observed several years earlier of the Air Staff's resurrection of aerospace rhetoric in 1997, "to justify exploitation of the aerospace environment as a unified whole, AFM 1-1 points to the fact that no absolute boundary exists between air and space. . . . But the distinction between military realms is based on the nature of the environment— not on the boundaries between them. The flawed logic of AFM 1-1 probably results from creating evidence to support a decision already made—specifically, consumption of space roles and missions by the Air Force."[51]

---

[48]*Long-Range Plan: Implementing USSPACECOM Vision for 2020,* Peterson AFB, Colorado: U.S. Space Command, March 1998, p. 73.

[49]McKinley, "The Guardians of Space: Organizing America's Space Assets for the Twenty-First Century," p. 39, emphasis added.

[50]Barry and Herriges, "Aerospace Integration, Not Separation," pp. 45, 47.

[51]The author added: "Unsurprisingly, an initial draft of AFDD 1, which clearly separated air and space without ever using the term aerospace, was disapproved. But the term dominates the latest draft version of AFDD 1 (14 May 1996), which is now on the verge of acceptance." (Major Bruce M. DeBlois, "Ascendent Realms: Characteristics of Air Power and Space Power," in Colonel Philip S. Meilinger, ed., *The Paths of Heaven:*

To be sure, one could hardly fault the Air Force's commitment to integrating the contributions of its air and space assets more closely within the service's overall operating repertoire. As then–vice chief of staff General Moorman summarized the direction of the Air Force in 1996, "an integrated air and space program that combines total battlespace awareness and knowledge with rapid and deployable communications to get information to the decisionmaker or shooter, fully integrated with highly capable, survivable aircraft and a fleet of unmanned aerial vehicles, both with precision munitions, is the wave of the future."[52] That was, both then and now, an entirely appropriate performance vision for tomorrow's U.S. Air Force as far as it went, and one could only welcome it as a statement of general principle.

Indeed, apart from the collapse of the Soviet Union in 1991, the unprecedented focus since Desert Storm on bringing U.S. air and space capabilities more closely together was arguably the pivotal development that made American military power preeminent in the world today. It played an important part in accounting for the substantially reduced sensor-to-shooter data cycle time which was recently displayed during the most intense portions of air and land force employment in phase one of Operation Enduring Freedom in Afghanistan. Thanks to this new focus, space has now been increasingly integrated into joint-force training and exercise schedules, Air Force Space Command now maintains a presence in support of every regional combatant commander worldwide, and a permanent space support cadre has been provided for every Joint Force Air Component Commander (JFACC). These are but three of the many salutary steps toward the closer integration of air and space that have been implemented by the Air Force since Operation Desert Storm.

That said, however, since the potential offerings of space promise to redound to the benefit not only of Air Force air power but of *all* force elements in *all* services, focusing solely on *air* and space integration

---

The Evolution of Air Power Theory, Maxwell AFB, Alabama: Air University Press, 1997, pp. 554–555.)

[52]General Thomas S. Moorman, Jr., USAF, "The Challenge of Space Beyond 2000," in Alan Stephens, ed., *New Era Security: The RAAF in the Next 25 Years*, proceedings of a conference held by the RAAF, Air Power Studies Center, RAAF Fairbairn, Canberra, Australia, June 1996, p. 173.

(or, in the Air Force's more recent preferred variant, "aerospace" integration) has come to be an overly restrictive paradigm for the sort of evolutionary change that is really called for. Now that air and space integration within the Air Force at the operator level is producing tangible results, the real question should be how best to integrate the Air Force's space offerings with *all* force employment and operational support functions across service lines. Yet as matters now stand, the Air Force has apparently devoted relatively little attention to its obligation, as the nation's military space custodian, to see to the closer integration of its space assets with the future needs of land and maritime as well as air operations. Moreover, rather than recognizing that air and space are, in fact, separate and distinct mediums when it comes to technology application, mission employment, and—most important—funding needs, formal Air Force doctrine on space until recently continued to insist that "the aerospace medium can be most fully exploited when *considered as a whole.*" It added that "although there are physical differences between the atmosphere and space, there is no absolute boundary between them. The same basic military activities can be conducted in each, albeit with different platforms and methods. Therefore, space operations are an integral part of aerospace power."[53]

In effect, the Air Force's reversion to the "aerospace" formula as its organizing theme for air and space beginning in late 1997 turned the clock back to the 1950s by applying a bureaucratically satisfying approach to a serious conceptual and resource apportionment challenge that has unfortunately remained unresponsive to such easy rhetorical solutions. In an apt coda to the story of an Air Force long divided over how to understand and embrace space, a former deputy chief of staff for operations at Air Force Space Command noted at the end of 1997 that the service's leadership had "simply not come to grips with whether to treat space as a continuum of air power or a separate domain." He added darkly (and also arguably both correctly and presciently): "The ultimate resolution [of this question] will likely determine whether space remains a part of the USAF or is ultimately

---

[53]AFDD 2-2, *Space Operations*, Maxwell AFB, Alabama: Air Force Doctrine Center, 1998, p. 1. Air Force chief of staff General John Jumper approved an updated and revised version of AFDD 2-2 on November 27, 2001.

organized as the fifth service within the [Department of Defense]."[54] Chapter Four considers in broad outline how the Space Commission ultimately elected in January 2001 to try to effect that resolution and what reactions its wide-ranging recommendations prompted within both the Department of Defense and the Air Force.

---

[54]Major General William E. Jones, USAF (Ret.), former deputy chief of staff for operations, Air Force Space Command, white paper on the creation of an air and space force within the USAF prepared at the request of Major General David McIlvoy, AF/XPX, December 22, 1997, p. 2.

Chapter Four

THE SPACE COMMISSION AND ITS IMPACT

As noted at the outset of this study, the congressionally mandated Space Commission was expressly established to deal with the national military space conundrum addressed in the preceding chapters. Chaired by Donald H. Rumsfeld, who had previously served as Secretary of Defense in the Ford Administration and who subsequently, just prior to the release of the commission's report, was again appointed Secretary of Defense by incoming President George W. Bush, the commission's membership consisted of uniformly qualified participants. Its 13 members included, among others, two former commanders in chief of U.S. Space Command, retired Air Force Generals Howell M. Estes III and Charles A. Horner; a former commander of Air Force Space Command and later Air Force vice chief of staff, General Thomas S. Moorman, Jr.; former Air Force chief of staff General Ronald R. Fogleman; former vice chairman of the Joint Chiefs of Staff Admiral David E. Jeremiah; former Assistant Secretary of Defense for Command, Control, Communications, and Intelligence Duane P. Andrews; and former presidential science adviser William R. Graham.

Although the commission was given a fairly broad charter, which included consideration of desired national goals in space, it elected in the end—no doubt recognizing that politics is the art of the possible—not to dwell on the question of *where* the nation should be headed with respect to the military exploitation of space, but rather on the more practical question of how the defense establishment should be organized and managed toward that end. Some analysts would find fault with that approach, arguing that U.S. planners should first have a clear notion of *what* needs to be done before proceeding to engage the second-order question of *how* we should go about doing it.[1] Yet there is an equally cogent case to be made for rectifying the most pressing organizational issues first, before grappling with the more controversial subject of where and how far the United States should move into the still largely undeveloped areas of space control and space force application. That argument would cite not only the organizational deficiencies that largely occasioned the Space Commission's creation in the first place, but also, as defense analyst Michael Evans has noted, the well-known propositions that "advances in military technology cannot be applied successfully without corresponding organizational innovation and flexibility" and that "it is through organizational responsiveness that technology is translated into superior strategic performance."[2] In the spirit of the latter propositions, the Space Commission was specifically asked by Congress to consider and offer recommendations on three alternatives to existing organizational arrangements for military space: namely, a separate and independent Space Force, a Space Corps within the Air Force, and a new Assistant Secretary of Defense and Major Force Program (MFP) for space. Although the commissioners brought different points of view to their tasking, they strove hard for consensus, and all of their conclusions and recommendations were unanimous.

---

[1]On this point, two commentators recently stressed "the importance of focusing on the first-order issue of developing a robust and comprehensive vision for United States space power rather than becoming mired in premature debates over the second-order issue of how to organize the management of national security space. . . . Any road will get you there when you don't know where you're going; a more effective and better funded organization will only get you lost faster in these situations." (Lieutenant Colonel Peter Hays, USAF, and Karl Mueller, "Going Boldly—Where? Aerospace Integration, the Space Commission, and the Air Force's Vision for Space, *Aerospace Power Journal*, Spring 2001, pp. 45–46.)

[2]Michael Evans, "Fabrizio's Choice: Organizational Change and the Revolution in Military Affairs Debate," *National Security Studies Quarterly*, Winter 2001, p. 3. Harvard political scientist Samuel Huntington likewise pointed out nearly two generations earlier how getting an armed service's organizational structure set correctly is an important precondition for that service's operational effectiveness, since that structure, whatever form it might take, is closely tied to a distinctive strategic concept and raison d'être. Huntington went on to note that "if a military service does not possess such a concept, it wallows amid a variety of conflicting and confusing goals, and ultimately suffers both physical and moral degeneration." (Samuel P. Huntington, "National Policy and the Transoceanic Navy," *Proceedings*, U.S. Naval Institute, May 1954, p. 483.)

WHAT THE COMMISSIONERS FOUND OVERALL

In by far its most overarching judgment, the commission flatly concluded that the Department of Defense was "not yet on a course to develop the space cadre the nation needs."[3] Because most of the nation's military space funding and space equities reside in the Air Force and because the commission was established in the first place out of congressional concern over the adequacy of the Air Force's stewardship of space, that reference to the Department of Defense was in fact a barely veiled reference to the Air Force. Although the report did not expressly criticize the Air Force, it did state candidly: "Few witnesses . . . expressed confidence that the current Air Force organization is suited to the conduct of [the nation's new space missions]. Nor was there confidence that the Air Force will fully address the requirement to provide space capabilities to the other services. Many believe the Air Force treats space solely as a supporting capability that enhances the primary mission of the Air Force to conduct offensive and defensive air operations. Despite official doctrine that calls for the integration of space and air capabilities, the Air Force does not treat the two equally." As if to show their hand further, the commissioners rejected the Air Force's long-standing contention that air and space represented a single and seamless "aerospace" continuum and observed that space was not just a "place" but also "a medium, much the same as air, land, or sea."[4]

The report offered both an assessment of the nation's institutional deficiencies with respect to military space and some recommendations to ameliorate the practical impact of those shortcomings. In the assessment portion of the report, the commissioners spotlighted three interconnected issue areas: cadre-building, funding, and organization. As for building, growing, and sustaining a cadre of truly space-competent professionals, it noted pointedly that unlike the combat aviation and submarine career fields, whose leaders have spent upward of 90 percent of their service careers in those fields, fewer than 20 percent of the general officers in key space positions

---

[3] *Report of the Commission to Assess United States National Security Space Management and Organization*, Washington, D.C., January 11, 2001, hereinafter referred to as *Space Commission Report*, p. 57.

[4] Ibid., p. 13.

have space career backgrounds. Most of the others have typically spent less than three years in space or space-related assignments. As a result, the report observed, today's most senior Air Force space leaders spend most of their time learning about space rather than actually leading.[5] This, the commissioners concluded, was a serious problem in need of fixing.

On this count, the commissioners agreed with other critics who have argued that the Air Force's long attachment to the aerospace construct—along with its recent insistence on making all its officers both air- *and* space-conversant by assigning non–space officers to space positions to enrich their knowledge of space and to better integrate space with air operations and vice versa—was threatening to have the long-term effect of producing jacks of all trades and masters of none. Many have faulted such well-meaning but arguably flawed education and training as not only detracting from the technical credibility of Air Force Space Command, but also undermining the morale of space officers by eliminating career paths for those who prefer to retain and develop their space expertise. A significant underlying problem is that the more senior space assignments are readily accessible to Air Force non–space personnel, whereas space officers cannot compete for command positions in the flying portion of the Air Force because they lack aeronautical ratings.

The commissioners further found that no single service had been assigned statutory responsibility to organize, train, and equip for space operations. In so doing, they lent tacit support to an argument often used previously by the Air Force leadership to counter charges that they were not adequately meeting their responsibilities of space stewardship. As Brigadier General Simon "Pete" Worden, then of the planning directorate at Air Force Space Command, recently expressed it, "While some would say that the Air Force has not been a good steward of space . . . the Air Force does not have an assigned responsibility to be the 'steward' of space." Worden added that the Air

---

[5]Ibid., pp. 43–46. As evidence of the rudimentary level of operator thinking about space and its potential a decade ago, General Horner commented after the Gulf War: "I was already aware of the danger of Scuds before we went to the Gulf, but it never occurred to me to use DSP [Defense Support Program missile launch-sensing satellites] to provide warning of Scud attacks. . . . But shame on me, I should have known." (Quoted in Lieutenant Colonel Steven J. Bruger, USAF, "Not Ready for the First Space War: What About the Second?" *Naval War College Review*, Winter 1995, p. 79.)

Force leadership had testified to the commission that it was more than ready to assume the mantle of being the nation's designated "space steward," but that "it must have that mission assigned to it, along with the resources to accomplish it."[6]

As for resource support, the commissioners noted that there is no existing Defense Department appropriation that identifies and aggregates funding for military space programs. Observing further that most of the funding for military space programs is in the Air Force and National Reconnaissance Office (NRO) budgets, they gave voice to "some concern" that although the Army and Navy are the defense community's largest users of space products and capabilities, the budget activities of those two services "consistently fail to reflect the importance of space," pointing up a "dichotomy between the importance of space to the Army and Navy versus the funding commitment these services make" which "needs to be addressed."[7] The commissioners seemed to be saying between the lines that although the Army and Navy are the main consumers of military space products, they were not shouldering their fair share of the funding burden for the space-related services provided to them.

On the matter of existing organization for military space, the commission clearly discerned a problem in the triple-hatting of the commander in chief of U.S. Space Command (CINCSPACE), who also served as the commander in chief of the North American Aerospace Defense Command (CINCNORAD) and commander of Air Force Space Command (AFSPC). The commissioners rightly spotlighted CINCSPACE as the principal advocate for the space needs of all the warfighting commanders in chief (CINCs) and as the one senior uniformed figure responsible for ensuring the security of the space environment. Yet they concluded that those preoccupations required him to pay more attention to the space tasks assigned by the president and Secretary of Defense, which necessarily left insuf-

---

[6]Brigadier General Simon Peter Worden, "The Air Force and Future Space Directions: Are We Good Stewards?" *Aerospace Power Journal*, Spring 2001, p. 51.

[7]*Space Commission Report*, p. 76. The report did acknowledge that the Army and Navy each fund service-specific space programs. The Army funds common-user and Army-distinct ground terminals, and the Navy funds the UHF follow-on program, the multiuser objective system, and Navy terminals.

ficient time for him to give due attention to his parallel duties at NORAD and Air Force Space Command.

The commissioners concluded from this undesirable situation that making CINCSPACE and the commander of Air Force Space Command two separate four-star generals rather than one would enable the commander of AFSPC to concentrate more fully on his "organize, train, and equip" duties mandated by the Air Force and Title X of the U.S. Code and also would allow CINCSPACE, for his part, to focus his full attention and energy on actually conducting space operations in support of the Secretary of Defense and the regional warfighting CINCs. Such a change, they concluded, would, in one stroke, solve a prior problem whereby the unified U.S. Space Command often appeared to be marginalized both by Air Force Space Command, which houses 90 percent of the nation's military space personnel and funding, and by the regional warfighting CINCs, each of whom has an assigned area of responsibility (AOR) and distinct operational and combat missions that are far clearer than those of the similarly unified U.S. Space Command.

To deal with these and other problems, the commissioners offered a number of unanimous recommendations. The first, and arguably an essential precondition for all the others to work, was that the president consider declaring and treating space as a U.S. national security priority, without which drift and a lack of focus and due funding support would be bound to persist. The commissioners further recommended amending Title X of the U.S. Code to assign the Air Force formal statutory authority to organize, train, and equip for offensive and defensive space operations. They also recommended that the Secretary of Defense formally designate the Air Force as the executive agent for space within the Department of Defense. In return for this groundbreaking dispensation, which essentially offered the Air Force on a silver platter a status it had sought in vain for nearly a half-century, the commissioners recommended that the unified U.S. Space Command be commanded by a four-star officer other than the commander of Air Force Space Command, that that position be open to any qualified four-star general in any of the four services, and that the position be nominative and not routinely rotated among the services.

As for the technical competence and organizational efficiency issues, the commissioners recommended giving Air Force Space Command full responsibility for providing resources to execute space R&D, acquisition, and operations. To do that, they added, the Air Force's Space and Missile Systems Center (SMC), hitherto a component of the separate and sometimes adversarial Air Force Materiel Command (AFMC), would need to be moved to AFSPC, thus consolidating all Air Force space functions into a single organizational entity so as to "create a strong center of advocacy for space and an environment in which to develop a cadre of space professionals."[8]

THE ISSUE OF A SEPARATE SPACE SERVICE

As noted at the start of this chapter, the Space Commission was empowered to offer recommendations on two oft-proposed alternatives for U.S. military space exploitation: a separate and independent Space Department and uniformed Space Force within the Department of Defense or, short of that, the creation of a more modest Space Corps within the Air Force, much along the lines of the Marine Corps within the U.S. naval establishment.[9] These alternatives have been pushed by their advocates for years out of concern for seeking greater leverage from space through a more efficient and more nurturing support infrastructure. Both have either implicitly or explicitly presumed that space mission-area development has not received its proper due with the Air Force as its de facto custodian; that there is a better approach toward underwriting continued military space exploitation *within* the Air Force than through the organizational and funding mechanisms currently in place; or that the nation's military space program is mature enough to strike out on its own toward mastering the fourth medium of warfare, either partly or completely detached from direct Air Force control.

---

[8]Ibid., p. 90.

[9]The Center for Naval Analyses, for example, recommended the creation of an independent U.S. space service in its 1995 study for the Commission on Roles and Missions of the Armed Forces, on the avowed premise that such a new service "would provide a pool of expertise and would anticipate the future evolution of space-based weapons." (G. A. Federici, B. Wald, et al., *Commission on Roles and Missions of the Armed Forces: Space Activities,* Alexandria, Virginia: Center for Naval Analyses, May 1995, p. 19.)

Similar expressions of concern have emanated from the Air Force itself, both from career space professionals who have sought to free space from the inhibiting bonds of traditional air power thinking and from more mainstream airmen, including some at senior leadership levels, who have grown increasingly perturbed over the long-term implications of the Air Force's having had to shortchange its air responsibilities, particularly in recent years, as a necessary condition for retaining its stewardship of space. Others have come from more outspoken critics, both within the Air Force and in influential circles outside it, who have become convinced that a cleaner break from existing practices will be essential if emerging technology opportunities are to be fully exploited in a timely way. All reflect a belief that the time for continued business as usual has passed and that military space exploitation by the United States has reached a point where it needs a decided assist.

The more radical of these proposed alternatives is the establishment of a separate and independent U.S. Space Force.[10] Such a new service would include its own civilian secretary, headquarters, and field staff. It would command, at least in principle, a place equal to that of the U.S. Army, Navy, and Air Force in terms of organizational stature and claims to a fair share of the annual U.S. defense budget. The Space Force's chief of staff would be a full and equal member of the Joint Chiefs of Staff. Such a separate and independent service would also presumably provide U.S. military space programs with a central acquisition executive having exclusive oversight authority and management responsibility for such programs.

A less drastic proposed alternative for better exploiting U.S. military space potential has been to create a semiautonomous Space Corps within the Air Force. As portrayed in one characterization, such an arrangement would be "modeled on the two-hundred-year-long evolution of the U.S. Marine Corps in both organization and function. The Marine Corps provides rapid-deployment forces in support

---

[10]I am grateful to Larry Valero, a doctoral candidate in the Department of War Studies, University of London, and RAND summer associate for 2001, for having marshaled a number of points regarding the Space Force, Space Corps, and MFP proposals addressed in this chapter. That research is presented in full in his unpublished paper, "A Historical Analysis of Bureaucratic Alternatives for U.S. Military Space Forces," August 2001.

of naval operations and relies on the Navy to provide all logistic and administrative support. The Space Corps would become [the Department of Defense's] single space entity within the Department of the Air Force. All [Defense Department] space assets, including personnel, space systems, and ground-based support systems would be transferred to this corps. This organizational structure would be able to leverage USAF logistical and support capabilities already in place and focus the Space Corps on space warfighting. . . . Existing space procurement, personnel, and [operations and maintenance] costs would transfer to the Space Corps budget."[11] The creation of such an entity would require establishing a separate headquarters unit reporting directly to the Secretary of the Air Force. The Space Corps commander, like the commandant of the Marine Corps, would be a full member of the Joint Chiefs of Staff.

The Space Commission heard testimony both for and against these alternatives. On the pro side, one argument cited the inhibiting effect the treatment of space power as a mere extension of air power has allegedly had on the development of a purer theory of space warfare that might offer better chances of making the most of the nation's military space opportunities. A casebook example of this view was expressed not long ago by a midcareer Air Force space scholar, Lieutenant Colonel Bruce DeBlois, who insisted that "one cannot build space power theory and doctrine in general upon air power theory and doctrine." Expanding on this point, DeBlois noted that while air warfare theories and doctrines, like those for land and sea warfare, can be helpful in informing the development of a vibrant theory of space warfare, space power in the end "clearly requires fundamental, bottom-up theoretical and doctrinal development. The most conducive requirement for such development remains a separate space corps or service."[12] Variations on this theme have been voiced by others in the space community in recent years. As one space officer observed of them, after all is said and done, "space-power separatists

---

[11] Ralph Millsap and D. B. Posey, "Organizational Options for the Future Aerospace Force," *Aerospace Power Journal*, Summer 2000, pp. 50–51.

[12] Major Bruce M. DeBlois, "Ascendant Realms: Characteristics of Air Power and Space Power," in Colonel Phillip S. Meilinger, ed., *The Paths of Heaven: The Evolution of Air Power Theory*, Maxwell AFB, Alabama: Air University Press, 1997, pp. 529–578.

maintain that space forces will reach their full military potential only when they free themselves from air power paradigms."[13]

Other arguments put before the commissioners on behalf of establishing a separate space service turned on the more practical concern for ensuring adequate bureaucratic support and funding flow for military space development. Because of the Air Force's current obligation to divide its attention and resources between its competing air and space responsibilities, the argument went, a separate and independent Space Force or Corps could be a stronger and more single-minded advocate for military space and its personnel. Moreover, the consolidation and centralization of all U.S. military space activities across service lines would minimize duplication of effort and reduce costs. Proponents of a separate space service added that such a move would "improve the visibility of space programs, increase the space budget, eliminate redundancy, and [better] promote the development of space professionals."[14]

In the end, the commissioners rejected these arguments and elected to give the Air Force the benefit of the doubt, at least for the near term. They concluded that, although the establishment of a Space Corps within the Air Force might be appropriate at some indeterminate future date, "a realigned, rechartered Air Force is best suited to organize, train, and equip space forces" for the more immediate years ahead.[15] The commissioners did not indicate which were the most convincing of the arguments they heard against establishing a separate space service at this still-embryonic stage in the evolution of the nation's military space capability. Surely high on the list, however, were the considerable start-up costs and additional bureaucratic overhead that would inevitably be associated with any such radical measure. The commissioners no doubt were also mindful of the divisiveness that could result from setting up a separate military space enterprise just at the point in the evolution of military space exploitation where the nation has begun to make substantial progress toward integrating space with other force elements in joint

---

[13]Major Shawn P. Rife, USAF, "On Space-Power Separatism," *Airpower Journal,* Spring 1999, p. 22.

[14]Millsap and Posey, "Organizational Options for the Future Aerospace Force," p. 48.

[15]Ibid., p. 89.

operations. Any creation of an independent space service today would almost surely threaten to insert a new wedge between space and the other mediums at just the time when the Air Force has finally grown serious about this issue and taken significant steps to break down the walls that have traditionally kept them separated.

In addition, the commissioners had ample ground for skepticism about the real-world prospects of eliciting additional discretionary funds for sustaining a newly established space service significantly over and beyond the existing budgetary limit on defense R&D and procurement. As matters now stand, because the nation's military space responsibilities reside largely within the Air Force, essential space programs compete almost exclusively with other Air Force programs rather than also with Army, Navy, and Marine Corps R&D and procurement accounts. But the latter would seem more appropriate, considering that the other services are no less beneficiaries of the contributions of space than the Air Force (indeed, are arguably more so). The compromises that this arrangement has necessitated for the Air Force's air interests since the 1980s have often been cited as a compelling reason for spinning off a separate and independent U.S. space service.

Yet as reasonable as it might sound in principle to presume that appropriations for a separate space service would come from budget trades not only with other Air Force accounts, as is the current practice, but with *all* military programs across service lines, the commissioners recognized that such an ideal solution was far more easily said than done. As an Air Force space officer commented in this regard, it would make sense, from a funding perspective, to create a separate space service *only* if doing so "would allow the budget to be split four ways, thus allowing air and space forces to command half of U.S. defense outlays." Yet such an arrangement, he cautioned, would probably not make a significant difference once one took into account "the power of established services to retain their share of the pie, the additional overhead costs in creating and maintaining a separate space service, and the very real questions regarding the nation's political will to militarize space even further."[16]

---

[16]Rife, "On Space-Power Separatism," p. 26.

At bottom, the commissioners concluded that the time for establishing a separate U.S. space service had not yet arrived, as attested by their unanimous judgment that the Air Force remains, at least for the near term, the most appropriate organization within which to continue to grow America's military space potential. The basis for that judgment is important enough to warrant further comment. Today's space separatists often compare the proposed creation of an independent U.S. space service to the earlier establishment of the U.S. Air Force as a separate service. In fairness to that comparison, there is indeed a discernible analogy in at least one respect between the current calls for the creation of a separate space service and the earlier arguments that eventually culminated in the establishment of the U.S. Air Force in 1947. During the 1930s and 1940s, the Army leadership naturally bridled at having to provide substantial funding for its Army Air Corps because aircraft competed with land-force needs for limited funds and because the Army was displeased that the Air Corps proclaimed its ability to achieve combat outcomes without the involvement of infantry and armor. In much the same fashion, there have been recurrent signs of similar tension in recent years between the Air Force's space community and the more aerodynamically minded parts of the Air Force, which have hitherto largely determined that service's spending priorities.

Yet although there is a superficial similarity between the two cases, the circumstances that surrounded the Air Force's attainment of independence differed considerably from those that prevail with respect to the American military space community today. The Army Air Force (AAF) in 1946 and 1947 could convincingly argue that it had taken the fight directly to the enemy in every theater of war, thanks to its possession of the needed wherewithal for imposing force on the enemy. Today's military space community, in contrast, clearly lacks such a capability at this stage of its evolution, notwithstanding claims by some that Operation Desert Storm was the first "space war."[17] Although America's space assets proved vital in supporting both the air campaign and coalition ground operations in southeastern Iraq and Kuwait during the 1991 Gulf War, they did not project power from space against the enemy directly. Indeed, although it took only 11

---

[17]See Gary Wagner, "Fighting the First 'Space War,'" *Space Tracks*, January 2001, pp. 9–11.

years from the invention of the airplane to the latter's first employment for force application, the nation has been in the military space
business for more than four decades with no space force application
yet in sight. U.S. space capabilities today are more analogous to the
nascent air power of the pre–World War I era, when the missions of
military aviation were limited to such support functions as battlefield
surveillance and reconnaissance, than to the more developed state of
the AAF on the eve of its attainment of independence from the Army.

The AAF had the needed political leverage to pursue its independence in 1947 because it had engaged successfully in combat and
had a record of accomplishment that both emboldened its leaders
and earned it the support of the White House and, eventually,
Congress. Although the most outspoken of today's space advocates
are no less insistent in their calls for the establishment of an independent space service, those calls do not yet have the persuasiveness
of those made by the USAF's founding fathers in the AAF during the
mid- and later 1940s. Moreover, the continued absence of a clear national determination to proceed with space weaponization constitutes yet another obstacle in the path of establishing a separate space
service worthy of the name. So does the absence of any assurance
that overall defense spending would increase in the wake of such a
development, thereby allowing an Air Force unburdened of its former space responsibilities to retain the lion's share of its prior R&D
and procurement allotments and to devote those exclusively toward
satisfying its presumably underfunded air needs. In the end, it is hard
to imagine how a space force with no capability to conduct space
control and space force application and with only support responsibilities might justify its existence as a separate service. As for the argument that a separate space service is needed to grow a proper
space doctrine, opponents of that idea counter that such logic puts
things backward, since doctrine derives from theory and experience
rather than the other way around, suggesting that "one must base the
creation of a separate space force on sound doctrine and concepts
first."[18]

In sum, the commissioners concluded that space does not yet meet
the test of independence because existing technology remains inca-

---

[18]Rife, "On Space-Power Separatism," p. 30.

pable of conducting direct military action from space. As two opponents of space separatism expressed it, "The Air Force was established as an independent force when air power had at least reached adolescence—only after combat-tested technology, doctrine, and leadership were well established. Military space is still in its infancy, with no unique mission, untested doctrine and personnel, and unfinished technology." Accordingly, while military space capabilities contribute to all warfighting functions in all terrestrial mediums, they have "yet to evolve into a full-spectrum warfighting force" in their own right.[19] According to that view, a separate service will be justifiable only when the engagement of targets both in space and on the ground from space becomes technically and politically feasible. Until space becomes weaponized and warriors are operating in and from it, critics of separatism insist, the nation's military space component will not win wars or be anything more than a support instrument for enabling more effective terrestrial operations.[20]

Although they foresaw an eventual need for a new U.S. military space organization, the commissioners declined to establish any definitive timeline for a space reorganization plan, should such a plan be deemed necessary or desirable in the future. In effect, the commission left it to the Air Force to determine how a duly realigned and rechartered Air Force organizational configuration would play out in actual practice. It concluded that the disadvantages of the more radical alternatives of a Space Force or Corps, at least for now, outweighed the advantages for numerous reasons, most notably that the nation's military space posture has yet to have attained a requisite critical mass of qualified personnel, a sufficient funding level, or a set of missions and associated operational requirements that would justify such a radical move.[21] However, in a clear tacit warning to the

---

[19]Millsap and Posey, "Organizational Options for the Future Aerospace Force," p. 52.

[20]Indeed, the nation's military space effort is still so embryonic that at least one senior Air Force general faulted those who would rush to have space declared a supported CINCdom when its principals have yet to fully articulate and demonstrate its current role as a supporting CINCdom. (Interview by the author, Headquarters U.S. Air Force, Washington, D.C., April 30, 1998.)

[21]It might be noted in passing, however, that some of these disadvantages, such as a lack of sufficient qualified personnel and funding, were precisely among the factors that contributed to the establishment of an Air Corps within the U.S. Army in 1926. My thanks to Rick Sturdevant, Office of History, Air Force Space Command, for bringing this to my attention.

Air Force, it also concluded that future U.S. military space needs "may" require the establishment of a separate space department and service "at some future date" and that nearer-term measures should be undertaken in such a way as "not to preclude" the later development of a separate space service "if that proves desirable."[22]

IMPROVING THE SPACE BUDGETING PROCESS

In addition to the question of establishing a separate space service, the Space Commission was also tasked to consider a third alternative often espoused for improving the day-to-day management of U.S. military space activities, namely, the appointment of an Assistant Secretary of Defense for Space who would be responsible for an attendant Major Force Program budget category for space that cut across service lines. In one oft-heard formulation, this alternative would roughly emulate the current MFP-11 arrangement that was created for the U.S. Special Operations Command (USSOCOM) established in 1986. Such an arrangement would provide a single budget mechanism for introducing greater transparency into the tracking and management of multiservice space procurement programs. Under this arrangement, the Assistant Secretary of Defense for Space would exercise budget responsibility and civilian oversight for the new MFP-12, as well as authority for overseeing the coordination of joint space requirements.

The precedents of MFP-11 and USSOCOM offer instructive insights into the argument for and promise of an MFP-12 budget arrangement for space. To review briefly the essential background of those precedents, the chairman of the Joint Chiefs of Staff, Air Force General David C. Jones, in 1980 established a high-level commission to explore the causes and consequences of the badly botched attempt to rescue American hostages from Iran earlier in April of that year. That commission's report spotlighted deep and systemic deficiencies in the organization and conduct of special operations activities in all four services. Similar shortcomings associated with the later U.S. intervention in Grenada in 1983 and the subsequent U.S. response to the terrorist hijackings of a TWA airliner and the *Achille Lauro* cruise

---

[22]*Space Commission Report*, p. 80.

ship in 1985 also drew congressional attention to the nation's special operations forces and to the question of whether or not they were adequately integrated and supported.

As a result of that attention, Congress in 1986 enacted the Nunn-Cohen Amendment, aimed at revitalizing special operations and correcting the deficiencies that had been identified in the nation's ability to conduct them. That legislation directed the president to establish a unified combatant command—USSOCOM—to ensure that the nation's special operations forces in all services met the highest standards of combat readiness. To provide for adequate funding for those forces, Congress further directed the Department of Defense to include a new special operations budget category, Major Force Program 11 (MFP-11), in its future-years defense plan.[23] That budget arrangement was noteworthy in that it provided USSOCOM with discrete funding authority for the development and acquisition of equipment, supplies, and services unique to special operations. The law further created a new position of Assistant Secretary of Defense for Special Operations and Low-Intensity Conflict, who would report to the Under Secretary of Defense for Policy, and a coordinating body within the National Security Council to advise the president on matters involving special operations and low-intensity conflict.[24]

Unlike the Space Force and Space Corps alternatives discussed above, an MFP-12 for space fashioned along the lines of MFP-11 for special operations would be strictly a procurement management and cost-tracking mechanism aimed at improving the efficiency of the nation's military space R&D and acquisition programs. Since a unified command for space—USSPACECOM—was already in place, no additional organizational initiative comparable to the creation of USSOCOM would be required. With such a provision, the space

---

[23]The other designated defense budget major force programs include strategic forces (MFP-1), general-purpose forces (MFP-2), intelligence and communications (MFP-3), airlift and sealift forces (MFP-4), national guard and reserve forces (MFP-5), research and development (MFP-6), central supply and maintenance (MFP-7), training, medical, and other personnel activities (MFP-8), administration and other associated activities (MFP-9), and support for other nations (MFP-10).

[24]Joel Nadel and J. R. Wright, *Special Men and Special Missions: Inside American Special Operations Forces, 1945 to the Present*, London: Greenhill, 1994, p. 113.

components of the individual services would retain their separate identity and integrity and would remain responsible for the organization, training, and equipping of their respective space assets and personnel, as well as for the management of their respective space career fields.

After assessing this option, the commissioners recommended establishing a Major Force Program budget category for space, yet one managed in a decentralized manner similar to the practices of MFP-1 through MFP-10, rather than in the fashion of MFP-11, which funds special operations through USSOCOM. Such an amended practice would produce an MFP-12-equivalent for space, yet not one applied in the same way as MFP-11, with its designated Assistant Secretary of Defense for Special Operations and Low-Intensity Conflict. The commissioners ruled out creating a similar position of Assistant Secretary of Defense for Space, on the ground that any such individual "would not have sufficient influence over the evolution of U.S. national security space capabilities" and thus the position would not be "likely to result in greater or more effective focus on space" within the defense community.[25]

One potential challenge facing the effective implementation of this recommendation could entail the satisfactory negotiation of memoranda of understanding and agreement with all concerned services to determine which space-peculiar activities in each would fall under the purview of the executive agent for military space and be deemed appropriate for inclusion in MFP-12.[26] By some accounts, USSOCOM has periodically encountered difficulty in adequately defining special-operations-unique items for MFP-11 to the satisfaction of all interested parties, a fact that has occasioned recurrent internal tensions between the service headquarters staffs and their respective special-operations components. If that experience is a relevant guide, one might anticipate similar problems from time to time in arriving at agreed determinations of space-unique R&D and procurement activities for MFP-12. The Air Force's then–senior plans

---

[25]*Space Commission Report*, p. 81.

[26]As a step in the direction of coming to effective grips with this concern, the Air Staff recently developed a notional baseline MFP for space. (Comments on an earlier draft by Major General Michael A. Hamel, USAF, commander, 14th Air Force, Vandenberg AFB, Calif.)

and programs executive, however, expressed confidence that this potential problem would *not*, in the end, be a serious impediment to the effective implementation of an MFP-12 for space.[27] In all events, the single greatest advantage of such a budget solution will be a centralization and clarification, for the first time, of overall U.S. military space spending, along with a removal of the confusion—sometimes bordering on opacity—that currently obscures how the nation's military space money is reported due to existing service and Office of the Secretary of Defense (OSD) accounting practices.

To be sure, such an arrangement, in and of itself, will not provide more overall funds for military space exploitation.[28] It will, however, dramatically improve the visibility and transparency of space spending in all services. It will also highlight conspicuous instances of redundant activity and indicate space mission needs that are not being adequately supported. As such, it represents a first step toward an eventual arrangement whereby budget trades on behalf of needed space programs may be made across service lines rather than solely within the Air Force budget. At a minimum, an MFP solution promises to create an expenditure-tracking situation in which the case for an increased overall budget limit for space—not only for the Air Force but for all services, as appropriate—can at least be more rigorously and effectively argued.

INITIAL AIR FORCE REACTIONS

There is no question that although it cooperated both willingly and seriously, the Air Force viewed itself as having been essentially targeted by the Space Commission and accordingly awaited its findings and recommendations with more than a little trepidation. As the commander in chief of U.S. Space Command, Air Force General Ralph E. Eberhart, candidly remarked, the formation of the Space Commission had been "an experience akin to a trip to the dentist"

---

[27]Conversation with Lieutenant General Joseph H. Wehrle, Jr., Deputy Chief of Staff for Plans and Programs, Headquarters USAF, Santa Monica, Calif., February 19, 2002.

[28]On this point, former Secretary of the Air Force F. Whitten Peters suggested that while the MFP approach will give decisionmakers a clearer picture and a spending trail of space allocations, making tangible improvements in space capabilities will not occur without more funds for space. (Amy Butler, "Pentagon Closely Studying Ramifications of Space Panel Suggestions," *Inside the Air Force*, April 13, 2001, p. 13.)

for the Air Force and was clearly "not something officials sought or looked forward to."[29] An even more pointed airing of that sentiment was made by then–Secretary of the Air Force Whitten Peters after the commission's report was released when he commented that "at the risk of confirming that I am a Luddite when it comes to space, let me say that I really do not understand what the big problem is that justifies a national commission."[30]

In a clear indication that he was on board with the commission's recommendations, however, General Eberhart hastened to add that the Air Force "may well be better off" when the fallout from the commission finally settled, and that the commission's creation and findings had clearly "helped us refocus, to chart the path ahead, and to truly realize what our destiny is" with respect to the Air Force's future in space.[31] Then–Brigadier General Michael Hamel, the Air Staff's director of space operations and integration, characterized the Space Commission's product as "a watershed report in terms of the evolution of space in the military," adding his belief that the reorganization moves prompted by the commission's report should lessen at least some management problems occasioned by a prior fragmentation of authority.[32] Recognizing that those proposed moves may have bought the Air Force some time with respect to its corporate hold over the space mission area, the since-retired Air Force chief of staff, General Michael E. Ryan, commented shortly after the report's release that an independent Space Force or Corps was not warranted for at least another 50 years.[33] Perhaps most concisely reflecting the official Air Force position adopted in the immediate aftermath of the report's release, the leader of the Air Force's review of the Space Commission's findings and recommendations, then–Major General Brian A. Arnold, director of space and nuclear deterrence on the Air

---

[29]Peter Grier, "The Force and Space," *Air Force Magazine*, February 2001, p. 52.

[30]Ibid., p. 51.

[31]Ibid., p. 52.

[32]*Inside the Air Force*, February 2, 2001, p. 1, and *Aviation Week and Space Technology*, May 14, 2001, p. 31.

[33]"Ryan Says Space Force Unwarranted for Next 50 Years," *Aerospace Daily*, February 9, 2001, pp. 217–218.

Staff, said of those findings and recommendations: "I don't see anything in there that we don't think we can do."[34]

Indeed, three months after the release of the Space Commission's report, General Eberhart indicated that Air Force Space Command had supported the commission's recommendations "in every respect."[35] He also noted that the Air Force chief of staff, General Ryan, had moved promptly to cut off any nonconcurring groups within the Air Force to telegraph clearly that the Air Force had accepted the commission's recommendations in principle and was now deep in the process of trying to determine how best to comply with them. Finally, Eberhart reported that the bureaucratically sensitive issue within the Air Force of transferring the Air Force Space and Missile Systems Center from AFMC to AFSPC had been worked out through a number of "productive sessions" between himself and the commander of AFMC, General Lester Lyles. The principal issue, he said, had nothing to do with any would-be heel-dragging from AFMC over an implied loss of turf, but rather with legitimate concerns within AFMC that AFSPC duly attend to career needs and opportunities for those SMC personnel who would be subsumed into AFSPC as a result of the transfer.

As for continued intra–Air Force sticking points, General Eberhart noted that similar concerns had been manifest at AFMC's depot in Ogden, Utah; within the space component of the Air Force's Electronic Systems Command; and at various other Air Force space-related functions residing outside AFSPC, all of which would need to be addressed in a similar manner. Still more vexing, he indicated that AFSPC was seeking oversight of the Air Force's science and technology program as it related to space and that "the jury [was] still out" as to whether the Air Force Research Laboratory would cooperate. Perhaps the biggest still-unsettled organizational challenge facing the Air Force, he suggested, entailed the relationship between the Under Secretary of the Air Force and director of NRO, on the one hand, and AFSPC and U.S. Space Command, on the other. The challenge here

---

[34]William B. Scott, "USAF Gives Nod to Space Report," *Aviation Week and Space Technology*, February 12, 2001, p. 63.

[35]General Ralph E. Eberhart, USAF, comments to a gathering of RAND staff, Santa Monica, Calif., May 9, 2001.

entails eliminating existing seams between the NRO and the director of operations at AFSPC and an essential migration of some NRO roles to AFSPC, which ultimately will require substantial trust between the Secretary of Defense and the Director of Central Intelligence. For the near term, Eberhart noted, how these issues are handled and ultimately resolved will be heavily dependent on the currently cooperating personalities involved. At some point, however, the new relationships will need to be institutionalized. For this, he said, there are already microcosms of the bureaucratic, organizational, and "turf" issues at stake in the analogous case of the individual uniformed service cryptologic functions and their relationship with the National Security Agency, which may well contain some instructive lessons to be pondered and applied.

THE BUSH PENTAGON'S POLICY DECISIONS

By law, as mandated by section 1624 of the National Defense Authorization Act for FY 2001, the former chairman of the Space Commission and later Secretary of Defense in the George W. Bush administration, Donald Rumsfeld, was required to provide Congress his assessment of the Space Commission's recommendations by April 12, 2001.[36] As part of that response, in a letter to the chairman of the Senate Armed Services Committee, Senator John Warner (R-Virginia), Rumsfeld granted the need for a "new and comprehensive national security space management and organizational approach" to promote and protect U.S. interests in space. He further reported the establishment of a Policy Coordinating Committee for Space within the National Security Council "to provide a senior, interagency forum to develop, coordinate, and monitor the implementation of the president's policy guidance for space activities." He also announced the creation of an executive committee co-chaired by the Secretary of Defense and the Director of Central Intelligence to review space-related intelligence issues of joint concern.[37]

---

[36]"Pentagon Says Rumsfeld's Space Report Response Will Be 'Complex,'" *Inside the Air Force*, April 27, 2001, p. 3.

[37]Secretary of Defense Donald Rumsfeld, letter to the Honorable John Warner, chairman, Senate Armed Services Committee, May 8, 2001.

Rumsfeld then enumerated the most important and potentially far-reaching of his decisions and intended actions on the commission's recommendations. Among other things, those decisions

- assigned responsibility to the Department of the Air Force to organize, train, and equip for "prompt and sustained offensive and defensive space operations"

- designated the Department of the Air Force as the executive agent for space within the Department of Defense (DoD), with DoD-wide responsibility for the planning, programming, and acquisition of military space systems

- directed the Secretary of the Air Force to make the commander of Air Force Space Command a four-star officer other than CINCSPACE and CINCNORAD

- discontinued the practice of requiring that CINCSPACE and CINCNORAD be flight-rated, thereby allowing for an officer from any of the four services "with an understanding of space and combat operations" to be assigned to that position

- directed the Defense Comptroller and Chief Financial Officer to establish a new space program, budget, and accounting mechanism to "increase visibility into the resources allocated for space activities" (in effect, creating an MFP-12)

- directed that headquarters and field commands be realigned to more effectively organize, train, and equip "for prompt and sustained space operations," with Air Force Space Command being assigned the responsibility for (and being duly funded for) executing space R&D, acquisition, and operations, as well as managing the space career field within the Department of the Air Force, thus removing any remaining space functions from Air Force Materiel Command and concentrating those functions exclusively in Air Force Space Command

- directed that the Under Secretary of the Air Force be dual-hatted as the director of the National Reconnaissance Office (NRO) and the Air Force's acquisition executive for space, thus aligning mainstream Air Force and NRO space programs and enabling both organizations to use each other's "best practices."

Concerning changes outside the corporate confines of the Air Force, Rumsfeld further

- directed the Army and Navy to continue to establish service-specific space requirements, to maintain a cadre of space-qualified officers, and to attend to R&D, acquisition, and deployment of service-specific space systems

- charged the director of the Defense Advanced Research Projects Agency (DARPA) and the service laboratories with undertaking R&D and demonstration of innovative space technologies and systems for military missions

- directed all service secretaries to enhance professional military education regarding space within their respective services at all levels "to ensure [that] our forces have a direct understanding of how to integrate space activities into military operations."

These decisions portended the most sweeping structural changes to have been made concerning the management of U.S. military space development and operations in many years. They also held out promise for a notable improvement in the U.S. military space posture in the coming years, since Secretary Rumsfeld's five articulated defense policy priorities (nuclear deterrence, ensuring the readiness of the deployed force, modernizing C3I and space capabilities, transforming the U.S. defense establishment, and reforming Pentagon processes and organization) all favor an increased focus on space and information technologies.[38] After the release of the Space Commission's report, Rumsfeld announced that a Policy Coordinating Committee for Space had been established in the NSC under national security director Franklin Miller to "help coordinate the civil and commercial and defense-related aspects of space."[39] He further confirmed that the Bush administration would commit $1 billion in R&D funding in FY02 to missile defense technologies, with decisions

---

[38]Robert Holzer, "IT, Space Top U.S. Military Priorities," *Defense News*, February 26, 2001, p. 22.

[39]Robert Wall, "Rumsfeld Revamps Space, Pushes 'Black' Projects," *Aviation Week and Space Technology*, May 14, 2001, p. 30.

yet to be made on how that allocation would be spent.[40] As for dis-
appointments, the Space Commission had recommended the creation of a Strategic Reconnaissance Office, which would consider not
just space-based intelligence, surveillance, and reconnaissance (ISR)
solutions, but also trade-offs among air, space, surface, and subsur-
face options. The services resisted that particular idea, and it was not
approved by Rumsfeld, at least as an overt entity. However, the newly
appointed Under Secretary of Defense for Acquisition, Pete Aldridge,
indicated that DARPA might be directed to take on more cutting-
edge space R&D.[41]

Clearly, an MFP-12-equivalent budget arrangement that would enable the tracking of all space-related spending was both intended
and directed by Rumsfeld. Under that arrangement, military space
initiatives and programs will continue to reside within the individual
service annual Program Objectives Memoranda (POMs). Yet the Air
Force, as the DoD's designated executive agent for space, will at least
now be able to monitor and track them in greater detail across the
board. In some cases, as before, individual services will want a specific space capability but will not want to pay for it. In others, as before, they will seek to hold onto existing equities and gain additional
ones. Until the wrinkles of the new budget-monitoring arrangement
are ironed out, the Joint Requirements Oversight Council (JROC) will
continue to be involved in adjudicating cross-service requirement
claims, so a system of de facto checks and balances should prevail.[42]

SOME NEAR-TERM IMPLEMENTATION QUESTIONS

Making the transition to the new arrangements outlined above will
definitely further underwrite the interests of U.S. military space development. However, needed changes will not come instantly or easily. The same day the Space Commission's report was released, one
of the commissioners, Senator Malcolm Wallop (R-Wyoming), said of
current U.S. military space organization and policy: "Right now,
there are lots of little individuals who will give you lots of little space

---

[40]"Rumsfeld Says $1 Billion Will Boost Missile Defense R&D," InsideDefense.com,
March 1, 2001.

[41]*Aviation Week and Space Technology*, May 14, 2001, p. 31.

[42]Eberhart, comments at RAND, May 9, 2001.

answers," but the community as a whole is "an enormous band of chieftains with no tribes."[43] Another commissioner, former Air Force chief of staff General Fogleman, frankly admitted that "some people within the Air Force [still] feel that . . . we got out the 10,000-mile screwdriver and started fine-tuning things that commissions ought not muck around with, but the fact of the matter is it was in our charter, so we did it."[44]

Fogleman added that until now, military space had "pretty much been on autopilot." Explaining the reason for the provision of a senior NSC monitor for space, he said that "if you go into the national security organization and apparatus as it existed [even recently], what you discover is that the individual who was responsible for space matters within the National Security Council was an Air Force lieutenant colonel who was doing it as an additional duty. So when we as a Space Commission started looking for a post office box and a telephone number, we couldn't find one. We took that as wrong if this is going to be a national security priority."[45]

Another early result of the commission's proposed reforms was the initiation of a transfer of the Air Force's Space and Missile Systems Center in El Segundo, California, from Air Force Materiel Command to Air Force Space Command. Ever since its establishment as the Western Development Division in 1954 to develop the nation's first ICBMs, this entity has been pivotal in military space acquisition. It currently is the principal nexus of U.S. military space systems development, in charge of developing, among other things, military communications satellites, the Global Positioning System (GPS), and missile defense functions.[46] It will now reside where it properly belongs in the interest of a more coherent U.S. military space program.

---

[43]"Panel Urges U.S. to Defend Space," *New York Times*, January 12, 2001.

[44]General Ronald R. Fogleman, USAF (Ret.), comments at a seminar on "Organizing for Future National Security Priorities in Space" jointly sponsored by DFI International and AF/QR, Washington, D.C., February 1, 2001.

[45]Ibid.

[46]Peter Pae, "Missile Base Is on an Upward Trajectory," *Los Angeles Times*, May 29, 2001.

Such a change will solve a major problem that had been caused by the previous separation of responsibilities for space systems acquisition and space operations between Air Force Materiel Command and Air Force Space Command, a practice that had tended to undermine the consideration of space as a mission area. Within the NRO, program managers enjoy full latitude to focus on the mission applications of their various systems and to make appropriate cost and schedule trade-offs over the life-cycle of those systems. In contrast, the mainstream Air Force space program did not benefit from that comparative advantage because of the duality of players (Air Force Space Command and those in the Program Element Office) who wielded influence over it. Its mission orientation was thus applied not from the top down but rather at lower levels and then folded into the acquisition, launch, or operations category as deemed appropriate in each case.

As for funding needs, General Fogleman remarked that all too often what commissions like the Space Commission typically hear from self-interested plaintiffs is that "if we just had more money, we could fix this problem." The former Air Force chief frankly allowed that "the commission did not bite on that as being necessarily true. What we did say is that if we get an overarching national policy and we get some coherent kind of flow to what we are doing, it may in fact require more money. It may. That money will probably flow if the right type of attention comes down from the top. The fact of the matter is that just throwing more money at a flawed organization or a flawed management system is not necessarily going to provide success. That was the approach the commission took."[47] On the MFP issue, Fogleman noted that he had been the Air Force's chief programmer at the time MFP-11 for special operations was created. As he recalled its practical effect, "the existence of that MFP gave visibility to special operations programs and, for the services who have been criticized for not supporting special operations, it took away that criticism. At long last, everybody could see what was happening. I think that the same thing will happen with an MFP [for space]."[48]

---

[47]Fogleman, DFI seminar.
[48]Ibid.

For that to happen, however, an essential next step (and one not expressly allowed for in the commission's recommendations) is the removal of the funding for multiservice space missions and functions from the Air Force's budgeting process, so that needed national security space funding can come from the *overall* defense budget rather than solely from the more limited Air Force budget. As long as space programs are traded off almost entirely against other competing Air Force mission needs, they will not receive either their due priority or the funding support they require. An all but certain side benefit of such a change in funding practice will be that once the other services are put on notice that space funding increases may come out of their allocations as well as the Air Force's, a new and long-overdue discipline will begin to influence and duly temper their hitherto often unconstrained generation of space "requirements" for the Air Force's budget to underwrite.

Clearly, the other services remain uneasy over the potential consequences that could ensue for them from the Air Force's having been designated the DoD's executive agent for space. General Eberhart candidly admitted three months after the release of the commission's report that the unified U.S. Space Command had been considerably slower to embrace the commission's recommendations than AFSPC had been because of the different service views and positions embedded within the joint command. For a time, Eberhart noted, those positions had "changed weekly" as the individual service views on the hot-button executive-agent issue shifted back and forth. The Army leadership was openly indicating its nonconcurrence. Other services argued, ultimately unsuccessfully, that executive-agent power should be vested in an Under Secretary of Defense for Space or in a reconfigured National Security Space Architect to keep the authority for military space development from becoming overly aggregated in Air Force hands.[49]

Later, an Army spokesman indicated that the Army supported the Air Force's new executive-agent status, but he warned against any consolidation of functions that might jeopardize the joint nature of space operations. The Army, more actively than the other services, is

---

[49]Eberhart, comments at RAND, May 9, 2001.

developing unclassified systems to disrupt an enemy's satellites.[50] Army Colonel Glen Collins, director of the Force Development and Integration Center at Army Space and Missile Defense Command, said that while NRO and the Air Force have the largest investments in space, the capabilities provided by the integration of those assets are "equally important to all the services. Any actions or decisions that do not protect the joint nature of our space forces . . . would cause irrevocable harm to the services' warfighting capabilities." He added that the Air Force's increased authority and responsibility for military space "must be balanced" by increased oversight from CINCSPACE, the Joint Chiefs of Staff, and the Office of the Secretary of Defense (OSD), and that "without this oversight, there is the potential that space could become focused on support to a single service, its style of warfighting, and to its priorities. This would be contrary to the best interests of the Army."[51]

Echoing such concerns, Rear Admiral Robert Nutwell, the Deputy Assistant Secretary of Defense for C3I, spoke for OSD in stressing that in assigning overarching authority for space to the Air Force, OSD intended to "ensure a voice" for the other services and space-related defense agencies. He added that "we also want to retain a role for each of the services in the innovation of space capabilities and generating new capabilities," especially for those services that are "just primarily customers of space capabilities in the force enhancement arena. Even though we want to empower the Air Force to be the champion and the principal implementer for space particularly, we need to preserve the proper oversight."[52]

A TIME FOR ACTION

As the Air Force entered the 21st century, the spectrum of views with respect to "where and whither military space" ranged from arguments that the time had come to start laying the groundwork for an independent U.S. space service to confident counterclaims by the Air

---

[50]These include laser dazzlers that can blind surveillance satellites, jammers to disrupt communication and surveillance satellites, and kinetic energy ASATs.

[51]Ann Roosevelt, "New Air Force Space Role Has Army Concerned," *Defense Week*, May 14, 2001, p. 1.

[52]Butler, "Pentagon Closely Studying Ramifications of Space Panel Suggestions," p. 13.

Force, including from many in the Air Force space community, that existing arrangements were more than sufficient for meeting near-term military space needs and that custodianship of the nation's military space effort was in responsible hands. Between these polar opposites, one could further identify a substantial cross-section of concerns that existing provisions for the orderly advance of U.S. military space exploitation could bear improvement—at least at the margins. At the root of these concerns was a mounting sense of need to ensure that continued space mission-area development would receive due support within the Air Force budget without compromising that service's no less important air-related mission needs along the way.

Within the Air Force, many were prepared to retain an open mind with respect to the question of whether the establishment of a separate space service might eventually become justified once the nation's military space applications reached sufficient maturity. Clearly, however, there was a prevailing view that the time for such a development was nowhere near at hand yet, considering that the Air Force had not yet *begun* to face up to defensive and offensive space control as prospective combat mission areas, to say nothing of space force application. Further, this view seemed to support the notion that, whatever alternative organizational and funding arrangements might ultimately be settled upon on behalf of space, the proper setting in which to push for developing and acquiring space control and, eventually, space force application capabilities was the existing Air Force space establishment. In the words of two proponents of this steady-on-course approach toward military space exploitation, the Air Force's initial evolution as an integral part of the Army until 1947 offered ample ground for concluding that "space should be allowed to mature within an established parent organization to determine whether it can develop and refine a unique warfighting capability."[53]

At the same time, a belief was growing within influential quarters *outside* the Air Force, including among both its critics and friends, that the Air Force needed a decided push toward making more of the space exploitation opportunities that now lay before it. Indeed, as

[53]Millsap and Posey, "Organizational Options for the Future Aerospace Force," p. 52.

noted in the introduction to this study, such concern lay at the heart of the creation of the Space Commission by Congress in 1999. Yet while many commissioners appeared strongly sympathetic to alternatives that recognized air and space as separate mediums and mission areas warranting their own dedicated organizational and funding support, the Air Force remained ever more deeply committed to its "aerospace integration" mantra and to the avowed conviction of its leadership that the atmosphere and space represented a single and inseparable aerospace continuum. This, in a nutshell, was the political and bureaucratic lay of the land on the eve of the release of the Space Commission's report in January 2001.

In their conclusions and recommendations, the commissioners seemed entirely content to allow the Air Force to remain the institutional nexus of the Defense Department's space expertise and activity for the indefinite future, albeit with that expertise duly reconstituted at some appropriate future point in an organizational structure that might eventually evolve into a Space Corps or some comparably autonomous institution. It seemed equally clear, however, that the commission's recommendation on that point was tacitly based on the presumption of a clean and unsentimental abandonment by the Air Force of its "aerospace" fixation, which had persisted throughout so much of its thinking and rhetoric since the late 1950s. Even before the commissioners issued this recommendation, many thoughtful critics of all persuasions on the relative importance of the Air Force's air and space priorities had concluded that the idea that the Air Force might somehow meld the very different air and space cultures to create "aerospace generalists" was seriously flawed.

In a major milestone in the maturation of Air Force thinking and policy on the relationship between air and space, the newly installed Air Force chief, General John P. Jumper, announced on October 16, 2001 a substantially changed direction in the Air Force's approach, declaring that "when I talk about space . . . I don't talk about aerospace, I talk about air *and* space" (emphasis added). Indicating in no uncertain terms that he had taken due note of the Space Commission's strong leanings, Jumper added that in his understanding, "space . . . is a separate culture. The physics that apply to orbital dynamics are different than what airmen experience in the air. And there's a culture that has to grow up that shows the same expertise in space as airmen showed after World War II in aerial combat. We have to respect that, and we have to grow that culture until it matures."[54]

Two months later, Jumper was even more emphatic in his avowal of the Air Force's need to reject once and for all its former aerospace mentality and to face up to the fact that air and space must be treated as separate and distinct mediums in the best interests of military space systems management, mission-area development, career cultivation, and funding support. To be sure, he reaffirmed the abiding importance of the Air Force's accomplishments to date in air and space integration when he underscored the continued importance of combining the effects of the two mediums in pursuit of asymmetric advantages for theater joint-force commanders. But he also recognized the closely connected fact that the Air Force had to accept that air and space operations entail fundamentally different ways of doing business. Yet he left no room for doubt that, in his view, the Air Force's decades-long infatuation with "aerospace" thinking had been a major part of the problem rather than a part of the solution to the nation's mounting military space exploitation predicament: "I carefully read the Space Commission report. I didn't see one time in that report, in its many pages, where the term 'aerospace' was used. The reason is that it fails to give the proper respect to the culture and to the physical differences that abide between the physical environment of air and the physical environment of space. We need to make sure we respect those differences. So I will talk about air and space. I will respect the fact that space is its own culture, that space has its own priorities that have to be respected."[55]

---

[54]Amy Butler, "Departing from Ryan's Rhetoric, Jumper Notes Unique Space Needs," *Inside the Air Force*, October 19, 2001, p. 15. In an important earlier benchmark of his developing thinking along these lines, during his tenure as the Air Force's Deputy Chief of Staff for Plans and Operations (AF/XO), then–Lieutenant General Jumper in 1996 changed that key office's name to Deputy Chief of Staff for Air and Space Operations. He was determined to provide an arrangement whereby any space officers who needed to vent operational space concerns would have both an incentive and the opportunity to proceed directly to AF/XO, the Air Staff's uppermost clearinghouse for all operational matters, rather than work those concerns through the acquisition establishment, the traditional Air Force clearinghouse for space. (Conversation with General Jumper, Nellis AFB, Nevada, June 24, 2002.)

[55]Peter Grier, "The Winning Combination of Air and Space," *Air Force Magazine*, January 2002, p. 75. In a predictable ratification of that policy shift, the name of the Air Force's professional quarterly, beginning with the Fall 2002 issue, was changed with little ado from *Aerospace Power Journal* to *Air and Space Power Journal*.

Those words represented a major, and possibly even historic, change in the Air Force's attitude toward space and how it should be approached both organizationally and operationally.

On this issue, General Eberhart indicated earlier that the Air Force leadership had made an easy peace with the commission's recommendation that the CINCSPACE and AFSPC command positions be separated, as well as with the dropping of the former requirement that CINCSPACE be a flight-rated Air Force pilot.[56] The North American Aerospace Defense Command (NORAD) director of operations billet is a statutorily flight-rated position, which satisfies the Canadian requirement for a rated officer at the appropriate level in NORAD and eliminates any requirement for CINCSPACE to be rated. Eberhart further suggested that the Air Force should continue to be able to compete successfully for the CINCSPACE billet because of its almost complete monopoly of space expertise among the four services. Yet it would be both necessary and proper for the CINCSPACE assignment to go to another service from time to time, if only to bear out the fact that all services are now legitimate contenders for that position. As for AFSPC, Eberhart indicated that the time had now come for routinely assigning commanders there who "grew up" in the space culture and who do not need to wear the two additional hats of CINCSPACE and CINCNORAD. Acceptance of this reality, he said, can only be healthy for the Air Force and the continued maturation of America's military space capability.

The Department of Defense finally made good on its earlier instructions to that end when Secretary Rumsfeld on October 18, 2001 directed the new Secretary of the Air Force, James Roche, to assign, within 60 days, a new Air Force four-star general to head up Air Force Space Command. General Eberhart had recommended such a move earlier in his testimony to the Space Commission and, in the end, warmly welcomed it, saying, "I can tell you that day in and day out I am very frustrated dividing my time and energy between those three hats [AFSPC, CINCSPACE, and CINCNORAD]."[57] In the same directive, Rumsfeld further instructed Roche to establish a space warrior

---

[56]Eberhart, comments at RAND, May 9, 2001.

[57]Amy Butler, "Rumsfeld Tells Roche to Pick New Four-Star for Air Force SPACE-COM," *Inside the Air Force*, October 26, 2001, p. 9.

career plan within 120 days and to assign the Program Executive Officer for military space directly to the Under Secretary of the Air Force, once that still-pending Bush administration nomination was confirmed. Shortly thereafter, the Senate approved the president's selection of former Lockheed Martin Corporation executive Peter Teets to be the Air Force's Under Secretary and the Pentagon's executive agent for military space, with acquisition milestone authority over all Department of Defense space programs, including those of the Army and Navy as well as of the Air Force and NRO. (Prior to that time, milestone authority for all major defense acquisition programs had resided solely with the Under Secretary of Defense for Acquisition). In addition, Rumsfeld directed the Pentagon's Comptroller to establish a "virtual" MFP for space so as to "increase visibility into the resources allocated for space activities."[58] The intent of that directive was to provide senior defense officials better insight into exactly how much money was being spent on space programs and in what way.

As might have been predicted, once the Air Force began pursuing its executive-agent role in earnest by developing a space program flow chart indicating Air Force, Navy, Army, NRO, and other defense-agency system requirements to be included in the space MFP and spotlighting any identified shortfalls, complaints arose from some Army and Navy quarters that the Air Force was seeking to wrest too much authority from other space-interested organizations. As one Army complainant put it, the Air Force's alleged interest in space-borne segments over the ground-terminal portions of space systems threatened to "take the equity out of the Army as a stakeholder."[59] Yet that same Air Force effort identified cross-service space funding deficiencies in the areas of communications, multitheater target tracking capability, missile warning, ISR, space control, science and technology, and "transformation," all of which added up to some $8 billion worth of underfunded military space activities, according to the Air Force's space operations and integration director, then–

---

[58]Quoted in Amy Butler, "Rumsfeld Issues Long-Awaited Guidance on DoD Space Realignment," *Inside the Air Force*, October 26, 2001, p. 6.

[59]Amy Butler, "Air Force's Notional Plan for Space Budgeting Process Draws Fire," *Inside the Air Force*, November 16, 2001, p. 17.

Brigadier General Hamel.[60] Moreover, as FY 2001 ended, it appeared that Department of Defense space programs might gain an overall increase of as much as $4.8 billion over future years if a pending draft Program Decision Memorandum dealing with so-called transformation issues was signed by Under Secretary of Defense Paul Wolfowitz.[61] The other services could hardly com-plain about those guardedly encouraging harbingers.

By early 2002, all of the essential pieces had fallen into place to signal the onset of a fundamental departure from the traditional American approach to military space exploitation—arguably a departure for the better. The Space Commission had delivered its recommenda-tions, the Secretary of Defense had duly acted upon them, and a newly incumbent Air Force chief had announced a decided farewell to the flawed aerospace construct. In so doing, he committed his ser-vice to a new approach to military space activity that recognized air and space, albeit both arenas of primary Air Force concern, as sepa-rate and distinct mission areas warranting separate and distinct or-ganizational attention and fiscal support.

Furthermore, a plan had been put in place to generate a new budget category for space that would allow for unprecedented accountabil-ity in the way the nation's defense dollars were spent on military space applications. Finally, the Air Force had committed itself to de-veloping and instituting a new space warrior career plan from the ground up. The only remaining near-term move on the military space chessboard was for the Air Force to make good on the Space Commission's recommendation to affirm Air Force Space Com-mand's stature as an operating command coequal with the Air Force's other operating commands, led full-time by a four-star commander with career space credentials and unencumbered by the obligations of serving also as CINCSPACE and CINCNORAD. That piece was finally moved into place when Secretary Roche announced on February 15 that General Eberhart would be unburdened of his AFSPC responsibilities while remaining CINCSPACE and CINC-

---

[60]Amy Butler, "USAF Identifies Key Space Activities DoD Has Not Yet Fully Funded," *Inside the Air Force*, November 16, 2001, pp. 17–18.

[61]Amy Butler, "DoD Space Program Could Get Additional $4.8 Billion Through FY07," *Inside the Air Force*, December 21, 2001, p. 1.

NORAD, and that command of AFSPC would go to General-select Lance Lord, a non-flight-rated missileer who had previously served as vice commander of AFSPC. The unfinished business for the Air Force that still remained included the implementation of these new space policy initiatives; the pursuit of a long-term space force enhancement strategy in which *all* consumers of the product might eventually share the cost burden; and—perhaps most challenging of all—coming to grips with the still undeveloped and politically sensitive but increasingly inescapable mission areas of space control and, when the right time for it comes, space force application.

Chapter Five

ON SPACE CONTROL AND SPACE FORCE APPLICATION

Until now, the Air Force has largely been limited in its space involvement to the two most basic mission areas of (1) space support, the launching of satellites and day-to-day management of on-orbit assets that underpin military space operations, and (2) space force enhancement, a broader mission category that includes all space operations aimed at increasing the effectiveness of terrestrial military operations.[1] These two mission categories have traditionally been politically benign, with no sensitivities attached other than cost considerations. Most would acknowledge that the Air Force has done commendably well at developing them in the nation's interest since the 1950s.

The space support mission, which makes all other space operations possible, has now matured to the point of considering acquisition of the Evolved Expendable Launch Vehicle (EELV) and pursuing single-stage-to-orbit technologies, in both cases with a view toward eventually driving down overall launch costs. The EELV, an Air Force partnership with industry, seeks to reduce the cost of space launch by at least 25 percent and to make access to space a more standard,

---

[1]The latter operations include satellite communications, space-based navigation, and a wide range of ISR functions that provide commanders and operators with information about weather, geodesy, terrain, and enemy forces, including real-time warning of ballistic missile launches. The most notable aspect of space force enhancement in recent years has been the steady tendency toward the use of space systems for directly enabling, rather than merely enhancing, terrestrial military operations, as attested by the increasing reliance by the Air Force and Navy on Global Positioning System (GPS) signals for guiding near-precision aerial munitions.

repeatable, and reliable process.[2] The space force enhancement mission is overdue for a concurrent replacement of entire constellations of existing space-based C4/ISR (command, control, communications, computers, information, surveillance, and reconnaissance) assets now entering block obsolescence. It also will eventually see a migration of such key air surveillance systems as the E-8 joint surveillance target attack radar system (Joint STARS) and E-3 airborne warning and control system (AWACS) to space. Such major replacement programs will be costly and will be hotly debated on need and affordability grounds. But they do not entail higher-level strategy and policy sensitivities.

That has not been the case for the two space mission areas of space control and space force application. The first involves ensuring that friendly forces can use space unmolested while denying the use of space, as circumstances warrant, to potential opponents. The second aims at directly striking terrestrial targets by means of space-based weapons.[3] Because the latter two mission categories envisage direct space combat functions, they have long been hobbled not just by cost considerations but also by a pronounced national ambivalence concerning space as an arena of warfare.

This was not a serious concern in years past because, despite a small number of nascent antisatellite (ASAT) and space defense programs, the Air Force's main interest in space was then directed largely toward developing the mission areas of routinely accessing space and using the satellites placed on orbit to support the national leadership and combatant commanders worldwide. It also was not a great preoccupation for the Air Force because threats to U.S. on-orbit assets were minimal to nonexistent and because technologies for potential use in both ground-to-space and space-to-earth combat were either in their infancy or altogether undeveloped.

---

[2]Statement by the Honorable Peter B. Teets, Under Secretary of the Air Force, to the Commission on the Future of the U.S. Aerospace Industry, Washington, D.C., May 14, 2002, p. 6.

[3]These four space mission areas (space support, force enhancement, space control, and force application) were first articulated and defined by AFSPC in its November 1983 Space Plan and were formally endorsed by the Department of Defense in 1987.

That is no longer the case today. Having been active in space operations for more than four decades now, the United States is more heavily invested than ever in space, both militarily and commercially, and potential opponents are increasingly closer to being able to threaten our space-based assets by means ranging from harassment to neutralization—and even outright destruction. Technologies offering promise for attacking near-earth orbital systems are no longer science fiction but now lie well within the realm of validation and exploitation, not only by the United States but also by potential adversaries. These developments have increasingly forced the American leadership to come face to face with the long-simmering question of whether it should continue treating space as though it were still a sanctuary from the use of force or accept instead that the time has finally come for the United States to seize the initiative in a measured way before others preempt us by aggressively testing the vulnerability of our most vital space systems.

WHY SPACE CONTROL NOW?

The most compelling reason for moving forward with dispatch toward acquiring at least the essential elements of a serious space control capability is that the United States is now unprecedentedly invested in and dependent on on-orbit capabilities, both military and commercial. Since these equities can only be expected to grow in sunk cost and importance over time, it is fair to presume that they will eventually be challenged by potential opponents. In 1997, then-CINCSPACE General Howell M. Estes III pointed out that with more than 525 satellites then on orbit (including more than 200 U.S. satellites) and with more than $250 billion likely to be invested by 46 nations in space assets by 2000, space had indisputably become an economic center of gravity and, hence, a major vulnerability of the United States and its allies.[4]

---

[4]For an argument that space in the coming century "will increasingly take on the lead role in international trade that sea-borne commerce has in centuries past," see Brigadier General Simon Peter Worden, USAF, "Space Control for the 21st Century: A Space 'Navy' Protecting the Commercial Basis of America's Wealth," in Peter L. Hays et al., eds, *Spacepower for a New Millennium: Space and U.S. National Security,* New York: McGraw Hill, 2000, pp. 225–237.

Some have questioned whether this aggregation of assets in space truly constitutes an economic center of gravity, even though there may be a thousand American satellites on orbit within ten years at a half-trillion-dollar investment. These skeptics counter that because satellites involve the movement of information rather than goods, they are not strictly comparable to the commercial ships that were plundered during the bygone era of rampant piracy on the high seas. On this point, it may well be, as Barry Watts has suggested, that we have not yet "found the right metaphors and historical analogies for thinking about the military use of near-earth space."[5] Yet what matters is that those satellites represent a tremendous U.S. dependency. It is thus entirely plausible that as the United States deploys ever more satellites and relies ever more on them for military applications, it will only be a matter of time before our adversaries are tempted to challenge our freedom of operation in space. In the security realm in particular, as two RAND colleagues have pointed out, a prospective opponent "will understandably view any space capability contributing to the opposing military as part of the forces arrayed against it in a theater. When the space capabilities represent an easier target than other critical nodes, we should expect interference with them. The natural consequence of space integration into military activity is a more hostile environment for space."[6]

Prompted by this concern, the U.S. Army, U.S. Strategic Command, and other joint agencies conducted a succession of high-level war games in recent years that focused expressly on the susceptibility of various U.S. space systems to disruption, denial, degradation, deception, and destruction. By one account, those experiences gave land, sea, and air commanders "a new appreciation for how dependent on space resources their operations have become."[7] In one Army-sponsored game, a scenario set in the year 2020 involving an invasion of Ukraine by "a neighboring state" featured the early neu-

---

[5] Barry D. Watts, *The Military Use of Space: A Diagnostic Assessment*, Washington, D.C.: Center for Strategic and Budgetary Assessments, February 2001, pp. 31–32.

[6] Bob Preston and John Baker, "Space Challenges," in Zalmay Khalilzad and Jeremy Shapiro, eds., *Strategic Appraisal: United States Air and Space Power in the 21st Century*, Santa Monica, Calif.: RAND, MR-1314-AF, 2002, pp. 155–156.

[7] William B. Scott, "Wargames Underscore Value of Space Assets for Military Ops," *Aviation Week and Space Technology*, April 28, 1997, p. 60.

tralization of many U.S. satellites by detonations of nuclear weapons on orbit aimed at disrupting intelligence and communications channels and at inhibiting any Western intervention. As one game participant later said of this gambit, "they took out most of our space-based capabilities. Our military forces just ground to a halt."[8]

Concern for the vulnerability of U.S. space-based assets was expressed with even greater urgency in the Space Commission's finding of a "virtual certainty" that a material threat to vital U.S. space equities will eventually arise. That finding led the commissioners to warn that the United States "is an attractive candidate for a 'space Pearl Harbor'" and must accordingly begin hedging now against hostile acts in and from space by developing and deploying what they called "superior space capabilities."[9] That conclusion was later echoed by Army Lieutenant General Edward G. Anderson III, the deputy CINCSPACE, who argued that "space is so critical now that if we don't do something about [our vulnerability] . . . we're going to have a 'space Pearl Harbor' and we'll deserve what we get."[10] Stressing the need to "ensure our continued access to space [and] deny space to others, if necessary," Anderson told the House Armed Services Committee that the nation runs "the very real risk of a 'space Pearl Harbor'" if this is not attended to in a timely manner.[11]

Such testimony raised an important question as to what a "space Pearl Harbor" might entail for the United States. At the darker end of the spectrum, it could occur frontally and as a stunningly rude surprise. The gravest threat in the near term would be a large number of U.S. and allied satellites being debilitated or destroyed by a major electromagnetic pulse (EMP) event or series of events staged by hostile forces in orbital space by means of nuclear weapon detonations. We already know something of the phenomenology of such a possible occurrence. In July 1962, Project Starfish Prime detonated

---

[8]Ibid.

[9]*Report of the Commission to Assess United States National Security Space Management and Organization*, Washington, D.C., January 11, 2001, hereinafter referred to as *Space Commission Report*, p. 100.

[10]William B. Scott, "Commission Lays Foundation for Future Military Space Corps," *Aviation Week and Space Technology*, January 15, 2001, p. 433.

[11]Walter Pincus, "U.S. Satellites Vulnerable to Attack, Officer Warns," *Washington Post*, June 21, 2001.

a 1.4-megaton thermonuclear weapon over Johnston Island in the Pacific Ocean at an altitude of 250 miles to test the effects of EMP on radio communications and radar. That event set off burglar alarms and burned out street lights in Oahu and further generated high-energy electrons that were trapped by the earth's magnetic field, producing an artificial radiation belt that damaged weather and observation satellites and destroyed seven satellites in seven months. The residual effects persisted until the early 1970s.[12] For years, the conventional wisdom among space optimists held that out of enlightened self-interest, if nothing else, no opponent would be so craven as to occasion such an omnidirectional and indiscriminate "scorched-space" cataclysm. The enormity of the terrorist attacks against the United States on September 11, 2001, however, coupled with the dawning realization of what the perpetrators of those attacks might have done had they been in possession of a nuclear device, went far toward discrediting that complacent counsel by confirming that at least some avowed mortal enemies of the United States are completely unbound by any such inclinations toward self-restraint.

At a lower level of potential destructiveness, a notional "space Pearl Harbor" might come in the form of a surprise hostile meddling with U.S. satellites by, for example, a ground-based laser attack that would cause irreparable damage to vital assets or otherwise interfere in some consequential way with an ongoing U.S. military operation. A disturbing hint of such a possibility was a 1997 Army test that temporarily blinded a U.S. satellite with a laser. In that test, a low-powered laser with little more wattage than a refrigerator lightbulb was fired at an Air Force MSTI-3 satellite on orbit 300 miles high. Pressed into service when the controversial million-watt Mid-Infrared Advanced Chemical Laser (MIRACL) melted one of its parts during an earlier test, the far weaker laser beam hit the satellite on three successive nights, suffusing the pixels on a focal plane array for several seconds.[13] That may not have been the first instance of such an event, moreover. Some people think that in October and

---

[12]R. C. Webb, "Implications of Low-Yield High Altitude Nuclear Detonation," Defense Special Weapons Agency (DSWA) presentation to an OSD/Net Assessment workshop on nuclear weapons and the revolution in military affairs, September 16–17, 1997, cited in Watts, p. 19.

[13]John Donnelly, "Laser of 30 Watts Blinded Satellite 300 Miles High," *Defense Week*, December 8, 1997, p. 1. MSTI stands for Miniature Sensor Technology Integration.

November 1975 the Soviets intentionally used intense radiation beams to interfere with three American satellites, although the U.S. government later publicly explained away the resultant degradation of those satellites as having been caused by natural phenomena.[14]

A particularly glaring U.S. space vulnerability is the constellation of Global Positioning System (GPS) satellites, thanks to our extraordinary dependence on that system. Although there is no public evidence that hostile jamming or other interference attempts have yet been made against GPS, it nonetheless presents a uniquely attractive target not only because of the extent of our reliance on it, but also because the GPS signal is faint and highly susceptible to jamming. Almost every high-end weapon in the U.S. military inventory relies on it for navigation and near-precision targeting, including the GBU-31 Joint Direct Attack Munition (JDAM), the powered GBU-15 electro-optically guided munition, unmanned aerial vehicles (UAVs), and certain Army ballistic missiles, among numerous others.[15] As strategist Colin Gray has cautioned, "people today who are easily impressed with the apparent difficulty a U.S. adversary would face in seeking to take down [GPS] should be exposed to the history of air power. . . . The technical-tactical challenges . . . eventually are overcome."[16]

Perhaps the most probable initial attempts against U.S. space-based assets will be made at the margins and incrementally, starting with a determined electronic "hacking" of those assets. At present, the United States is poorly equipped to deal even with the problem of accurately characterizing an attack in the event of such an attempt. There are proposals on the books for installing threat-warning sensors on future U.S. satellites to detect, identify, and classify attacks of various sorts. Most producers of commercial satellites, however, remain unconcerned about such potential threats to their products and are disinclined to spend the considerable sums that would be

---

[14]Paul B. Stares, *The Militarization of Space: U.S. Policy, 1945–1984*, Ithaca, N.Y.: Cornell University Press, 1985, p. 146.

[15]See John A. Hancock and Robin M. Pettit, "Global Positioning System—Our Achilles' Heel?" *Proceedings*, U.S. Naval Institute, January 2002, pp. 85–87.

[16]Colin S. Gray and John B. Sheldon, "Spacepower and the Revolution in Military Affairs: A Glass Half-Full," in Peter L. Hays et al., eds., *Spacepower for a New Millennium*, p. 244.

required to install threat-warning systems on their satellites.[17] As matters now stand, a satellite failure could be the result of natural radiation, a technical malfunction, a collision with space debris, or a deliberate attack, whether physical or electronic. To cite but one example, the U.S. Galaxy IV satellite in geostationary orbit above the United States began to roll aimlessly on May 19, 1998, leaving 35 million personal pagers in the United States dead and many self-service gasoline pumps unable to accept credit cards for nearly a day. It was the worst failure in space communications history up to that point. Fortunately, it proved to have been the result of a processor error and was eventually fixed. But it could just as easily have been the work of a mischievous hacker or a more malevolent agent.[18]

No military or commercial satellites are yet known to carry sensors to detect an attack by lasers, electromagnetic energy, or a kinetic-kill device. At present, the United States relies solely on passive measures for protecting its on-orbit assets against such threats. These measures include hardening and shielding against radiation, orbital maneuvering capabilities to evade attacks, and the use of such means as data encryption and antijamming provisions. Hardening of satellites and other onboard protection means offer an interim defense against potential threats. However, those measures are expensive and can be countered by a determined attacker. That is why CINCSPACE General Ralph E. Eberhart remarked that space control is "still at idle," referring to an aircraft's lowest throttle position, and that "it's time to move that up."[19] He also commented that even though the mere mention of "space control" leads many people's thoughts to turn instantly to "weapons in space," the pillars of space control "start with space surveillance." Beyond that, Eberhart added, with respect to the active denial of enemy space capabilities, there are multiple ways of doing the job without actually

---

[17]During the Schriever 2000 wargames, a satellite company executive said to Major General Lance Smith: "Protection? That's what insurance is for." (Quoted in Major M. V. Smith, USAF, "Ten Propositions Regarding Spacepower," M.A. thesis, School of Advanced Airpower Studies, Maxwell AFB, Alabama, June 2001, p. 24.) In fairness to industry here, the U.S. government has shown equally little inclination to pay for even modest electronic hardening of commercial satellites.

[18]John T. Correll, "Destiny in Space," *Air Force Magazine*, August 1998, p. 2.

[19]"World News Roundup," *Aviation Week and Space Technology*, February 25, 2002, p. 24.

destroying equipment on orbit: "There are lots of things you can do. You can use nonkinetic means." Most important of all in his view, however, is getting beyond the time not so long ago when "we couldn't [even] talk about it," a self-imposed restriction which he saw as "terribly naïve."[20]

UNDERSTANDING THE SPACE CONTROL MISSION

There is nothing particularly exotic about space control as a mission area. Conceptually, it is analogous to the long-familiar notions of sea and air control, both of which likewise involve ensuring friendly access and denying enemy access to those mediums. Viewed purely from a technical perspective, there is no difference in principle between defensive and offensive space control operations and operations conducted in any other medium of warfare. It is simply a matter of technical feasibility, desirability in principle, and cost-effectiveness for the payoff being sought. Yet the idea of space control has been slow to take root in the United States ever since the earliest days of the space age. The reason has long been a pervasive lack of government and popular consensus as to whether actual combat, as opposed to passive surveillance and other terrestrial enabling functions, should be allowed to migrate to space and thus violate the status of space as a weapons-free sanctuary, quite apart from the more practical question of whether preparing for space combat is even needed yet at this still-embryonic stage of space weapons development.[21]

To be sure, high-level leadership declarations have repeatedly acknowledged that the nation's space capabilities will routinely support U.S. military operations as feasible and appropriate. That has been the case with each successive U.S. National Space Policy since

---

[20]Quoted in Peter Grier, "The Combination That Worked," *Air Force Magazine*, April 2002, p. 32.

[21]The core issue here, it bears emphasizing, is not the "militarization" of space, even though this has long been a favorite whipping boy of critics. In fact, space has been "militarized" ever since the late 1950s by the constant presence of Soviet and American intelligence-gathering satellites on orbit. Rather, the sensitivity that attaches to the space control and, even more so, space force application missions has to do with their implied prospect of actually putting munitions in space and thereby migrating armed conflict itself into space.

1958, as well as with other national security documents that have periodically emanated from the White House and the Office of the Secretary of Defense and with the various service and joint vision statements of more recent years. All of these documents have repeatedly and consistently underscored the criticality of space for providing services geared to maintaining and exercising the nation's military core competencies to the fullest.

Yet these declarations have typically paid only lip service at best to the goal of ensuring U.S. freedom of operations in space. Not only that, they have been repeatedly belied by a sustained record of inaction on hard investments in space control mission development. Little has changed in this respect since the late 1950s. High-level military space guidance remains much the same today as it was when the Eisenhower administration endorsed the first national space policy in 1958. The principal unifying theme of that guidance has long been promoting the use of space for "peaceful purposes," while granting in principle that such use also includes defense and intelligence-related R&D and operations. Yet in practice, service programs proposed for actually developing and testing systems for possible space control applications have typically been resisted both within and outside the government.

By the same token, efforts to address space control needs programmatically have typically been either delayed or canceled outright as a result of a widespread determination to treat space as inviolate, irrespective of the nation's verbal commitment to space control. Most recently in this regard, then–Secretary of Defense William S. Cohen noted in a memorandum to U.S. military leaders accompanying the new Department of Defense Space Policy in July 1999 that "purposeful interference with U.S. space systems will be viewed as an infringement on our sovereign rights."[22] That document, in effect, declared that space control was an essential precondition for the United States to maintain information dominance. Yet the same Clinton administration of which Cohen was a key member two years earlier used the line-item veto to kill the Air Force's spaceplane proposal, as well as a kinetic-energy Army ASAT program, both of which

---

[22]John Donnelly, "Cohen: Attack on U.S. Satellite Is Attack on United States," *Defense Week*, July 26, 1999, p. 2.

were expressly geared to offering first-generation approaches toward enforcing space control.[23]

Accordingly, the space control mission area remains almost completely undeveloped in any operationally meaningful way. True enough, the coalition's air attacks against Iraqi satellite ground stations during the 1991 Gulf War could be rightly construed in hindsight as having entailed a successful first-generation attempt at conducting offensive space control because their intent was to deny Iraq access to the product of commercial satellite systems. Apart from that, however, no true space control systems have yet been deployed by the United States. About all we can do today to deny an enemy access to the data stream flowing from space is to jam or physically destroy satellite ground-control stations with aircraft or special operations forces or to use ground-based lasers in a crude effort to disrupt satellites that might be used against us. To all intents and purposes, as space-power advocate Steven Lambakis has pointed out, any security the United States may enjoy in space today—apart from that incurred as a happenstance by-product of deterrence—has been "by default, not because there is a deliberate policy framework and well-resourced, organized, and strategically guided military force to guard national space interests."[24]

In large part out of its growing appreciation of that fact, the Air Force leadership in recent years has been at the forefront of measured advocacy of more determined investment in space control. During his incumbency as CINCSPACE, General Estes pressed especially hard for aggressively pursuing concrete space control measures, declaring that "the writing is on the wall. If we don't [devote] some attention to

---

[23]That use of the line-item veto was interpreted by then-CINCSPACE General Howell M. Estes III as an effort by President Clinton to send a message to Russia's President Boris Yeltsin that the United States was not interested in starting a new arms race in space. Estes added that in his personal opinion, the vetoes were meant "to try to send a signal back to Russia in a public way that we were not going to develop systems for space control in terms of not creating systems to put their sensors at risk." He further suggested that those vetoes were but "a little bump in the road" on the way to space control because, given the "importance of the space control mission to this country's national security, we will continue to move down this road." See "Estes Sees Need for Continued ASAT Planning," *Aerospace Daily*, December 4, 1997, p. 1.

[24]Steven Lambakis, *On the Edge of Earth: The Future of American Space Power*, Lexington, Ky.: University of Kentucky Press, 2001, p. 1.

[space control] now, when the time comes, we'll wish we had—because it'll be a crisis that causes a huge government reaction. I want [us] to start working on it now, in a measured way, so we don't find ourselves in a crisis [where] chances are greater that we'll make the wrong decision."[25] More recently, General Eberhart similarly insisted that the Air Force and the nation need to embrace the space control mission more seriously: "I don't think we would be good stewards of space capabilities if we only thought about 'integration.' We should also be spending resources and intellectual capital on space control and space superiority." Eberhart repeated the increasingly heard refrain that space control will become ever more important "as our economy becomes more reliant on space." He further declared: "If we only look at space in terms of 'integration,' in my view, we'll fall into the same trap we fell into with the airplane. We [initially] thought of it in terms of intelligence, surveillance, reconnaissance, communication, and weather [support]. If we only think of space in these ways, [it's just] a 'higher hill' as opposed to a center of gravity."[26]

This insistence by the Air Force leadership, aided in considerable part by a worsening security situation in recent years, has been accompanied by encouraging signs that further progress toward serious space control mission development may finally be at hand. The Space Commission clearly backed the space control mission in its January 2001 report by noting that "the loss of space systems that support military operations or collect intelligence would dramatically affect the way U.S. forces would fight," indicating a "need [for them] to be defended to ensure their survivability."[27] The commissioners further noted that the threat to U.S. freedom of operation in space "does not command the attention it merits from the departments and agencies of the U.S. government." They went on to warn that a continued "failure to develop credible threat analyses could have serious consequences for the United States." They flatly con-

---

[25]William B. Scott, "CINCSPACE Wants Attack Detectors on Satellites," *Aviation Week and Space Technology*, August 10, 1998, p. 22.

[26]Ibid.

[27]*Space Commission Report*, p. 32.

cluded that because "we know from history that every medium . . . has seen conflict, reality indicates that space will be no different."[28]

Seemingly accepting this counsel, the George W. Bush administration's Quadrennial Defense Review (QDR) for 2001 noted not long afterward that the emergence of space and information operations as the predominant aspect of the nation's commercial and military space involvement had raised "the possibility that space control—the exploitation of space and the denial of the use of space to adversaries—will become a key objective in future military operations."[29] The QDR added that "future adversaries will . . . likely seek to deny U.S. forces unimpeded access to space." It further noted that such counterspace alternatives as space surveillance, ground-based lasers, space jamming capabilities, and proximity microsatellites are becoming increasingly available to potential U.S. opponents, making it an "essential objective" of U.S. defense transformation "not only to ensure the U.S. ability to exploit space for military purposes, but also, as required, to deny an adversary's ability to do so."[30] Consequently, the QDR declared, the Department of Defense "will pursue modernization of the aging space surveillance infrastructure, enhance the command and control structure, and evolve the system from a cataloguing and tracking capability to a system of providing space situational awareness."[31] Although these expressions fell short of promising hard funding for such mission needs, they nevertheless were important bellwethers of administration concern and intent.

SOME INITIAL SPACE CONTROL ALTERNATIVES

The first point that bears emphasizing in any consideration of next steps toward space control is that the initial requirement for developing such a capability is simply better space surveillance, the sine qua non of any would-be space control regime. A ready availability of functioning ground- and space-based systems to

---

[28]Ibid., pp. 18, 22.

[29]The Honorable Donald H. Rumsfeld, *Quadrennial Defense Review Report*, Washington, D.C., Office of the Secretary of Defense, 2001, p. 7.

[30]Ibid., p. 31.

[31]Ibid., p. 45.

monitor what is on orbit, where those items are at any given moment, and what they are capable of doing is a precondition for *any* significant space control capability. The Space Commission did the cause of space control a favor by reminding readers of its report that the need to come to better grips with the space surveillance challenge does not contravene the argument of successive administrations that the United States should endeavor to preserve the space weapons regime established by the Outer Space Treaty concerning the "traditional interpretation of the Treaty's 'peaceful purposes' language to mean that both self-defense and non-aggressive military use of space are allowed."[32]

At present, the United States enjoys only a modicum of real-time space situation awareness, since it only tracks objects that are already known to be on orbit. The next step toward acquiring the essential elements of a space control capability will be securing the ability to search space in short order so that U.S. space monitors can better know what is being put into orbit and by whom. Such a capability will probably be based initially on improved ground- and space-based optics, supplemented by better and more proliferated ground-based radar "fences" which will detect anything that transits their field of regard.[33]

Beyond improved surveillance and situation awareness, much more can be done to develop an operational space-control repertoire merely by using existing ISR and strike assets to engage a potential enemy's most immediately accessible and exposed space system nodes, such as ground-based satellite uplinks and downlinks. As for follow-on measures toward acquiring a more active space control capability, those who would seek the benefits of such a capability without transgressing the taboo against migrating armed combat into space have proposed a mode of operations called "flexible negation" in lieu of direct attack. Flexible negation involves such measures as jamming, spoofing, and blinding enemy satellites and disabling enemy ground support stations. The underlying idea is to temporarily disable a satellite rather than to damage or destroy it,

---

[32]*Space Commission Report*, p. 37.

[33]William B. Scott, "CINCSPACE: Focus More on Space Control," *Aviation Week and Space Technology*, November 13, 2001, p. 80.

and to do so in a manner that might provide the attacker a fair amount of deniability. It is an inescapable fact that any use of kinetic-kill alternatives would create a host of associated problems, not only because a direct attack on a satellite could be construed as an act of war but also because any physical destruction of a hostile satellite would create a severe on-orbit debris problem that could badly backfire on the United States and its allies by strewing low orbital space with potentially lethal shrapnel. As two Air Force space professionals soberly observed, "satellites that die an explosive death become a lot of space debris. Space debris is fundamentally an unguided, hypervelocity kinetic-energy weapon" and, at a minimum, a hazard to space navigation.[34]

Primarily for that reason, "flexible negation" was the preferred approach of the Clinton administration to space control, emphasizing relatively benign, nonlethal, and reversible imposition options. As then–Deputy Secretary of Defense John Hamre explained the concept: "We fully believe that 'negation' in space—preventing the bad guys from using space against us—is fully authorized under international law. But we do want to take steps and actions that don't create instability in the world. This [space control] area is, frankly, on the edge, and we do not want to take steps that are precipitous and that could create greater problems for the U.S." Hamre added: "There is a range of things we can do. It isn't simply blowing up satellites in space." The latter, he said, would make it "much, much harder for us to get international cooperation" on such important matters as frequency and orbital slot allocation. "We could spend an enormous amount of money on space destruction capabilities that our leaders would never authorize us to use, for fear of international [backlash] and the problems it might create. So our preference is that we design a negation program around tactical denial of capability, not permanent destruction."[35] Representative examples of such a tactic might

---

[34]Lieutenant General Roger G. DeKok and Bob Preston, "Acquisition of Space Power for a New Millennium," in Peter L. Hays et al., eds., *Spacepower for a New Millennium*, p. 85.

[35]William B. Scott, "U.S. Adopts 'Tactical' Space Control Policy," *Aviation Week and Space Technology*, March 29, 1999, p. 35. It should be noted here that the United States is hardly a newcomer to the space situation awareness business. As far back as the early 1960s, the Ballistic Missile Early Warning System (BMEWS) fenced the Arctic, the

include the selective jamming of an enemy's satellite data stream and denying an enemy the use of GPS signals in a localized zone.

Beyond these nonintrusive flexible negation alternatives, a more direct and aggressive approach being explored for disrupting enemy on-orbit assets might feature the use of "micropaint" satellites, which could rendezvous with those assets and fire paintball-like material at them to blind them. Yet another option might entail small, highly maneuverable microsatellites that could rendezvous with enemy satellites and negate them by blocking their field of view, spot-jamming their transmissions, or burning out their wiring with lasers. Once developed, such space control activities will be dominated by both passive and active space defense capabilities, which will be natural extensions of today's multisensory tracking systems, antisatellite weapons, and embryonic decoy and deception technologies and concepts.

FORCE APPLICATION AND THE ISSUE OF WEAPONIZATION

Space force application, an area of interest farther down the list of priorities than the more pressing matter of space control (leaving aside the related but separate case of ballistic missile defense), is rightly regarded as representing the ultimate use of space for military purposes. Among other things, it envisages the use of space-based directed-energy and kinetic-energy weapons against missile targets, kinetic-energy weapons against ground targets, and conventional weapons against ground targets. A recent RAND study defined space weapons as "things intended to cause harm that are based in space or that have an essential element based in space," with the degree of

---

Navy Space Surveillance System (NAVSPASUR) fenced the continental United States, and Baker-Nunn cameras and imaging radar provided fairly prompt space object identification. All this was triggered by Defense Support Program (DSP) launch detections and was augmented by additional phased-array and mechanical tracking radars in the space surveillance network. Once this capability had matured, neither the Soviets nor the Chinese launched anything that U.S. sensors did not detect, track, identify, and catalog within about 20 minutes. The fact that the United States needs to get better and faster at the space situation awareness game should not be taken to suggest that it neglected that mission area during the first four decades of the space age. I am indebted to Lieutenant Colonel Forrest Morgan, USAF, for reminding me of this important piece of Air Force space history.

sought-after harm ranging from temporary disruption to permanent neutralization or disruption.[36]

U.S. space systems do not currently have any ability to employ direct force against an opponent. Once such an ability becomes economically, technically, and politically feasible, however, the development of the force application mission, often referred to more colloquially as the "weaponization of space," will complete the nation's transition to a true military space power.[37] It could ultimately lead to the use of such exotic technologies as space-based lasers to intercept ballistic missiles and destroy or neutralize other satellites. It may also involve the use of space-based nonnuclear hyperkinetic weapons against terrestrial targets, ranging from hardened bunkers, munitions storage depots, underground command posts, and other heavily defended objects to surface naval vessels and possibly even armored vehicles and other ground targets of interest.

Numerous force application concepts have been seriously proposed and considered. The first national-level war game dedicated primarily to military space operations—Schriever 2001, conducted by the Air Force Space Command's Space Warfare Center—sought to explore a range of operational requirements for space force application. One alternative considered was the use of so-called common aerospace vehicles against ground-based lasers situated deep within enemy territory, with the intent of engaging a class of targets that must be serviced very quickly, something the United States currently lacks an ability to do with its existing nonnuclear projection forces.[38] (The extended distances involved would preclude the effective use of

---

[36]Bob Preston, Dana J. Johnson, Sean J. A. Edwards, Michael Miller, and Calvin Shipbaugh, *Space Weapons, Earth Wars*, Santa Monica, Calif.: RAND, MR-1209-AF, 2002, p. 23. This well-informed primer on space weapon concepts currently being considered describes their attributes, categorizes and compares them, and explores the political implications of their possible acquisition and deployment—all at an unclassified level.

[37]Lest there be unintended confusion here, it bears stressing that many defensive and offensive space control functions could also involve "weaponization" of various sorts. The difference at issue is between weaponization against enemy space systems and weaponization against more classic terrestrial targets of independent strategic, operational, or tactical interest.

[38]William B. Scott, "Wargames Zero In on Knotty Milspace Issues," *Aviation Week and Space Technology*, January 21, 2001, pp. 53–54.

bombers and cruise missiles to prevent enemy lasers from negating U.S. satellites.)

In a similar spirit, Air Force officials have reported that they could launch a demonstration space-based laser by 2010. It would permit the downing of an in-flight ballistic missile within about 18 months, at a projected cost of around $4 billion. A constellation of six such satellites, using technology similar to that on the Air Force's airborne laser currently in advanced development, would be needed to make the system operationally effective. The projected cost would be $70 billion to $80 billion.[39] To cite but one more of the numerous weapons concepts that have been considered, the Defense Science Board has urged the initiation of a demonstration project to validate the feasibility of deploying highly accurate hypervelocity rods made of heavy material to engage ground targets through the atmosphere from space.[40]

As in the case of space control, the issues associated with space force application are fairly simple and straightforward from a narrow military viewpoint and largely entail matters of technical feasibility, strategic desirability, and cost. Apart from their political dimensions, the importance of which cannot be overstated, decisions about the merits of developing and deploying space-to-earth weapons could be based simply on a trade-off assessment of the operational efficiencies of space-based weapons and their terrestrial counterparts. The advantages and disadvantages of space-to-earth weapons will, of course, depend on the specific characteristics of the systems in question. In most cases, however, the comparisons will turn on a weighing of differences in such familiar variables as speed, range, lethality, flexibility, vulnerability, and acquisition and sustainment costs.

The overarching problem connected with this mission area, however, is that—at least today—far greater political sensitivities attach to it than those associated with the less provocative notion of space con-

---

[39]Peter Pae, "Doubts Trail 'Son of Star Wars' Proposal," *Los Angeles Times*, May 23, 2001.

[40]Defense Science Board, *Joint Operations Superiority in the 21st Century: Integrating Capabilities Underwriting Joint Vision 2010 and Beyond*, Washington, D.C., Office of the Under Secretary of Defense for Acquisition and Technology, October 1998.

trol. It is revealing that media representatives in attendance at Secretary of Defense Rumsfeld's May 2001 press conference (called to discuss the bureaucratics of military space reorganization in response to the Space Commission's recommendations) seemed to want to discuss only the hot-button issue of space "weaponization." To preempt any possible media charges of hidden administration weaponization intent, Rumsfeld came forearmed with the space policy statement issued in 1996 by the Clinton administration, which declared that the Department of Defense would "maintain space control capabilities to ensure freedom of action in space and, if directed, deny such freedom to adversaries."[41] Rumsfeld further emphasized that his proposals had "nothing to do" with weaponization, but rather concerned organizational arrangements within the Department of Defense "that put a focus on the important issues relating to space, which [hitherto] have been spread throughout the department in a way that has made it difficult to get the right kind of focus and the right kind of emphasis."[42] Yet many simply refused to accept that message. Opined one critic with a predisposition to presume the worst, even though Rumsfeld admittedly claimed that his proposed reforms "had nothing to do with any intention to deploy antisatellite systems or weapons, such protestations were cold comfort to the very countries that the United States seeks to assuage about its missile defense program."[43]

As baseless and unfair as that particular charge and others like it may have been, the fact remains that there is no more fundamental or more unresolved a military space issue in the United States today than the long-festering question of whether space should be kept free of weapons at every reasonable cost or actively exploited to the fullest extent of its ability to underwrite the nation's security. From a purely operational viewpoint, there is no difference between combat functions that would be carried out from space and those that al-

---

[41]John Diamond, "Rumsfeld Hedges on Space Arms," *Chicago Tribune*, May 9, 2001.

[42]Quoted in Amy Butler, "Air and Space Ops Chief Refutes Accusations of Political Subversion," *Inside the Air Force*, May 18, 2001, p. 1. Later, in a press interview, Rumsfeld bridled at the media's effort to portray his reorganization briefing as a weapons-in-space briefing: "I couldn't believe it. I had to spend the whole dadburn press conference trying to dig out from that." (Thomas E. Ricks, "Post Interview with Defense Secretary Donald H. Rumsfeld," *Washington Post*, May 20, 2001.)

[43]Paul B. Stares, "Making Enemies in Space," *New York Times*, May 15, 2001.

ready occur routinely in the land, naval, and air environments. The *technical* differences between attacking land, naval, or aerial targets with terrestrially based weapons and doing the same with weapons delivered from space are, by and large, distinctions solely involving tactics, techniques, and procedures.[44] Yet the American political establishment and its elected leaders have not yet made up their collective minds as to whether space should be deemed just another operating domain like the more familiar, air, land, and maritime environments or instead should somehow be treated as "different" and protected from conversion into yet another potential battle arena.

To summarize the arguments regarding space weaponization briefly: What might be called the "sanctuary school" continues to insist that because the United States is the country most dependent on space both militarily and commercially, it has the most to lose by rushing to weaponize before a clear need for doing so has been established. Among other things, this school bases its case on an asserted absence of imminent threats to U.S. freedom of space operations and a belief that weaponization could appear aggressive to others and accordingly could trigger a space arms race and other destabilizing consequences—such as inducing others to take asymmetric responses like acquiring nuclear weapons. At bottom, it holds that a premature deployment of space force application systems not only would provide the United States with few security gains to offset these penalties but might have implications that could be highly unwelcome, especially should the United States seek a truly hegemonic space-based force application capability.[45]

Opposed to this argument is the school of thought whose proponents actively seek the weaponization of space at the earliest opportunity, with more than a few already busy at work laying the doctrinal and

---

[44]This is not meant by any means to trivialize the *political* salience of putting offensive space-to-ground weapons on continuous station in earth orbit. As noted in Chapter Three, enemies and allies alike would understandably have every reason to perceive American space-based offensive weapons orbiting constantly overhead as no different in principle than armed American bombers routinely transiting their airspace. There is no prima facie reason to believe that most countries would readily countenance our doing with space-based weapons in normal peacetime conditions something we would never presume to do with air-delivered weapons.

[45]I am indebted to my colleague Karl Mueller for the framing of this characterization of sanctuary thinking.

technology foundations for such a development. At the root of this thinking is an implicit belief that timely and effective space weaponization would naturally be a good thing for the Air Force and for the larger interests of U.S. security. Among those of this persuasion both in and out of uniform, some would undoubtedly concede that although space weaponization is probably undesirable in principle, it also is ultimately bound to happen, since those who are inimical to the United States will sooner or later come to view space weapons as offering an attractive and lucrative means for threatening U.S. interests.

Others would argue more matter-of-factly that the United States should prepare *now* not only to deny the use of space to potential enemies for military purposes, but also to make whatever offensive use of space as may be advantageous, on the premise that continued U.S. unilateral restraint would do little to dissuade present and potential rivals from pursuing weaponization options of their own whenever it seemed feasible and suited their purposes. At bottom, the most extreme of the would-be space weaponizers argue that the United States should press ahead with acquiring space force application capabilities as soon and as extensively as practicable while time remains. Their reasoning is that if we prepare in a timely and effective way not only to control who uses space and how, but also to exploit it offensively in support of U.S. strategy, no potential challenger will ever be able to catch up with us.

IS SPACE WEAPONIZATION INEVITABLE?

The foregoing discussion raises the important yet ultimately intractable question of whether the migration of combat operations to orbital space is bound to take place sooner or later out of sheer inexorability. Many regard such an eventual development simply as a given. As former Air Force General Joseph Ashy declared during his incumbency as CINCSPACE, "it's politically sensitive, but it's going to happen. Some people don't want to hear this, and it sure isn't in vogue . . . but—absolutely—we're going to fight *in* space. We're going to fight *from* space, and we're going to fight *into* space when [U.S.

and allied assets on orbit] become so precious that it's in our national interest."[46]

This widespread belief in the eventual inevitability of space weaponization stems in part from air analogies and, in particular, from a conviction that the space experience will naturally repeat the air experience. As General Estes, for example, argued while serving as CINCSPACE, "the potential of aircraft was not recognized immediately. Their initial use was confined to observation . . . until one day the full advantage of applying force from the air was realized, and the rest is history. So too [will it be] with the business of space."[47]

In fact, the United States possesses the essential wherewithal in principle to begin weaponizing space today. Reduced to basics, it is only a question of leadership choice, societal acceptance, and which particular force-employment alternatives to pursue first. Yet it also is true that the United States retains the power of the initiative in this respect and has at least some basis for guardedly hoping that if it continues to show restraint, others may also. The unanswerable question concerns when—not whether—our opponents will decide to become militarily proactive in space to counter U.S. dominance.

Regarding this issue, the United States faces a difficult policy conundrum. As the world's leading democratic country, its leadership is bound by an understandable obligation to do everything reasonable to maintain the moral high ground. Yet that leadership cannot afford to remain so passive as to allow itself to be caught by a "space Pearl Harbor" surprise. An important question thus entails whether proceeding to lay down at least the essential wherewithal for moving, as need be, to weaponize space sooner would risk incurring fewer downside consequences than waiting until later. The deputy commander-in-chief of U.S. Space Command, General Anderson, recently put the dilemma this way: "Right now there is no need to deploy weapons in space, but . . . we are tasked with the responsibility for examining force application. It is reasonable that we should do that. . . . This is not easy technology. It is something that does take

---

[46]William B. Scott, "USSC Prepares for Future Combat Missions in Space," *Aviation Week and Space Technology,* August 5, 1996, p. 51.

[47]General Howell M. Estes III, USAF, address to the Air Force Association annual symposium, Los Angeles, October 18, 1996.

time. You can't wait until you decide you need it and then not have it. It seems to me we would be failing our obligations to the nation."[48]

Most would agree that space weaponization is not inevitable in the *near term*. Indeed, there is scant observable evidence to suggest that the military use of near-earth space will be substantially different in 2020–2025 than it is today, at least regarding the development and fielding of new technologies and systems that would broaden the use of our on-orbit assets from force enhancement to force application— unless, of course, some unforeseen trigger event occurred to provoke it. It naturally follows that any U.S. space weaponization that eventually occurs, whether preemptive or reactive, will most likely be threat-driven rather than as a result of prior unprovoked choice. Former Air Force chief of staff General Michael Ryan suggested as much when he stated: "I don't think you'll see us moving real fast until some threat occurs—a huge threat, a threat that makes a big dollar difference. Then you'll see a shift in policy."[49]

For the time being, the idea of placing offensive weapons in space for use against terrestrial targets remains contrary to declared national policy, and there is no indication that the nation is anywhere near the threshold of deciding to weaponize space. Any truly serious steps toward acquiring a space force application capability will involve a momentous political decision that the nation's leadership has not yet shown itself ready to make. As the Air Force's former deputy chief of staff for air and space operations, then–Lieutenant General Robert Foglesong, noted, "if the policy decision is made to take our guns into space, that will be decided by our civilian leadership."[50] Until that threshold is reached, any talk of space weaponization will remain not only politically moot but needlessly provocative, and military space activity will remain limited to enhancing terrestrial operations and controlling the ultimate high ground.

Yet to say that space weaponization is not around the corner is scarcely to say that it is out of the question altogether. As Colin Gray

---

[48]"Interview with U.S. Army Lieutenant General Edward Anderson," *Jane's Defence Weekly*, July 11, 2001, p. 32.

[49]William Matthews, "To Military Planners, Space Is 'The Ultimate High Ground,'" *Air Force Times*, May 18, 1998, p. 12.

[50]"If Ordered, AF Ready to Arm Space," *San Antonio Express-News*, May 11, 2001.

has pointed out, such a development "may be slow to arrive, but slow to arrive is a light year removed from impracticable. . . . Speculation about the efficacy of seapower in the 17th or early 18th century could have pointed to problems entirely comparable to those which [skeptics of weaponization cite] to suggest that spacecraft will enjoy a continuing sanctuary status in orbit."[51] In a similar reflection of what might be called space weaponization fatalism, General Estes likewise observed that "some day in the not so distant future, space will have evolved to the point where the movement of terrestrial forces will be accomplished only at the pleasure of space forces, much in the same way that the movement of land and sea forces today can only be accomplished at the pleasure of air forces."[52] By this logic, the eventual weaponization of space is only a matter of time—albeit a span of time that is, at least to a degree, within the power of the United States to control by its near-term conduct and by the character and pacing of its eventual actions.[53]

NEAR-TERM IMPLICATIONS FOR THE AIR FORCE

It is now widely accepted within the Air Force and among other observers of the space scene that if the Air Force intends to evolve into an "air and space force" worthy of the name, it will soon need to start acquiring at least the beginnings of a serious space control capability, just as it did in the realm of counterair operations during the formative years of air power's development. Fortunately, the climate for taking the next steps toward space control has become increasingly favorable. The nation's leadership, by numerous indications (including the Space Commission's recommendations and the most recent QDR), finally seems disposed to lend a receptive ear toward that end. Moreover, the terrorist attacks against the United States on

---

[51]Gray and Sheldon, in Hays et al., eds., *Spacepower for a New Millennium*, p. 243.

[52]Quoted in Correll, "Destiny in Space," p. 2.

[53]To note one conceivable possibility in this respect, the distinction between space force enhancement and space force application could become increasingly blurred over time when one considers that the GPS satellites, for example, which already guide a JDAM to its target, are, in fact, participating very directly in the application of force, much like a strike aircraft's laser designating a target upon which it is dropping a laser-guided bomb. Whether a system like GPS is considered part of a weapon or a mere force enhancer is partly a matter of perception, which will be greatly affected by how the United States elects to characterize it. I am grateful to Karl Mueller for this insight.

September 11, 2001 irreversibly altered the conventional wisdom about the character of the external threats the nation faces. Those attacks confirmed beyond doubt that America's enemies, especially fanatically hostile nonstate enemies, possess the will, if not yet the means, to go to any achievable lengths to harm the most vital U.S. interests. As a result, the long-standing popular reluctance to migrate even defensive force-employment functions to space under any conditions may be gradually losing its former tenacity.

True enough, with the end of the cold war now more than a decade behind us, the United States still lacks a peer opponent of sufficient technological virtuosity to warrant our proceeding aggressively toward offensive space weaponization today. That said, several state actors in President George W. Bush's declared "axis of evil" are working diligently toward acquiring the means for accessing space in a spoiler role. While deterrable to a point, they also possess both the motive and the determination to exploit any such means to the hilt at the earliest opportunity. It follows that the Air Force, now more than ever, needs a measured approach toward moving systematically beyond space support and space force enhancement to further developing and ultimately mastering the space control mission. To do this successfully will require being more careful than ever to avoid projecting any appearance of prematurely overreaching with respect to space "weaponization" and instead concentrating unswervingly on laying down the essential building blocks for realistically enforceable and credible space control, while deferring any active involvement in force application initiatives until a clear justification for them has arisen and the associated enabling technology and political will have matured to a point where their time has arguably come.

Some Air Force commentary in recent years on the would-be virtues of space weaponization has seemed surprisingly oblivious of the real sensitivities that still attach to the idea of combat operations from space in many quarters, as well as of the no-less-real political costs and potential consequences for our national interests that could accrue from making space force application a premature goal of U.S. strategy.[54] One such example was the space applications volume of

---

[54]See Karl Mueller, "Space Weapons and U.S. Security: Why and How to Avert a Dangerous Potential Revolution," unpublished paper, School of Advanced Airpower Studies, Maxwell AFB, Alabama, September 28, 1997.

the Air Force Scientific Advisory Board's widely publicized *New World Vistas* study of 1995. This study categorically stated that the Air Force should "broaden the use of space to include direct force projection against surface, airborne, and space targets," without the least apparent consideration of possible political or strategic ramifications.[55] Fortunately, those in positions of higher Air Force leadership have been more measured and discreet when it comes to this most touchy of space issues. General Estes, for example, in stressing the need for moving ahead smartly in the space control arena, was keenly mindful of the issue's political delicacy when he candidly admitted: "We've got to be real careful how we do this. It's a sensitive issue. . . . I don't know how else to tell you . . . because we're talking about doing things in space that upset people."[56] He also took studious care to decouple space control from space force application, to emphasize that the first does *not* automatically imply the second, and to highlight the importance of attending to first things first: "We [also] have to be able to surveil, protect, and negate under this space control mission. . . . I believe it's obvious to all—*short of deciding we're going to weaponize space*—that we understand we must be committed to space control, that we must be able to prevent [adversaries'] use of space and protect our use of space. And if protection goes to negation, then we need to be prepared to do that."[57]

Most of all, the Air Force should recognize that although the nation may indeed be nearing a tectonic shift in public attitudes with respect to migrating combat functions into space, it will take astute leadership, both civilian and military, to ensure the necessary transition toward a robust American space control capability in a seemly way. That will not occur until that leadership first forges a new national consensus on the still-sensitive issue. As John Logsdon, a re-

---

[55]*New World Vistas: Air and Space Power for the 21st Century,* Space Applications Volume, Washington, D.C., USAF Scientific Advisory Board, 1995, p. 164.

[56]John Donnelly, "Commander: Clinton's Vetoes Won't Halt Space Weapons," *Defense Week,* December 15, 1997, p. 3.

[57]Ibid., emphasis added. A spokesman for AFSPC's directorate of plans and programs conceded candidly, however, that in order to pursue space control seriously, "seventeen consecutive miracles are going to have to happen to get us there," since Air Force space activity has to compete for funds not only with the other services but also within the Air Force. "Air Force Space Command Developing Strategies for Satellite Protection, Warfare Advances," *Florida Today,* June 22, 2001. AFSPC currently spends $12 to $15 million of its $8.8 billion annual budget researching space control concepts.

spected space scholar at George Washington University, aptly observed in this respect, "it may well be that the time has come to accept the reality that the situation of the past half-century, during which outer space has been seen not only as a global commons but also a sanctuary free from armed conflict, is coming to an end. But decisions about how the United States should proceed to develop its space power capabilities and under what political and legal conditions are of such importance that they should be made only after the full range of concerned interests have engaged in thoughtful analysis and discussion."[58]

In light of that, an important challenge facing the Air Force entails helping to inform such analysis and discussion by taking the lead in articulating the issues authoritatively, while disavowing any immediate programmatic commitment to space force application and, at the same time, keeping the argument for space control unswervingly fixed in its public message as the nation's most pressing priority for expanded space mission development. The Air Force's executive agent for military space, the Honorable Peter Teets, set a helpful precedent in that respect when he suggested that the time may have arrived for the Department of Defense to consider developing space-based weapons, at least to protect its on-orbit equities. "Given the dependence of U.S. military forces on space-based assets, illustrated every day over Afghanistan," he said, "it is critical that the Pentagon find ways to protect those assets. I believe that weapons will go into space. It's a question of time. And we need to be at the forefront of that."[59]

---

[58]Quoted in Butler, "Air and Space Ops Chief Refutes Accusations of Political Subversion," May 18, 2001, p. 1.

[59]"Defense Department Should Consider Developing Space-Based Weapons, Teets Says," *Aerospace Daily*, March 7, 2002.

Chapter Six

THE ROAD AHEAD

As this study has documented in detail, there have been two distinguishable schools of thought throughout most of the Air Force's history with respect to whether air and space should be treated as two separate operating mediums and mission areas or as a single and seamless "aerospace" continuum. The introduction of the "aerospace" construct by Air Force chief of staff General Thomas D. White in 1958 was principally the outgrowth of a perceived need to help ensure the Air Force's institutional survival. As such, it was a product of artful sloganeering that was never really backed up by any deep thought or systematic, operationally focused analysis. Instead, it was, for the most part, merely an inspired catchword for an Air Force roles and missions claim that caught on and persisted in Air Force declaratory pronouncements for years thereafter. Rampant uncertainty and confusion actually marked the Air Force's groping attempt to make sense of space during its first formative decade, when it had far more immediate and pressing preoccupations. Recalling that time, former Air Force chief of staff General Lew Allen, under whose watch Air Force Space Command was finally created in 1982, said that in 1958, "the Air Force clearly was determined to get involved in space but didn't know yet what it wanted to do. . . . Everybody was enthusiastic about space, but no one had yet defined what it was all about."[1]

---

[1] General Lew Allen, Jr., USAF (Ret.), U.S. Air Force oral history interview, Maxwell AFB, Alabama, Air Force Historical Research Agency, January 1986, p. 28. On the point about institutional survival, General Allen further recalled (p. 192) that the Navy was anxious to organize its own space activities and create a space structure, which "contributed to the Air Force looking a little backward in not doing so."

Although the ensuing "aerospace" idea tended to predominate in Air Force doctrinal rhetoric and expressed positions in the roles and resources battles, at the operational level the fielded Air Force almost from the outset saw and treated space instead as a distinct and unique mission area in its own right. During the early years of the 1960s and 1970s, space was a domain of Air Force activity clearly apart from the air environment. That activity was highly compartmented and heavily shrouded in secrecy, with a predominant focus on systems development and national leadership support in connection with the missions of nuclear deterrence and retaliation.

By the early 1980s, however, a recognition had gradually arisen throughout the operational Air Force that the nation's growing military space communications, surveillance, and sensor capabilities had an important contingency-support contribution to offer not only to the president and the Secretary of Defense to ensure against the most grave national crises, but also more routinely to joint-force commanders in regional theaters around the world. Numerous Air Force leaders, uninhibited by "aerospace" thinking, accordingly came to regard space as a medium and mission area in and of itself. Because space was understood as being separate and distinct from the air medium, it naturally followed, in the judgment of those leaders, that the Air Force needed a separate and dedicated operational command for space in order to develop and grow the special competence required to build and operate space systems.

Simply put, Air Force Systems Command came to be viewed as doing things of an operational nature in space which it had no business doing. Such activity, according to this growing perception of the Air Force's leading commanders, made no more sense than having the Aeronautical Systems Division in Dayton, Ohio, running Air Force fighter wings or the Electronic Systems Division at Hanscom Field, Massachusetts, developing concepts of operations for and flying the E-3 airborne warning and control system (AWACS).[2] The establishment of Air Force Space Command (AFSPC) in 1982 and, three years later, the unified U.S. Space Command was directly traceable to that logic. As AFSPC's first commander, General James V. Hartinger, re-

---

[2]General W. L. Creech, USAF (Ret.), presentation to the commander and senior headquarters staff, Air Force Space Command, Peterson AFB, Colorado, April 15, 1999.

marked several years later in hindsight, "we thought we were looking at space with a different perspective. Space is a place, like the land, the sea, or the air. It's a theater of operations, and it was just a matter of time until we treated it as such."[3]

In 1996, however, a major move occurred at the behest of the incumbent Air Force chief of staff, General Ronald R. Fogleman, to redefine air and space as a single medium and mission area and to commit future Air Force planning and programming toward that end, with the idea that space would eventually replace the atmosphere as the Air Force's main operating arena. The 1996 Corona conference of senior Air Force leaders which ratified that move all but expressly promised that spacemen would eventually inherit the Air Force—and most of the Air Force's space officers believed it. General Michael E. Ryan, who succeeded General Fogleman as chief, regarded the Corona formulation as excessively divisive of the service's air and space communities because of its clear implication that the latter would eventually supplant the former. Yet his closely related stress on "aerospace integration" served to entrench ever further the idea of air and space as constituting a single and seamless continuum.

In 2000, the Space Commission heard the Air Force's argument on behalf of the "aerospace" construct and did not buy into its premises and assumptions. The idea that space is simply an extension of the vertical dimension did not prevail with the commissioners. Instead, they concluded that space is a separate medium and mission area, just like the air, land, and naval operating environments. Secretary of Defense Donald Rumsfeld, who had chaired the Space Commission until his selection to head the George W. Bush administration's Pentagon, issued appropriate directives to the Department of Defense and to the Air Force alike to implement most of the commission's recommendations. Not long thereafter, on succeeding General Ryan as Air Force chief of staff, General John P. Jumper moved with both conviction and dispatch to disavow the "aerospace" construct and to portray space as separate and unique, warranting its own organizational infrastructure and career track. That ended decisively, at least for the moment, the long-running intra–Air Force to-ing and fro-ing

---

[3]General James V. Hartinger, USAF (Ret.), U.S. Air Force oral history interview, Washington, D.C., USAF Historical Research Center, Office of History, Headquarters USAF, September 1985, p. 167.

over whether the preferred mantra of the day was "air *and* space" or "aerospace."

That recent change in mindset on the proper understanding of space is overwhelmingly in the Air Force's interest and should be made a permanent fixture of Air Force thinking and rhetoric. To be sure, the now-discredited aerospace construct had never been a unanimous preference of the Air Force leadership. As noted above, a number of senior Air Force leaders who helped to sire AFSPC understood explicitly that air and space were separate mediums and mission areas warranting separate organizational support and funding treatment. This became increasingly apparent as the Air Force began putting ever more of its investment dollars into space in the absence of a commensurate increase in the Air Force's overall budget limit, making intra–Air Force budget trades ever more obvious and painful.

Yet the Air Force's continuing insistence on the notion that no conceptual boundary existed between air and space, notwithstanding its understandable intent to ensure the Air Force's long-term institutional livelihood, had a perverse effect: It worked against that service's interests by threatening to increase funding for space at the expense of the Air Force's no less important *air* responsibilities, all other things remaining equal. As far back as the 1970s, the Air Force had acquired a wholly new mission set in space that fully warranted separate and dedicated funding. Indeed, as AFSPC was being established, there was serious discussion among the four-stars as to whether the Air Force should seek an arrangement in which all the services would contribute their fair share for the percentage of the nation's military space product they consumed. "User pays" arguments began to be aired among the Air Force leadership, along with discussion of a common DoD stock fund for space into which all of the services would pay, as appropriate, to support the overall national military space effort.[4]

However, the Air Force leadership never actively pursued such an arrangement. Nor did it ever make a serious effort actually to petition the Office of the Secretary of Defense (OSD) to be formally designated the nation's executive agent for military space. Had its leaders

---

[4]Telephone conversation with General W. L. Creech, USAF (Ret.), January 20, 2001.

been so inclined, the Air Force might have reached out during the early 1980s to get space formally defined as a separate and independent mission area under its corporate purview. Instead, it simply asserted a *claim* to both air and space while never being officially given the space mission area as a separate tasking. As a result, military space continued to be paid for solely out of the Air Force's preexisting budget allocation, and Air Force space, both predictably and of necessity, ended up facing the eventual prospect of being underwritten at the expense of other Air Force accounts, notably the service's force-projection air accounts—at the same time as "must-pay" space investments in the interests of all the services and other users grew at a rate greater than that of the Air Force's overall annual budget dispensation.[5] As just one straw in the wind in this respect, the Air Force laboratories at Wright-Patterson AFB, Ohio, were not long ago put on notice by the Air Staff that the air portion of their R&D charter would experience significant cuts in the next budget cycle and that they would need to step up their space-related research activities with the resultant funds that will flow from future Program Objectives Memoranda (POMs) and budget apportionments.[6]

Fortunately for the Air Force, in rejecting the aerospace construct, the Space Commission in effect gave the Air Force something no other service had ever before been granted, namely, *two* formally mandated mission areas—air *and* space. The commission also acknowledged, in its recommendation of a Major Force Program (MFP) budget category for space, that the space mission rightly demanded dedicated organizational oversight and funding. Finally, it provided what the Air Force had yearned for without fulfillment for more than 40 years, namely, formal designation as the nation's executive agent for military space. With the Space Commission's findings now published and Secretary Rumsfeld committed to implementing the bulk of its recommendations, the Air Force has lately found itself with respect to space somewhat in the unexpected position of the

---

[5]In contrast, by way of suggesting what might have been a feasible alternative approach, the National Aeronautics and Space Administration (NASA), from its inception, made a successful division of air and space into two mediums and mission areas in its organization and budgeting.

[6]Telephone conversation with General W. L. Creech, USAF (Ret.), April 26, 2002.

proverbial dog that chased a truck for years to no avail and finally caught it. Now it must decide what to do with it.

Already, the Air Force leadership has taken the first steps toward realizing the promise held out by the Space Commission. That leadership has not only willingly but enthusiastically accepted its assigned role as executive agent for military space, thanks to what Under Secretary of the Air Force Teets recently described as "some remarkable changes made in the last year to refine and improve the way we organize space capabilities and execute space activities for national security purposes."[7] As a result, it has gained the formal recognition as the nation's military space steward that accompanies that role. With most of the bureaucratic and structural concerns described in Chapter Four now resolved, at least for the near term, the Air Force faces a clear horizon with respect to next steps in implementation. Five pressing space-related issues remain outstanding and in need of focused attention. They entail continuing with the operational integration of space with the three terrestrial warfighting mediums while ensuring the organizational differentiation of space from Air Force air; effectively wielding the Air Force's newly granted military space executive-agent status; realizing a DoD-wide budget category for space which imparts transparency to how much money and manpower are going into space each year and for what; achieving signal progress toward fielding a meaningful space control capability, while decoupling that progress cleanly from any perceived taint of force-application involvement; and making further progress toward developing and nurturing a cadre of skilled space professionals within the Air Force ready and able to meet the nation's military space needs in the coming decade and beyond.

OPERATIONAL AND INSTITUTIONAL IMPERATIVES

To begin with, considering that *all* the uniformed services and *all* force elements benefit equally from what space has to offer, it would behoove the Air Force to make peace once and for all with the fact that "air and space integration," narrowly construed, was and re-

---

[7]Statement by the Honorable Peter B. Teets, Under Secretary of the Air Force, to the Commission on the Future of the U.S. Aerospace Industry, Washington, D.C., May 14, 2002, p. 1.

mains an inappropriate peg on which to hang its future role in space. To be sure, a closer meshing of the Air Force's air and space capabilities was not only desirable but absolutely essential during the initial years following Operation Desert Storm. During the Gulf War, the remarkable space support that was provided to the coalition's terrestrial force elements, notably including coalition air power, was made possible only by what one Air Force space officer later characterized as "ingenious adaptation, resourcefulness, and ad hoc procedures."[8] Recognizing that such jury-rigged arrangements would hardly suffice to meet the needs of a future joint force commander faced with a no-notice contingency, in the decade after Desert Storm AFSPC took numerous steps to make the contribution of the nation's military space assets more routinely accessible to air warfighters at all levels, from the Joint Force Air Component Commander (JFACC) all the way down to individual operators working within tactical confines.

To cite two examples, the establishment of Space Warfare Center (SWC) Detachment 1 at Nellis AFB, Nevada in 1996 offered a means of providing space-derived imagery, communications, weather, and navigation support to aircrews in Weapons School training and at Red Flag, a quarterly large-force training exercise, much like that which has increasingly become available to aircrews in actual global contingency operations. Funneled through the new Nellis Combined Air Operations Center (CAOC), this new space-derived information flow has included the delivery of target imagery and threat location information directly into the cockpits of airborne aircraft in the advanced training environment. As just one illustration, a data burst from assets in space to a Block 50 F-16CJ equipped with the Improved Data Modem can cue the pilot in real time to a threatening radar-guided surface-to-air missile site.[9] Similarly, SWC's Detachment 2 at Langley AFB, Virginia has begun to support the recently established CAOC-X there, to teach CAOC staffs how to employ on-

---

[8]Lieutenant Colonel Steven J. Bruger, USAF, "Not Ready for the First Space War: What About the Second?" *Naval War College Review,* Winter 1995, p. 7.

[9]I had an occasion to observe this capability in operation at first hand during an F-16CJ sortie flown in support of the mission employment phase of the USAF Weapons School's Class 98A at Nellis AFB, Nevada, on June 12, 1998. During this high-intensity and highly realistic large-force graduation exercise, we successfully engaged and negated a simulated SA-3 site entirely through off-board cueing from a national asset on orbit.

orbit space assets during peacetime, in much the way as Red Flag has long sought to provide participating aircrews with the functional equivalent of their first ten combat missions through peacetime training.[10]

Moreover, whereas the Air Force in years past was slow to insert space expertise and a space exploitation capability into its Air Operations Centers (AOCs), that erstwhile deficiency has since been significantly redressed. During the tenure of General Howell M. Estes III as CINCSPACE in 1997, space support teams were permanently assigned to regional joint-force headquarters worldwide, where career space officers (often space weapons officers) routinely served a full tour of duty on the regional CINC's staff.[11] Previously, those with such expertise stayed at Air Force Space Command in Colorado Springs and only ventured into regional theaters as needed for training exercises or actual contingencies. Today, the Air Force has disbanded its space support teams, opting instead to imbed space weapons officers as appropriate in various planning and execution cells throughout its AOCs worldwide. In a similar spirit, at Vandenberg AFB, California, a new Space Operations Center analogous to the familiar and proven AOC opened in 2000 at 14th Air Force to monitor the status of on-orbit satellites, missile warning assets, and launch system plans and schedules. Directives to 14th Air Force wings are now routinely communicated by the new daily Space Tasking Order (STO), analogous to the familiar Air Tasking Order, as part of an ongoing effort to normalize and align space units more closely with air operations.[12]

---

[10]William B. Scott, "Detachment Brings 'Space' to Nellis Air Operations," *Aviation Week and Space Technology,* January 15, 2001, pp. 453–454.

[11]Beginning with its first space division class in 1996, the USAF Weapons School at Nellis AFB has routinely been graduating some 24 space weapons officers a year. These space-division graduates learn how to integrate existing space capabilities into air combat operations and to translate the potential of those capabilities into a language planners and aircrews can readily understand. (William B. Scott, "USAF Space Weapons Officers Find Unique Niche in Air Warfare," *Aviation Week and Space Technology,* January 15, 2001, pp. 454–455.)

[12]William B. Scott, "Air Force Opens New Space Center," *Aviation Week and Space Technology,* November 24, 1997, p. 71. For more on SWC and its pivotal role in extending the offerings of space to terrestrial warfighters in all services, see Benjamin S. Lambeth, *The Transformation of American Air Power,* Ithaca, N.Y.: Cornell University Press, 2000, pp. 238–242.

Yet despite the significant progress borne out by these examples toward making the contributions of space more routinely accessible by terrestrial warfighters, the Air Force's narrow focus on "aerospace integration" toward the end of the 1990s remained overly parochial and inward-looking—and was so perceived by the other services in the joint arena. Accordingly, the time has come to start thinking in terms of integrating space more fully with *all* the services in a joint context. Since the potential offerings of space promise to redound ultimately to the benefit of all terrestrial force elements, not just to that of Air Force air power, it seems incontestable in hindsight that merely "air and space" (or "aerospace") integration was a paradigm that precluded the kind of evolutionary change actually called for. Not only was the Air Force's insistence that air and space constituted a seamless continuum increasingly self-destructive over time, its stress on "aerospace integration" was also misfocused on integrating space solely with Air Force air functions when what was needed was a conceptual framework aimed at permitting better integration of U.S. military space capabilities with all the force employment functions of all the U.S. services.[13]

Toward that end, what seems most indicated today for managing the seams between space and the air, land, and maritime environments is a perspective focused on *operational integration* accompanied by *organizational differentiation*. Through such a bifurcated approach, space can be harnessed to serve the needs of all warfighting components in the joint arena while, at the same time, being rightly treated as its own domain in the areas of program and infrastructure management, funding, cadre-building, and career development. After all, AFSPC was established to give the Air Force's space professionals a proper home in which to develop the required special competence in

---

[13]It would be ideal if the Air Force could approach what needs to be done by way of conceptual, doctrinal, and organizational improvements with a clean slate, designing an approach to becoming a bona fide space power much as Douhet and Mitchell freely theorized about air power. But too much bureaucratic and organizational turf has already been claimed, which unfortunately will limit the Air Force leadership to suboptimal action at the margins. As Barry Watts has pointed out, although the United States currently enjoys a considerable head start over any other potential military competitors in space, "it also is encumbered by powerful stakeholders with limited interest in organizational or conceptual transformation." (Barry D. Watts, *The Military Use of Space: A Diagnostic Assessment*, Washington, D.C.: Center for Strategic and Budgetary Assessments, February 2001, p. 72.)

space mission execution. That rationale needs to be sustained and further entrenched, not lost in a vain effort to meld Air Force air and space professionals in a manner that risks making dilettantes of all. It is well enough in principle for the Air Force to strive to give its air and space communities a more common language and vocabulary, as well as a better mutual appreciation of what each community does. But beyond a point, as General Jumper has observed on numerous occasions, the military space career field is a unique culture that needs cultivating in its own right both in the Air Force's and the nation's best interest.[14]

To be sure, in working toward the further refinement and maturation of a distinctive and duly backstopped space career field within the Air Force, air and space professionals at all levels must understand that while the organizational differentiation of space from air will be crucial for the promise of space to be most fully realized for joint warfighters, any emergent "space culture" that may ensue from it must *not* be isolated from the mainstream Air Force, as it was during the long years when it was in the clutches of the systems and acquisition communities, but rather must be rooted from the start in an unerring focus on the operational level of war. Toward that end, such post–Desert Storm initiatives as the establishment of a space division within the USAF Weapons School at Nellis and the subsequent inclusion of a Space Warfare School at AFSPC's Space Warfare Center at Schriever AFB, Colorado represent important steps in the right direction. They should be further nurtured and substantially broadened because both aim expressly to produce operationally literate space warfare professionals and to proliferate operationally minded space expertise where it is most needed throughout the Air Force and in key joint warfighting centers worldwide. Beyond that, as Air Force

---

[14]A recent article roundly scored the Air Force's experiment with a career management approach called Developing Aerospace Leaders (DAL) and its associated stress on "broadening" assignments across the air and space career fields, on the ground that such "broadening" will inevitably come at the cost of a loss of critical officer technical skills in both fields at precisely the time the service needs those skills the most. (See Lieutenant Colonel Steven C. Suddarth, USAF, "Solving the Great Air Force Systems Irony," *Aerospace Power Journal*, Spring 2002.) Since that article's publication, in keeping with the Air Force's shift away from aerospace thinking to a renewed emphasis on air *and* space, there have been signs that the Air Force leadership was having second thoughts about the merits of the DAL approach, which was very much a product of the aerospace mindset prevalent at the time of its creation.

space professionals become ever more conversant with the operational imperatives of joint warfighting, they have a collective obligation to bend every effort to rise above the fault lines and fragmented subcultures that unfortunately still persist within their *own* community (the National Reconnaissance Office, the nascent information-operations guild, and the myriad niches of the C4/ISR world, for instance). Only then can they form a more coherent and interconnected center of space excellence able to speak credibly about what space brings to joint-force employment—not just across the chasm that still separates them from Air Force airmen but also between and among themselves as they develop and mature in their own right.[15] The initiative for following through on such needed and overdue measures, which typify the essence of what is meant by the operational integration of space with other warfighting elements, lies squarely at the feet of today's Air Force space community and its senior leaders.

By the same token, those on the more traditional side of the Air Force with career roots in the fighter, bomber, and other flying communities also have a solemn obligation to understand and internalize the fact that the Air Force is now fully in the space business as much as it ever was in the force-projection air business. If the Air Force is to vindicate the generous charter it was given by the Space Commission, it must press for needed space systems modernization with every bit the same energy and passion that it shows for such centerpiece programs as the F-22 air dominance fighter (recently redesignated F/A-22 to capture the aircraft's significant ground-attack potential and intended all-weather day and night deep-strike mission portfolio). The Secretary of the Air Force, the Honorable James Roche, could not have been more emphatic on this point when he recently declared that the Air Force "is entering a new era of air and space power" and that as the service continues to evolve to meet the requirements of this new era, "we must ensure [that] our space forces and equipment and concepts of operations remain as innovative and capabilities-based as those we are now developing for our air-breathing systems." Continuing in the same vein, Secretary Roche

---

[15]I am grateful to Major General Michael A. Hamel, USAF, commander, 14th Air Force, Vandenberg AFB, Calif., for calling my attention to these latter points during a conversation in his office at Vandenberg on July 29, 2002.

added that "space capabilities in today's world are no longer [just] nice to have. They are becoming indispensable at the strategic, operational, and tactical levels of war."[16]

CEMENTING THE EXECUTIVE-AGENT MANDATE

The assignment of executive-agent status to the Air Force for military space by Secretary Rumsfeld in May 2001 was not only appropriate, it was arguably a generation late in coming. Ever since the 1970s, if not before, the Air Force has had a legitimate claim to stewardship of military space. By virtue of years of unquestioned institutional dominance in the space mission area, it commands a monopoly on space resources, infrastructure, equipment, and expertise that no other service comes close to matching. The Air Force owns 90 percent of the nation's military space personnel, manages 85 percent of the nation's military space budget, wields 86 percent of the nation's military space assets, and operates 90 percent of its military space infrastructure. It is on *that* basis, not as the result of any self-arrogated "birthright" to space or its long-asserted claim that space is merely a linear extension of its mandated air domain, that the Air Force has earned such stewardship.[17] Indeed, as Chapter Two detailed, space has been anything *but* an Air Force "birthright." On the contrary, ever since the late 1940s, the Air Force had to claw its way aggressively, and often against significant Army, Navy, and civilian bureaucratic resistance, toward its newly acquired status as the nation's formally designated executive agent for military space.

---

[16]The Honorable James G. Roche, Secretary of the Air Force, "Transforming Our Air and Space Capabilities," remarks to the Air Force Association National Convention luncheon, Washington, D.C., September 18, 2002. This comment seemed unmistakably to reflect the Space Commission's observation that, for all its talk in the recent past about "air and space integration," the Air Force had not been generally perceived by many as treating its air and space mission taskings with equal commitment. It also seemed to be a reminder that in recommending that the Air Force be formally assigned responsibility for two operating arenas (air *and* space), the commissioners had intended to send a signal that the Air Force was duty-bound to show equal devotion to both mission taskings—not just in its own interest but also in the national interest.

[17]Nor, it should be noted, did the Air Force's claim to the space mission area draw strength from any intimation that space is somehow a greater servant of Air Force air power than of other force elements, since all services and force elements benefit from the offerings of space—land and maritime forces arguably even more, in relative terms, than the Air Force.

Now that it has been granted such status, the Air Force should have every incentive to vindicate its designation as the nation's military space steward by moving proactively to fulfill its new role. In that regard, how the executive-agent role, now vested in Under Secretary of the Air Force Teets, is understood and played out by the civilian and uniformed Air Force leadership will be crucial. A key initial question concerns what executive-agent status for military space entails in principle and how the Air Force can best fulfill it in practice. Simply put, there is no government manual, at least yet, that explains what an executive agent for military space is and does. The absence of any agreed and formalized baseline for the charter would appear to give the Air Force great latitude to interpret and test the charter's boundaries. It seems almost axiomatic that the better the Air Force understands, articulates, and executes its new executive-agent role, the longer it will succeed in postponing the eventuality of an independent U.S. space service.

Because the Air Force, as the nation's designated executive agent for military space, must maintain oversight of all military space activity even if other services assume an increased space mission burden, a particular challenge will be for it to both be and *appear* to be evenhanded and effective in exercising such oversight. An important part of that challenge will entail accepting individual service control of service-specific space systems rather than further splintering the execution of operational functions through needless duplication of effort. Because the executive agent is authorized to track all U.S. military space activities (not to wield *cognizance* over them, but certainly to maintain awareness and recognition of them), it should have a compelling interest in understanding Army and Navy space systems and programs in every significant technical and fiscal detail. To help ensure such informed awareness, the Air Force might do well to invite formal Army and Navy input to ensure that it is performing the executive-agent role to the satisfaction of those services. One way to do that might be to elicit senior Army and Navy space representation at AFSPC on a permanent basis.

Beyond that, it bears noting that the Department of Defense, having designated the Air Force the executive agent for military space, has an obligation to delimit the boundaries of the executive agent charter by setting forth the Air Force's various powers and responsibilities and ensuring that the charter is clearly understood by all concerned elements throughout the department. It goes without saying that an "executive agent" without an adequately broad and clearly defined mandate can hardly function effectively as DoD's designated clearinghouse for military space matters. At a minimum, the space executive agent should be able to claim coordinating and monitoring responsibility for all space-related activities to be included in the space MFP (see the next section), since the MFP budget category for space will rise to its potential and fulfill its promise only if *all* space-related funding is included therein.

Fortunately, since the release of the Space Commission's report, OSD has moved on three important fronts to develop and promulgate initial guidelines for the definition and implementation of space executive-agent authority throughout DoD. First, following up on his earlier letter of May 8, 2001 to the chairman of the Senate Armed Services Committee indicating his planned responses to the Space Commission's recommendations, Secretary Rumsfeld issued an all-hands memorandum to the most senior principals in the defense establishment (including the service secretaries, the chairman of the Joint Chiefs of Staff, the under secretaries of defense, and a few others) on October 18, 2001. It announced his decisions with respect to military space management and organization and his guidance as to "how best to ensure [that] the Department of Defense is arranged and focused" toward effective implementation of those decisions.[18] Heading his guidance list was a directive to the Under Secretary of Defense for Acquisition, Technology, and Logistics, Pete Aldridge, to develop a plan for delegating milestone decision authority for all DoD space acquisition programs to the Secretary of the Air Force, along with approval to redelegate that authority to the Under Secretary of the Air Force. Under Secretary Aldridge followed through on that directive not long thereafter in a memorandum dated February 14, 2002, which delegated milestone acquisition decision authority to the Secretary of the Air Force. Although Aldridge's memorandum expressly ruled out any applicability to "highly sensitive classified programs" as defined by Title X of the U.S. Code (namely, those satellite programs conducted and operated under the

---

[18]The Honorable Donald H. Rumsfeld, "Memorandum on National Security Space Management and Organization," Washington, D.C.: Office of the Secretary of Defense, October 18, 2001.

NRO's auspices), it empowered the Secretary of the Air Force, "in coordination with the Secretaries of the Army and the Navy," to "implement further actions with regard to space acquisition streamlining."[19] In so doing, it gave the Air Force an unprecedentedly powerful tool, at least in principle, for exercising its executive-agent status. For that reason alone, in conjunction with the long-overdue hard-wiring of the Air Force's Space and Missile Systems Center (SMC) to AFSPC (finally consummated the year before), Aldridge's empowering memorandum represented a momentous step in the maturation of America's military space capability.

Second, the OSD director of space policy in late February 2002 circulated a draft DoD directive on executive-agent implementation for review and comment by the senior working-level principals in OSD's acquisition and C3I secretariats, the Office of the General Counsel in OSD, the Army, Navy, and Air Force, and the Directorate of Plans (J-5) on the Joint Staff, with courtesy copies also provided to the National Security Space Architect and the office of the Deputy Director of Central Intelligence. As explained in the cover memorandum, the draft directive was meant to clarify "the lines of authority, specific responsibilities, and coordination requirements between the executive agent for space and DoD components."[20]

Among other things, this detailed document (important enough to have been included as an appendix to this study for further reference) outlined the Air Force's upcoming roles in the space policy and planning arena. It stipulated in particular that the Air Force "shall establish appropriate DoD-wide processes for the development, coordination, integration, review, and implementation of space system plans, budgets and acquisition programs in conjunction with other military departments and defense agencies."[21] The directive further

---

[19]The Honorable E. C. Aldridge, Jr., "Memorandum on Delegation of Milestone Decision Authority for DoD Space Systems," Washington, D.C.: Office of the Under Secretary of Defense, February 14, 2002.

[20]Marc J. Berkowitz, Director, Space Policy, "Action Memorandum on the DoD Directive 'Executive Agent for Space,'" Washington, D.C.: Office of the Under Secretary of Defense for Policy, February 26, 2002.

[21]"Department of Defense Directive 'Executive Agent for Space,'" Washington, D.C.: Department of Defense, February 25, 2002, p. 2.

empowered the Secretary of the Air Force, as the principal repositor of DoD's space executive-agent authority, to ensure that all executive-agent responsibilities are assigned and carried out, to "strongly represent DoD-wide space interests" in the planning, programming, budgeting, and acquisition processes; to harmonize all requirements for space programs generated by the other services through the Joint Requirements Oversight Council; and to recommend proposed space-related planning and programming guidance to the DoD Comptroller and Under Secretary of Defense for Policy.[22]

At bottom, the draft directive gave the Air Force what one account rightly called "sweeping new authority in the planning, programming, and acquisition of military space systems."[23] As of the end of November 2002, unlike the earlier signed implementation tasking outlined above, it remained in the grips of intradepartmental coordination and accordingly had not yet been formalized as DoD policy. All the same, it represents a crucially important step forward within DoD that should be warmly welcomed by the Air Force because it gives the service all appropriate authority in principle to act effectively on its recent empowerment as DoD's executive agent for military space. Indeed, about the only major area of Air Force concern left unspecified in the implementation directive—and it is a significant one—entails the relationship of Air Force Space Command to the Air Force secretariat and the breadth of AFSPC's authority within the executive-agent context. The Under Secretary of the Air Force, as DoD's newly designated executive agent for space, may wish to inquire into this subject as an early order of business in pursuit of greater specificity and clarity.

Third, with respect to the pivotally important issue of DoD space funds management, the above-cited draft directive authorized the Air Force to "periodically review the space program, budget, and accounting mechanism" recently established by the DoD Comptroller, which the directive described as a "virtual" MFP, and to recommend to the DoD Comptroller suggested changes to the content of that "virtual" MFP. The directive as currently written leaves room for

---

[22]Ibid., pp. 3–4.

[23]Anne Plummer, "Draft Memo Outlines Air Force Role as Executive Agent for Space," *Inside the Pentagon*, March 7, 2002, p. 1.

much ambiguity and uncertainty in its cryptic allusion to a "virtual" MFP for space, offering little specificity as to what such a "virtual" MFP might entail in practice. Unless it amounts to a de facto MFP in all but name, any such "virtual" budget category will surely be destined to fail as an identifying and controlling mechanism for cross-service military space programs.

Encouragingly, in what may be indicative of things to come, a subsequent DoD report to Congress on the department's implementation of the Space Commission's recommendations expressly defined the "virtual" MFP as consisting of some "180 program elements grouped into space control, space force application, space force enhancement, space support, and other space. Included in the 'virtual' [MFP] for space are research, development, test and evaluation, systems, user equipment, people, organizations, and infrastructure whose primary [or] dedicated mission is space or a space-related ground system. The 'virtual' [MFP] for space identifies program elements from the Air Force, Army, Navy, Defense Information Systems Agency, and Defense Advanced Research Projects Agency."[24]

Although these program elements remain, as before, service-specific, their aggregation in this new and unprecedented manner for all to comprehend in a single look should give the space executive agent an unprecedented ability to identify cross-service program overlap and redundancies. That in itself represents a major step in the right direction toward a more rational management of DoD spending on military space. That said, however, irrespective of how right-minded and informative it may sound in and of itself, a DoD report to Congress does not constitute guidance with binding authority over DoD. That report most definitely offered at least the beginnings of a good and workable definition of what a space MFP, whether called "virtual" or something else, should include by way of programs and related space activity. However, it must be promulgated as formal, top-down OSD guidance to the services with all due specificity if it is to be on point with respect to needed improvements in DoD-wide space funds management. One can only hope that the terms of refer-

[24]"Commission to Assess United States National Security Space Management and Organization (Space Commission) Implementation," Washington, D.C.: Department of Defense, interim report to the Committees on Armed Services of the U.S. Senate and House of Representatives, May 2002, pp. 5–6.

ence in DoD's report to Congress describing the "virtual" space MFP will survive the internal DoD coordination and staffing process. For as now written, they offer real promise of putting teeth into the Space Commission's recommendations with respect to military space budget accounting. This too may be a topic that the Under Secretary of the Air Force may wish to pursue further as a matter of special priority in the course of testing his newly assigned executive-agent authority.[25]

UNSETTLED FUNDING ISSUES

Of all the uncertainties that currently affect the Air Force's prospects for realizing the near-term promise of military space, none is more critical than the most basic question of how and at what opportunity cost those prospects will be financed. Echoing an argument voiced for years by many airmen (and not just those in the space career field), the Space Commission categorically concluded in January 2001 that America's military space capabilities are "not funded at a level commensurate with their relative importance."[26] This predicament is traceable largely to the fact that military space funding comes almost entirely out of the Air Force's budget, even though all of the uniformed services benefit from the space products ultimately provided.

Not surprisingly, the Air Force has thus become increasingly hard-pressed to uphold both its air and its space mission responsibilities with only a constant one-third share or so of overall annual defense

---

[25]One might note in passing that the executive agent for military space also has an important educational responsibility—to groom tomorrow's Air Force executives for military space. Another important responsibility entails measured advocacy of all four of the DoD's space mission areas (space support, force enhancement, space control, and force application), with predominant emphasis today on the first three. Yet another involves providing reasoned explanations of the increasing risk faced by the nation's most vital on-orbit assets as a result of present and potential threats.

[26]*Report of the Commission to Assess United States National Security Space Management and Organization*, Washington, D.C., January 11, 2001, p. 97, referred to hereinafter as *Space Commission Report*. Areas noted as underfunded included space situation awareness; enhanced protection and defensive measures for on-orbit assets; modernized launch; and a more robust science and technology program, including space-based radar, space-based laser, hyperspectral sensors, and reusable launch technology.

total obligational authority (TOA). One reason why the other services have been so readily acquiescent in the Air Force's dominance of military space is almost surely that the Air Force's shouldering of virtually the entire military space funding burden has essentially allowed them a free ride. One should hardly be surprised that the other services would have such an unlimited appetite for space support and such an unbounded roster of space "requirements" when they do not have to pay for those costly force-enhancement benefits.

As General Estes pointed out in 1997, the Air Force will never make good on its various long-term planning statements if it does not begin investing greater sums in space.[27] However, Estes also acknowledged that in an era of unusually tight budgets, the nation's space priorities must be balanced against equally vital nearer-term air-related mission support needs. He further acknowledged that few Air Force leaders would suggest that the Air Force can afford to abandon its existing core air mission responsibilities simply to free up more money for space.[28]

Given the current zero-sum competition between military space priorities and the Air Force's other spending requirements, it is inescapable that should DoD continue its current resource apportionment practices with respect to space, the Air Force will, in the words of one former senior space officer, find itself faced with "the untenable option of capitalizing space with its increasingly limited resources."[29] This is not to say that the space and air mission areas are in direct competition with one another for Air Force funding support and that every additional dollar invested in space somehow automatically implies a loss for the USAF's air force-projection capability. To the contrary, investments in military space programs over the past two decades have contributed materially to a greatly disproportionate expansion of the overall leverage of the Air Force's

---

[27]William B. Scott, "'Space' Competing for USAF Funds," *Aviation Week and Space Technology,* December 1, 1997, p. 69.

[28]Conversation with the author at Headquarters U.S. Space Command, Peterson AFB, Colorado, June 18, 1998.

[29]Major General William E. Jones, USAF (Ret.), former deputy chief of staff for operations, Air Force Space Command, white paper on the creation of an air and space force within the Air Force, prepared at the request of Major General David McIlvoy, AF/XPX. December 22, 1997, p. 11.

numerically smaller combat-aircraft inventory—in terms of such key attributes as flexibility, survivability, situation awareness, responsiveness, target-attack accuracy, and lethality, among others. Nevertheless, while it would be wrong for this reason to portray space and air as involving stark either/or choices for the Air Force leadership, it remains a fact that, unless current DoD budget-balancing priorities for R&D and procurement are changed, it will become increasingly difficult to do proper justice to both mission areas as each assumes ever greater importance over time.

A particularly aggravating factor in this respect is that space applications have become increasingly expensive as the defense establishment has become increasingly dependent on them and ever more invested in them.[30] One seemingly intractable cause of this is the persistently high cost of space launch, which has imposed an inherent limit on the sustainable rate of expansion of U.S. military assets on orbit. The constant-dollar price of getting a satellite to low earth orbit (LEO) has not changed much over the past two decades. The average cost per pound to LEO for most commercial satellites now on orbit is between $3,600 and $4,900, depending on the altitude and character of the orbit. The cost per pound for getting a payload all the way out to geostationary earth orbit (GEO) is considerably higher than that, averaging $9,200 to $11,200.[31] Furthermore, the prospect for any substantial diminution in launch costs over the next 10 to 15 years remains dim because of the unalterable physics of chemically fueled, rocket-based launch. There is little new technology now on the near-term horizon that offers any promise of circumventing this constraint.

To be sure, offsetting the low likelihood of even a marginal reduction in the cost per pound for putting payloads on orbit, miniaturization has slowly but inexorably increased the functionality of each payload pound on orbit, making possible the development and launching of smaller satellites. As one Air Force officer recently noted, "These

---

[30]For example, the first MILSTAR satellite, launched in 1995 nearly five years after the cold war's end, cost roughly the same as the entire operating revenue of Intelsat, the commercial provider, and five times the entire Defense Department outlay for commercial satellite time in 1997. ("New Space Race," *Jane's Defence Weekly*, August 26, 1998.)

[31]Watts, *The Military Use of Space: A Diagnostic Assessment*, p. 7.

things aren't the size of a school bus any more, they're the size of a bread box."[32] A decade ago, military satellites typically weighed between 5,000 and 20,000 lb. Now those going to LEO increasingly weigh between 500 and 2000 lb. This means that the cost-per-pound issue may turn out to be less pressing in the future than it has been hitherto. The ever-decreasing size and weight of satellites further portends the ability to put more fuel aboard them, since they cannot be refueled in space. This will enable larger orbit changes as needed during contingencies and crises.[33]

Compounding the continued high cost of space launch is the fact that the Air Force is facing an impending acquisition and funding problem of the first order, created by the block obsolescence of many on-orbit systems now in service and the imminent emergence of a new generation of systems now at the threshold of being fielded as replacements. Virtually every major U.S. military space system is facing a planned upgrade or replacement over the coming decade, at an estimated cost of some $60 billion. These include the next-generation Global Positioning System (GPS), all military communications satellites, a space-based infrared system (SBIRS) to replace the Defense Support Program (DSP) constellation of missile-launch sensors, and a space-based laser technology demonstrator.[34] There also is the looming prospect of space capabilities within the grasp of potential adversaries that could threaten some U.S. satellite functions and accordingly beg for defensive and counteroffensive space control measures—as well as the tantalizing potential of such new capabilities as space-based radar, laser communications, and hyperspectral sensing, all of which can significantly enhance overall terrestrial force combat effectiveness. The problem is that these technology opportunities have arisen at a time when the Air Force is also facing an unprecedentedly expensive replenishment cycle in its fielded *air* assets. All of these options are competing for scarce re-

---

[32]"SAB Releases Its Space Surveillance Recommendations," *Inside the Air Force*, December 12, 1997, p. 12.

[33]There is a practical limit, however, to how small many categories of military satellites can be made, since solar panels require a large surface, necessitating size and weight, in order to produce sufficient electrical power.

[34]*Space Commission Report*, p. 15.

sources within the Air Force budget, and hard choices will have to be made and impediments removed if those options are to be realized.

A core challenge here entails devising an equitable funding arrangement that will adequately underwrite the nation's military space needs in the interest of all services, but not at the unacceptable expense of the Air Force's Title X–mandated air responsibilities. To correct this aberration, military space funding must somehow be drawn from the totality of the U.S. defense budget—including not only Air Force air programs but also Army helicopters, Navy carrier aviation, and Marine aviation, along with offset decrements to submarines, surface ships, tanks, howitzers, and all other military procurement programs across the board. The reason is that military space is not just another Air Force service-specific function such as airlift and close air support, which serve other categories of military operations and other services. Rather, it constitutes a separate and distinct mission arena in its own right that promises over time to become as costly to underwrite to its fullest potential as the land, maritime, and air arenas are today.[35]

As long as U.S. military space funds are provided for as they are now—that is, almost entirely within the Air Force's R&D and procurement budget—those in the Office of Management and Budget and in Congress will retain every inclination to continue their familiar and historic "service budget balancing" practices, and the other services will be more than content to go along. Unless and until there is a change in the way military space capitalization is paid for, it will continue to come almost exclusively out of the Air Force's annual resource allocations. Valiant attempts to "persuade" the other services to pony up their fair share for the benefit they accrue from the nation's on-orbit systems, something the Space Commission clearly concluded was overdue for attention, will go nowhere.

---

[35]With respect to this important and still-unresolved issue, a position paper written by the Air Staff as the Space Commission was hearing testimony from the services declared candidly that "the Air Force recommends consideration of budget mechanisms that would more equitably distribute the costs of space services throughout the Department of Defense" and that such an arrangement might better "help DoD space users focus on their requirements and establish priorities in their respective uses of space services." ("Air Force Position Paper on Space Commission Issues," Washington, D.C.: Headquarters USAF, August 14, 2000, p. 5.)

In one sense, the Air Force has no one but itself to blame for this predicament owing to its recurrent insistence in the annual budget wars since the 1950s that a seamless "aerospace" continuum was its exclusive operating domain. But it has nonetheless been both unfair to the Air Force and irrational from a broader defense planning perspective that funding for national military space systems should come almost exclusively out of the Air Force's procurement accounts at the expense of Air Force air power and other investment needs. In contrast, the nation's land and sea systems (including the air components of those systems) have been much less burdened by such draconian trades. On reflection—especially given the growing centrality of space to every service's operating repertoire—it is simply unreasonable for a single service to be expected to bear the burden of the nation's military space costs alone. As matters stand, said former CINCSPACE General Charles Horner, "space is sick, and the only way it's going to get well is at the expense of air programs."[36] Earlier, Horner maintained that if the Air Force continued to cling to its "aerospace" fixation, "then trade-offs [would] be made between air and space, when in fact the trade-off should be made elsewhere."[37] Horner stressed that next-generation space investment needs and the F/A-22 "are too important to trade off against each other" and that the "fundamental problem" is to "expand air power *and* expand space power, obviously at the cost of the surface forces."[38]

This naturally raises the hot-button issue of whose program interests across service lines should be forced to suffer in order to finance an accelerated migration of American military capabilities into space. It

---

[36]"Will the Air Force Lose Its Space Program?" *Air Force Times*, February 8, 1999, p. 7.

[37]"Air Force Space System Control Questioned," *Space News*, September 8, 1997, p. 2.

[38]Brendan Sobie, "Former SPACECOM Chief Advocates Creation of Separate Space Force," *Inside Missile Defense*, November 19, 1997, p. 24. As a possible way to ease the pain at least at the margins, Air Force General Richard B. Myers, then–vice chairman of the Joint Chiefs of Staff and former CINCSPACE, suggested that military space exploitation needed to rely increasingly on the commercial sector. As that sector expands, the Air Force could consider divesting some of its infrastructure in launch and surveillance in order to concentrate on more pressing concerns. "If industry can do it," said Myers, "we probably shouldn't. Let industry do it, help industry to do it, buy products from industry, and focus on things that only people with a big R&D budget can do." (Linda de France, "Myers: Future of Military Space Requires Use of Civilian Capabilities," *Aerospace Daily*, May 8, 2001.)

is all but axiomatic that the four uniformed services, let alone the Air Force by itself, are incapable of reapportioning the defense budget in favor of more equitable support to Air Force air and space interests at the expense of competing service R&D and procurement accounts, since doing so would require the services to set aside, with inconceivable magnanimity, the overarching imperative of maximizing their own program equities in the roles and resources arena. Trade-off decisions of that magnitude are what the most senior U.S. civilian defense leaders are paid to make, based on prior determinations of national need that lie well beyond the purview of the uniformed services.[39]

Until the space MFP budget category recommended by the Space Commission and directed by Secretary Rumsfeld is better defined and more fully in place, there will be a need for greater top-down discipline by OSD in controlling the space requirements of the other services and more closely adjudicating those requirements by the JROC, so that identifying and budgeting for new space needs will reflect fiscal reality. Toward that end, the evolving MFP-12 mechanism should prove salutary in that it will enable the Defense Comptroller, as well as other supervising entities, to view the entire space funding scene. The specific purpose of this action is to size the space-related budget and scrub excess service requirements that may have worked their way into that budget by singling out and deleting those that represent overlap or redundancy, as well as capabilities that might be desirable in a perfect world but do not emanate from any clear and compelling operational need. Such DoD oversight, in part through the MFP-12 mechanism, should provide a means for putting senior officials in all the services on notice that everything they ask for in space will henceforth, in effect, entail a trade-off against everything else they ask for in the other MFPs. That provision alone should help bring greater rigor to the space requirements process, since with it, OSD will command far better visibility and awareness of the trade-

---

[39]There is nothing preordained or permanent about the manner in which American defense TOA is currently divided. That is strictly a matter of senior civilian leadership choice and congressional consent. At one point during the early 1960s, because declared national strategy demanded it, the Air Force's share of the overall U.S. defense budget was 43 percent. (Major General John T. Chain, Jr., USAF, AF/XOO, remarks at the Air University Air Power Symposium, Maxwell AFB, Alabama, February 23, 1981, p. 3.)

offs between MFP-12 (or the space "virtual" MFP) and MFP-1 through MFP-11.

As a first step toward coming to better grips with the funding conundrum outlined above, it was absolutely crucial to have space ratified by the Secretary of Defense as a separate and distinct military mission area in its own right. What is now needed is a funding arrangement that promises to remove national and multiservice space systems from the Air Force's budget and relocate them in a DoD-wide budget category, which MFP-12 essentially will be, so that the other services will henceforth have to make due contributions for their service-specific space ambitions and requirements. Such an arrangement would help ensure that the air operations portion of the Air Force's Title X responsibilities can compete on more reasonable terms with the programs of the other services. The Air Force executive agent for space will thus set the direction of the national military space effort, and AFSPC and the Air Staff will facilitate rather than dictate its execution. In due course, through MFP-12, space should become a more joint domain of activity, and all the services should be able to develop space expertise and work on joint problems, with the net result that no service should get crowded out at budget allocation time for sought-after space equities that serve its specific needs.

As for implementation, the Space Commission recommended that Congress be asked to amend Title X of the U.S. Code to give the Air Force statutory authority over the space mission as well as air mission areas. Upon reflection, OSD chose not to follow up on that recommendation out of understandable concern over the legal Pandora's box it might open.[40] As a result, the air mission area is now assigned to the Air Force by Title X, whereas the space mission is assigned by executive authority. Nevertheless, the Air Force's space executive-agent role has a Title X context, even if it lacks Title X authority. By the same token, the planned MFP for space has a Title X flavor, even if it is set in an executive-agent context. As this budget-tracking mechanism becomes more institutionalized and better understood, it will make space increasingly joint, thus allowing all

---

[40]General Ralph E. Eberhart, USAF, commander in chief, U.S. Space Command, comments to a gathering of RAND staff, Santa Monica, Calif., May 9, 2001.

services to develop space expertise and to work on their service-specific space problems as they deem appropriate. Since service-specific programs will, at least for the time being, remain within the various service budgets, those programs may not invariably show up in MFP-12 as a matter of routine practice. That is why the Air Force executive agent for space must maintain a detailed and thorough awareness of them, given his responsibilities for monitoring and tracking military space activities across service lines.

Although this arrangement will be insufficient, in and of itself, to un-burden the Air Force of its current budget-trade dilemma, it may of-fer at least the initial building blocks for a more permissive funding solution. Ultimately, if U.S. military space involvement is to be prop-erly funded over the coming decade and beyond without unduly compromising the Air Force's continuing Title X air responsibilities, DoD will need to settle on a more equitable arrangement. "Fee for service," one option sometimes suggested, is, by most expert opinion, not the right answer for multiple reasons. That said, this is-sue warrants creative and solutions-oriented thought by the Air Force's space executive agent and by OSD's concerned principals, along with determined and energetic action by both, as appropriate, to realize the full promise of MFP-12. On this point, Under Secretary Teets sounded a clear note of optimism when he recently spoke of a new "receptivity to change [among senior Pentagon leaders] and an environment where, perhaps, additional resources can be brought to bear to achieve some great objectives."[41]

NEXT STEPS IN SPACE MISSION DEVELOPMENT

With the most important organizational and management hurdles now either successfully negotiated or at least identified, the next round of the military space debate should concern investment pri-orities and program sequencing. The Defense Science Board (DSB) concluded in February 2000 that the United States currently enjoys undisputed space dominance, thanks in large part to what the Air Force has done over the past four decades to build a thriving Ameri-

---

[41]William B. Scott, "Milspace Comes of Age in Fighting Terror," *Aviation Week and Space Technology*, April 8, 2002, p. 78.

can military space infrastructure.[42] Air Force contributions toward that end expressly cited by the DSB included a robust space launch and support infrastructure, an effective indications and warning and attack-assessment capability, a unique ground-based space surveillance capability, global near–real time surveillance of denied areas, the ability to disseminate the products of that capability rapidly, and a strong C3 infrastructure for exploiting space systems. For all the criticism the Air Force has endured from some quarters in recent years for not having done more to underwrite the nation's military destiny in space, the fact is that in space, as in life itself, one must develop good crawling skills before walking. That the Air Force has progressively made space such an effective enhancer of terrestrial military operations by all services should be roundly applauded, not faulted.

Furthermore, the Air Force's alleged failures to proceed more aggressively with military space programs and associated space spending have not invariably been the result of its own choices. First, as noted earlier, more than a few Air Force space initiatives, notably including space control-related initiatives, have been terminated in recent years by executive or congressional action. As noted in the previous chapter, it was not the Air Force but the Clinton White House that used the line-item veto in 1997 to kill both the spaceplane and Clementine II, a spacecraft intended to be launched in 1999 into an asteroid in a test of technologies aimed at exploring the feasibility of diverting errant asteroids that might someday threaten to collide catastrophically with the earth. (The reason given for the latter's cancellation was that the project could be perceived as a violation of the Anti-Ballistic Missile Treaty and might also have been a thinly disguised precursor to a space weapons project.)[43]

One may further recall that as one part of Congress was publicly berating the Air Force for its alleged failures of space stewardship, another part canceled its plan to demonstrate a space-based radar capability. The Discoverer II program sought to explore the feasibility

---

[42]Cited in E. C. Aldridge, Jr., "Thoughts on the Management of National Security Space Activities of the Department of Defense," unpublished paper, July 6, 2000, p. 3.

[43]Leon Jaroff, "Dreadful Sorry, Clementine: Washington Brushes Off the Asteroid Threat," *Time*, October 27, 1997.

of a cost-effective approach to fielding a high-range-resolution space-based radar analogous to Joint STARS and capable of providing both a ground moving target indicator (GMTI) and synthetic aperture radar (SAR) capability. The proposal was to orbit two satellites to show the practicality in principle of migrating the Joint STARS mission to space. It was terminated not by the Air Force but by Congress.

On top of that, as explained in the preceding chapter, there has been for years a pronounced and continuing national disinclination to tamper with the status quo concerning space force-application initiatives and "weaponization." There also remains a persistent absence of national agreement over present and emerging threats to U.S. space-based assets. On this point, in a forceful call for bolder U.S. measures toward acquiring a serious space control capability, space-power advocate Steven Lambakis cited the "awkward absence of a collective, politically sanctioned vision for space," adding that "while space control is viewed as a logical outgrowth of a commitment to freedom of space, it has been neither a mission area that the citizens of the U.S. truly believe in nor one that energizes present U.S. strategic thinking."[44] The resultant "debate" over U.S. military space policy, he concluded, has been entirely predictable and has turned on decades-old arguments about preserving space as a sanctuary and not generating new instabilities. It has been further aggravated, one might note, by a natural media tendency to sensationalize and to assume the worst, as was evident in the press agitation over the presumed hidden agenda for national missile defense (described in Chapter Four) occasioned by Secretary Rumsfeld's perfunctory announcement in May 2001 of his planned organizational reforms for military space.

These facts have invariably made all calls for space force application initiatives and, by association, for even more relatively benign space control measures, both provocative and polarizing. So long as such a disinclination to grapple with the nation's rock-bottom security needs in space persists and the nation continues to adhere to an ambivalent military space strategy, space will remain only a support-

---

[44]Steven Lambakis, *On the Edge of Earth: The Future of American Space Power,* Lexington, Ky.: University of Kentucky Press, 2001, p. 38.

ing enabler of terrestrial operations. Worse yet, as long as steps to-ward acquiring effective defensive and offensive space control capabilities continue to be held in check by political irresolution and popular indifference, the nation will run an increasing risk of being caught by surprise someday as a result of its space vulnerabilities being exploited by a hostile party—whether or not in a notional "space Pearl Harbor."

In light of that, a prime imperative for the Air Force should be to continue leading from the front by advocating a disciplined space control mission-development road map and investment strategy. Such an approach might usefully start out by describing, in a clear and convincing way, the growing vulnerability of existing and planned U.S. space assets to present and potential threats. It might also emphasize, in the words of two RAND colleagues, that preparing to defend critical space capabilities and to attack those of opponents "is not a call for space fleets, although some such forces may be needed eventually," but rather "is a prescription for [enhanced] situational awareness incorporating space and theater perspectives coupled with responses employing the full range of means currently available in joint military operations."[45]

To help preempt potential domestic opposition to such prudent initiatives, the Air Force might accentuate the substantial divide that separates space control from space force application and stress that the *latter* mission area, not the former, chiefly entails the dreaded specter of offensive "space weaponization." In contrast, not only does the former not envisage the use of force from space against terrestrial targets, and hence any prospect of U.S. global "space hegemony," it has become increasingly indispensable if the nation is to protect its on-orbit assets *merely in order to remain secure in the space enabling game*. It bears stressing that unlike the controversial and provocative force-application mission, space control has been consistently approved as a legitimate venue for U.S. military space activity by every high-level guidance document since the first U.S. national space policy was enunciated by the Eisenhower administration in 1958. It remains poorly understood even in high circles to

---

[45]Bob Preston and John Baker, "Space Challenges," in Zalmay Khalilzad and Jeremy Shapiro, eds., *Strategic Appraisal: United States Air and Space Power in the 21st Century*, Santa Monica, Calif.: RAND, MR-1314-AF, 2002, p. 178.

what extent the services have all become so heavily dependent on space-based force enhancement assets, not only for providing routine C4/ISR support, but also for a growing number of critically important terrestrial target attack functions, including the operation of unmanned aerial vehicles (UAVs) such as Predator and Global Hawk, the real-time provision of space sensor target data directly into the cockpits of engaged combat aircraft, and the accuracy of near-precision satellite-guided munitions, to note only three among many.[46] In practice, this already deep and steadily growing national dependence on key space-based enabling equities warrants arguing ever more insistently for effective space control measures, including offensive measures that do not include kinetic kill, with its associated hypervelocity space debris problem.

Beyond the need to move more vigorously into the space-control mission area, the Air Force also faces much unfinished business in the less contentious force-enhancement arena which, as discussed earlier in this chapter, has been prompted by the aging of many on-orbit systems now in service and the imminent emergence of a new generation of systems now at the threshold of being fielded. In the years ahead, space-based radars may take over much of the battlefield surveillance role currently performed by such aircraft as the E-8 Joint STARS, although there are reasons to believe that it may be 2020 or beyond before fielding a militarily effective constellation of GMTI and SAR satellites will be feasible.[47] These options will soon be competing for resources within the Air Force R&D budget, and hard

---

[46]Not only do satellites enable the remote piloting of Predator and Global Hawk, they support an increasingly broad array of data-intensive U.S. systems in various weapons employment modes. Just one Global Hawk reportedly consumes about 500 megabits per second of satellite-provided bandwidth, nearly five times the total bandwidth consumed by the entire U.S. military during Operation Desert Storm. The vulnerability and, hence, attractiveness of this growing U.S. space-based dependence to hostile attack should be readily evident. For more on this, see Greg Jaffe, "Military Feels Bandwidth Squeeze as the Satellite Industry Sputters," *Wall Street Journal*, April 10, 2002.

[47]AWACS will take even longer because that mission is substantially more demanding technologically than GMTI/SAR. For a detailed treatment of the magnitude of these challenges, see Lieutenant General Roger G. DeKok, USAF, and Bob Preston, "Acquisition of Space Power for a New Millennium," in Peter L. Hays et al, eds., *Spacepower for a New Millennium: Space and U.S. National Security*, New·York: McGraw Hill, 2000, pp. 80–84.

choices will have to be made and impediments removed if they are ultimately to be realized.

In considering an orderly transfer of C4/ISR functions from air to space, one must bear in mind the inherent and natural conservatism of military organizations. Such organizations are characteristically inclined to implement change only slowly and incrementally, since to do otherwise would risk compromising their ability to execute decisively at a moment's notice. Accordingly, an instructive lesson from the study of organizational history is that one should not try to change too much at once. This time-honored adage has a direct bearing on how the Air Force should approach the migration of its surveillance and battle-management capabilities from air to space. Legacy air-breathing systems such as Joint STARS and AWACS, which have been acquired through multiple billions of dollars of investment, cannot be summarily written off if they have substantial service life remaining—however well-intended the various arguments for mission migration to space may be. It may make better sense to think of space not as a venue within which to replace existing surveillance functions wholesale, but rather as a medium offering the potential for expanding the Air Force's existing surveillance envelope by more fully exploiting both the air *and* space environments.

It also may help to think in terms of "windows" in which to commence the migration of surveillance missions to space. For example, at certain predictable points in their life cycles (called Service Life Extension Program phases), airframes face the need for major investment for recapitalization. The same holds true for engine replacement, aircraft reskinning, structural integrity upgrades, and so on. The point, as one former Air Force senior space manager observed, is that "a system-wide planning process injected into resource allocation deliberations offers the opportunity to transition from large airframe dependency to legitimate space alternatives as space demonstrates the potential to achieve greater operational utility with fewer expended resources."[48]

Until a more equitable cross-service military space funding arrangement is put into place, the Air Force will continue to confront a

---

[48]Jones, memo to McIlvoy, p. 12.

mission-development dilemma. Should it move *too* fast toward expanding its percentage of funding support for space, it will run the danger of further undercutting its support to its equally important air obligations. Alternatively, should the Air Force be perceived as dragging its heels with respect to funding the nation's military space needs out of a determination to do right by its mandated *air* force-projection obligations, it will risk appearing to have willfully violated the Space Commission's trust and thereby run the danger of eventually being asked to turn over its stewardship of space to a separate Space Corps or Space Force.

In light of this mission-development dilemma, it would seem that the next round of Air Force investment in space-based enabling applications should entail an orderly evolution. A question of particular importance in this regard entails which existing air-based ISR missions (notably Joint STARS and AWACS) should be migrated to space and in what order. A preeminent challenge the Air Force faces in this respect is to determine how to divest itself of existing legacy programs in a measured way to generate the funds needed for taking on tomorrow's challenges one manageable step at a time. That will require careful trade-off assessments to determine the most appropriate technology and medium—air or space—toward which its resources should be directed for any mission at any given time.

Stated differently, just because a C4/ISR mission *can* be performed from space does not necessarily mean that it *should* be. Functions should not be migrated to space just because it is technologically possible. Any transition to space should also be paced by a prior determination that the mission or function in question can be performed more cost-effectively from space than from the air.[49] That, in

---

[49]For example, in the case of supplanting AWACS with a space system, as former AFSPC commander and later Air Force vice chief of staff General Thomas Moorman explained some years ago, "you must develop a global system to have sufficient revisit rates to be useful. Additionally, if you are putting a radar capability in space, it has to be at low altitude because of a power aperture problem. You can't get the resolution at geosynchronous [orbit] or something like that. As a consequence, the combination of having to have a global capability with a high revisit rate and power for resolution means that you have to buy a large number of satellites. Depending on the altitude, it could be between 25 and 40 satellites. That may be a very expensive way to do the AWACS job." (General Thomas S. Moorman, Jr., "The Challenges of Space Beyond 2000," in Alan Stephens, ed., *New Era Security: The RAAF in the Next Twenty-Five Years*, Proceedings of a Conference held by the Royal Australian Air Force, Canberra,

turn, will mean laying down a firm technology base first, and then identifying reasonable transition points at which a migration of effort can be rationally justified. In this, the nation does not need a crusade so much as a careful and studied phasing of migration. Some space advocates within the Air Force go so far as to insist that if one does not support moving the Joint STARS mission capability to space forthwith, one has not taken due heed of the Space Commission's recommendations. Yet however much some may deem the migration of existing air force-enhancement capabilities to space to be a command duty for ensuring the Air Force's future in space, not every investment area need entail a crash effort like the Manhattan Project, which developed the first American atomic bomb. Space proponents in the civilian defense leadership and in Congress, as well as within the Air Force itself, can best help this process by *enabling* Air Force change rather than trying to force it. For the nearer term, it may make more sense—and may be far more cost-effective—to pursue a seemly blend of air- and space-based ISR capabilities, linking the digital information gathered and processed by aerodynamic systems through space rather than moving the platforms themselves to space, at least as a first order of business.

Most important of all, it will be essential for the survivability of any new C4/ISR assets migrated to space to be protected by appropriate measures beforehand. This means that attention to potential system vulnerabilities must be paramount in any migration planning. If we move to migrate new assets to space before first ensuring that a credible space control enforcement regime is in place to protect them and to hold any possible enemy threat systems at risk, we will simply compound our existing vulnerabilities—all the more so if those assets supplant rather than merely supplement existing air-breathing capabilities. It would make no sense whatever to migrate Joint STARS and AWACS to space if the resultant on-orbit capabilities were any less survivable than Joint STARS and AWACS are today. It follows that getting more serious about space control is not an issue apart from force-enhancement migration but rather represents a sine qua non for such migration. Otherwise, in transferring our

---

Australia, June 1996, p. 174.) A more recent Air Force assessment has concluded that, quite apart from the vulnerability issue, it may take as many as 48 to 60 satellites on orbit to accomplish the space-based radar mission. (Conversation with General W. L. Creech, USAF [Ret.], July 15, 2002.)

asymmetric technological advantages to space, we will also run the risk of burdening ourselves with new asymmetric vulnerabilities. This is yet another reason why seeking the beginnings of a credible space control capability should represent the next U.S. military space mission-development priority.

SOME UNRESOLVED ORGANIZATIONAL QUESTIONS

Finally, we come to two notable organizational and management concerns with respect to military space that have yet to be fully accommodated. The first of these involves reconciling the theater needs of a joint force commander and his subordinate component commanders with the global focus and coverage of the nation's military space assets while still retaining unity of command of the nation's air and space forces. One proposed solution is to centralize military space tasking at the unified level so that all force elements would receive all of their combat tasking from CINCSPACE (now the commander of U.S. Strategic Command since the disestablishment of USSPACECOM on October 1, 2002).[50] This would mean, in effect, a joint force space component commander (or JFSCC), most likely either in the person of the USSTRATCOM commander or else his senior designee reporting directly to the joint force commander. A problem with this proposal is that it cuts against the grain of further air and space integration. It also raises some troublesome coordination questions between air and space, much as those that exist today between air and land. Alternatively, the existing JFACC could be designated the supported commander for space operations within his specific theater, in effect making him a joint force air *and* space component commander, or JFASCC. He would thus be the point of contact for space concerns for a joint-force commander (JFC). One might imagine other solutions as well, including ad hoc arrangements tailored to meet a JFC's specific space support needs for any given contingency. In all events, the organizational integration of space in joint-force operations at the most senior command level remains an area of joint doctrine and practice in need of further thought.

---

[50]Briefing by then–Major General William R. Looney III, USAF, commander, 14th Air Force, at the Air Force Doctrine Symposium, Maxwell AFB, Alabama, April 6, 2001.

A second organizational interface that could benefit from further remedy is the long-standing relationship between the Air Force and the National Reconnaissance Office (NRO), as well as between the Air Force and the ultimate consumer of NRO's product, the national intelligence establishment. A promising step toward that end was Secretary Rumsfeld's acceptance in May 2001 of the Space Commission's recommendation that the Under Secretary of the Air Force be designated not only the nation's executive agent for military space, but also the director of the NRO. Yet the fact remains that although the Air Force largely staffs the NRO and provides the launch and support services for its various reconnaissance assets on orbit, it is only an agent in the service of the intelligence community when it comes to the control and exploitation of those assets.

On this delicate point, the Space Commission went out of its way to emphasize that the nation's security-related space capabilities are controlled jointly by the Secretary of Defense and the Director of Central Intelligence (DCI), that the DCI necessarily provides much of the intelligence required by the services for the conduct of military operations, and that "neither [of these individuals] can accomplish the tasks assigned without the [support of the] other."[51] How such enhanced mutual support between the NRO and its principal patron might be achieved in practice will obviously be up to those directly involved. The overarching goal, however, must be to shorten the ties between the NRO's assets and all other U.S. C4/ISR systems in the interest of providing more timely support to joint-force commanders. Everything the Space Commission concluded with respect to the need for better integration of all military space assets with terrestrial force elements in all services was intended to apply equally to those assets launched by the Air Force under NRO auspices.

As for what specific arrangements might work best toward better harmonizing that relationship, the commissioners gently reminded both the Secretary of Defense and the DCI that "there is no systemic organizational impediment to such [improved] alignment or to meeting the need for increased attention to critical issues," and that it was simply a matter of the priorities of both and "how they choose to delegate and oversee responsibilities for space-related con-

---

[51] *Space Commission Report*, p. 64.

cerns."[52] Toward that end, it seems reasonable to suggest that the Under Secretary of the Air Force, in light of his dual-hatted status as executive agent for space and NRO director, would be entirely within his assigned charter to identify such integration opportunities, bring them about on his own when they lie within his breadth of authority, and seek the approval of the DCI as appropriate when they do not— or when an ambiguous situation might obtain. In all events, whenever the product of NRO assets is likely to be of immediate use to joint-force commanders and their subordinate component commanders, making that product readily accessible to those warfighting principals should be a goal of the Under Secretary under the new arrangement endorsed and supported by both the Secretary of Defense and the DCI.

From an operator's perspective, the core issue concerns getting *all* the nation's security-related space assets working more harmoniously in the interest of joint-force commanders worldwide. Toward that end, the current Air Force chief, General Jumper, is deeply committed to bringing about what he calls the "horizontal integration" of all warfighting instruments, including not just the overhead enabling systems operated by the Air Force but ideally those under the purview of the other services and the DCI as well. He envisions, among other things, linking together the entire spectrum of available ISR sensors so they might provide, through better information-sharing and significantly reduced data cycle time, a richer situation picture to senior commanders faced with immediate contingency-response demands. Without singling out the NRO's assets in particular, he has identified as a part of the generic problem what he has labeled "proprietary systems," whose data are first interpreted by "tribal representatives sitting in front of their tribal work stations" before being provided to operators who might most immediately and usefully benefit from them.[53] This impacted process invariably makes both the sharing of time-sensitive information and sensor-to-shooter links needlessly slow and cumbersome.

---

[52]Ibid., p. 65.

[53]Ron Laurenzo, "Jumper: Talking Is Key to Transforming," *Defense Week*, March 25, 2002, p. 16.

On this point, Jumper recently commented in testimony before the defense subcommittee of the House Appropriations Committee that if such institutional roadblocks were eliminated or at least minimized, "the result would be a cursor over a target, not a conversation between two tribal representatives."[54] After all, when it comes to making the most of the nation's space-based force-enhancement capabilities in accommodating the exacting demands of time-sensitive targeting, both DoD-owned space assets and those operated by other government agencies need to be synergistically linked on the input side with the full spectrum of the joint-force commander's force-employment infrastructure—without bureaucratic firewalls obstructing the expeditious sharing of time-sensitive information. Shorn of pleasantries, the real need is to ensure that the information gathered by NRO assets—acquired and launched by the Air Force yet controlled by the DCI—continues to accrue primarily but not solely to the intelligence agencies in the interest of shortening the sensor-to-shooter connection.[55]

As the Air Force continues to grapple with such organizational issues, it should be on guard against pressing for premature moves in a

[54]George C. Wilson, "Air Force's Jumper Catches a Tailwind: The Revolution in Aerospace Jumps Forward with a New Air Force Chief," *National Journal*, March 16, 2002. Elsewhere, Jumper has noted how bureaucrats of all varieties have long been taught as a first order of business to defend their institutional prerogatives, when what is more urgently needed is to get the nation's combat and combat-support assets all working from a common script with a view toward "the integration of space, standoff precision . . . and information." (Ibid.) As if to underscore this point, he recently stressed at an Air Force Association–sponsored gathering of some 800 government, military, and industry officials: "For this decade, the buzz word is integration. . . . I've talked about it before and I will talk about it again. We will get it right." (David Hughes, "USAF Aims to Forge C2ISR into a 'Weapon,'" *Aviation Week and Space Technology*, May 6, 2002, p. 54.)

[55]As an Air Staff paper written at the height of the Space Commission's hearing of service testimony carefully expressed this important point, "as a direct result of the Air Force–NRO partnership, the resources of the intelligence community space systems play an increasingly important role in the direct support of military operations. Though the 'cultural' gaps are narrowing, differences in military and intelligence community user priorities, security constraints, and separate resource processes continue to result in more of a 'cooperative coexistence' than a truly integrated space architecture. Specific challenges remain in . . . operational integration into joint warfighting." ("Air Force Position Paper on Space Commission Issues," p. 2.) For more on this serious and still-unresolved concern, see Preston and Baker, "Space Challenges," in Khalilzad and Shapiro, eds., *Strategic Appraisal: United States Air and Space Power in the 21st Century*, pp. 158–159, 176.

spirit of appearing to be "doing something" before the time is ripe. A potentially divisive issue of this sort within the joint arena emerged in 1997 concerning whether space should be formally designated an Area of Responsibility (AOR), with CINCSPACE as its commander. Early that year, U.S. Space Command issued what it called an "informational" proposal suggesting Joint Chiefs of Staff considera- tion of space as a possible sixth AOR, on a par with the extant five unified commands (Central, European, Atlantic, Southern, and Pa- cific).[56] USSPACECOM officials were quick to insist that they were not calling at that point to have space established as an AOR but were merely suggesting that the time had come to give it serious and sys- tematic thought. Nor was there any hint of interest at USSPACECOM in new definitions that would artificially separate air and space. In- stead, USSPACECOM sought to have space declared CINCSPACE's AOR in principle so that the command could proceed with the kind of war planning and doctrinal development needed for preparing to conduct military operations in space once the time for them came. All the same, the Air Staff in the end rightly rebuffed that initiative, in part because it would have required a prior agreed definition within the joint arena of the border between the space AOR and the regional AORs, which would have been difficult to achieve even in the best scenario, since space is, by definition, global in coverage, embracing all the regional AORs.[57]

TOWARD THE AIR FORCE'S FUTURE IN SPACE

Today, there is no question that the Air Force is the nation's dedi- cated and acknowledged military space service. Vice Admiral Herbert A. Browne, a recent deputy commander in chief of the unified U.S. Space Command, attested to that when he commented not long ago that "we already have a Space Force—it is the Air Force."[58] For its part, the Space Commission was emphatic in its judgment that the argument for a separate space service had not yet been convincingly

---

[56]William B. Scott, "Pentagon Considers Space As New Area of Responsibility," *Avia- tion Week and Space Technology*, March 24, 1997, p. 54.

[57]"Command Plan Revision Will Not Declare Space a CINC's Regional Area," *Inside the Pentagon*, November 27, 1997, p. 1.

[58]Quoted in Ralph Millsap and D. B. Posey, "Organizational Options for the Future Aerospace Force," *Aerospace Power Journal*, Summer 2000, p. 48.

made. On the contrary, after careful deliberation, it concluded that the Air Force continues to serve responsibly as the nation's military space custodian. As an Air Force space officer incisively observed several years before the commissioners reached that conclusion, those who would wrest space from the Air Force and invest it in a separate institution must first prove at least one of two hypotheses: First, that the requirements for developing unique space-related expertise are not being adequately met by current arrangements (or that that expertise is not being properly utilized), and second, that *only* a separate and independent U.S. space service would be capable of providing the military space leverage the nation requires. Proving the first and more controversial hypothesis, he added, would require "proving that the United States Air Force has not served as a satisfactory steward for our nation's military space power."[59] That would be a tall order, not least because the DoD and Congress never assigned the Air Force any formal responsibility for space stewardship until the spring of 2001.

With the Space Commission's recommendations and OSD's resultant empowerment of the Air Force now formally promulgated, the charter for the Air Force to move ahead in space seems firmly in hand. To fulfill that charter, the Air Force needs to continue embracing the endowment it was so generously given by the Space Commission. This means, first and foremost, accepting and internalizing the important, indeed fundamental, contrasts between air and space, as well as the need for clear organizational differentiation between the two mediums, along with their continued operational integration. As noted earlier, it is all well and good for Air Force air and space professionals at all levels to be encouraged by their leadership to think like a fellowship of like-minded airmen up to a point. Yet those professionals should not be treated as though they were interchangeable. On the contrary, they live in separate cultures, have separate job responsibilities, and thrive on separate skill sets. Some distinctive "tribes" within the Air Force are not only unavoidable but desirable—and even essential.

---

[59]Major Shawn P. Rife, USAF, "On Space-Power Separatism," *Airpower Journal,* Spring 1999, p. 25.

Indeed, the Space Commission's recommendations and Secretary Rumsfeld's determination to act on them may prove, in the long run, to have been crucial pivots for resolving at least a portion of the nation's military space funding predicament. Those recommendations led to a number of important—even game-changing—breakthrough developments in the Air Force's interest. For one thing, they provided the Air Force with executive-agent authority over all U.S. military space activities, as well as the improved budget-tracking mechanism for space that went along with that authority—two hitherto elusive goals the Air Force had coveted for decades. They also gave the Air Force a new mission responsibility: That service now has *two* assigned mission areas, air *and* space, an outcome far preferable to the single "aerospace" mission area that not only hindered the development of a robust space doctrine but also needlessly compounded the Air Force's space funding dilemma.

Yet at the same time, the Space Commission also telegraphed a clear message to the Air Force that it had about five to ten years to get the space mission right or else risk being asked to relinquish it to a separate entity charged with that responsibility.[60] In so doing, the commissioners concluded that needed efforts in the realm of military space exploitation "are not being pursued with the vision and attention needed," adding that if such efforts are not satisfactorily pursued by the Air Force in the near future, "U.S. interests in space may well ultimately call for the creation of a Space Corps or a Space Department" to carry out the "organize, train, and equip" functions associated with military space. In an unmistakable shot across the Air Force's bow, the commissioners further noted that giving the Air Force MFP budget authority for space and granting formal designation as the nation's executive agent for military space were "recommended to lay the foundation for such future steps" should they be deemed necessary—with the timetable to be "dictated by circumstances over the next five to ten years."[61]

Viewed in hindsight, the since-superseded vision promulgated at the 1996 Corona conference that characterized the Air Force as an insti-

---

[60]See William B. Scott, "USAF Warned to Bolster or Lose 'Space Force' Franchise," *Aviation Week and Space Technology*, January 29, 2001, p. 55.

[61]*Space Commission Report*, pp. 93–94.

tution rapidly becoming an "air and space force" on an evolutionary path to becoming a "space and air force" may be said to have been exactly half right: Today, the Air Force is well beyond the initial stages of not only becoming but actually *being* a bona fide "air and space force." Yet the time the nation finds itself at the brink of possessing a true "space and air force" (probably somewhere nearer to the midpoint of the 21st century) may also be the time when a separate U.S. space service will have finally earned its right to independence. After that, the Air Force may retain niche space equities to support its continued *air* force-application responsibilities, much as the Army, Navy, and Marine Corps retained niche air equities to support their *surface* warfighting responsibilities after the Air Force gained its independence from the Army.

In arguing the case for the evolution of a full-fledged "space and air force" within the confines of the existing Air Force, one thoughtful Air Force space professional visualized such a notional force as follows: "If space-based force application approaches the full potential of its technological capabilities (i.e., the ability to find, fix, track, and destroy virtually anything in the terrestrial environment), the debate over a separate space service will become obsolete because air power, as we understand it today, will become obsolete. Space power will be able to do virtually everything that air power does today—and do it faster and with less risk. Predominantly space forces (with air in an auxiliary role) will subsume the roles and missions of air forces, and the reins of power within the U.S. aerospace force will, by rights, transfer from the combat pilot of today to the space operator of tomorrow."[62] Similarly, former CINCSPACE General Estes has predicted that "over time, the projection air mission will continue to migrate to space, and the Air Force will become heavier on space and lighter on projection air"—a forecast that precisely reflects the logic of the 1996 Corona formulation.[63] The one drawback to this otherwise bold vision, and it is an important one, is that even if space-based forces eventually acquire combat capabilities of such caliber by the mid-21st century, there will still be mobility and lift functions, as well as surveillance and attack functions, that can only be performed by air assets. That being the most plausible prospect for at

---

[62]Rife, "On Space-Power Separatism," p. 28.

[63]Letter to the author by General Howell M. Estes III, USAF (Ret.), October 1, 2002.

least the midrange future, although one can readily imagine the Air Force evolving naturally into a transitional "air and space force," a more fully developed "space and air force" seems counterintuitive—almost analogous to the tail wagging the dog.

So long as space continues to perform primarily in a supporting force-enhancement role, one can imagine defensive and offensive space-control operations drawing on the established expertise in intelligence, targeting, battle-damage assessment, and other familiar air-related operational techniques and procedures already well-developed and extant within the Air Force. But if space is expected to eventually assume additional and unique mission burdens, such as space-to-earth force application, then the space operations and management structure will need to evolve to accommodate those new functions. Once the current space-support role transitions into space missions that address national objectives but are independent of terrestrial forces (including terrestrial air forces), such as space-based missile defense and force application against terrestrial targets from space, there will be increasingly strong pressures for the establishment of a semiautonomous Space Corps within the Air Force or even a separate space service altogether. As a former Air Force space general presciently commented in late 1997, "at the point when political consensus is reached to weaponize space, either based on the emergence of a compelling military threat or to counter the impact of adversary space forces on U.S. and allied security interests, the same debate that resulted in establishing a separate [U.S. Air Force] air component is inevitable. At this point, the Air Force is totally unprepared for this dialogue."[64]

It is perhaps not too soon, even now, for today's Air Force leaders to devote some thought to how their successors a generation or more downstream might best anticipate that challenge and how the service might best divest itself of the bulk of its space equities when that day of reckoning eventually comes. The alternative would be for tomorrow's Air Force to feel somehow cheated by that inexorable development, much as the Army felt wrongly cheated by the Air Force's attainment of independence in 1947, rather than instead feeling thankfully freed to continue fulfilling its historic role as the

---

[64]Jones, memo to McIlvoy, p. 2.

nation's full-service air arm as space rightly goes its own hard-earned way. Yet whatever the longer-term inevitability of offensive space-to-ground weaponization and the consequent emergence of a separate U.S. space service may be, the prevailing worldwide consensus today against such weaponization, the countervailing Air Force investment priorities of greater near-term importance, and the lack of technically feasible and cost-effective weapon options will all but surely foreclose any realistic chance of the Air Force's acquiring a significant space force-application capability for at least the next 15 years.

As for the nearer-term future, the Air Force now has a clear path marked out for it, thanks to the many ripple effects that were set in motion by the Space Commission's recommendations of 2001. As noted at the beginning of this chapter, it now faces five challenges with respect to space:

- Continuing the operational integration of space with the three terrestrial warfighting mediums while ensuring the organizational differentiation of space from Air Force air.

- Making good on defining and realizing the Air Force's newly granted military space executive-agent status.

- Dealing with what the Space Commission characterized as an inadequate DoD-wide space funding situation.

- Prioritizing next steps in space mission development, most notably including the need to start moving more briskly toward developing and deploying a serious space control capability before the nation's growing space vulnerabilities are tested, perhaps severely, by hostile forces.

- Making progress toward honoring a key recommendation of the Space Commission by taking more aggressive steps to develop and nurture a cadre of skilled space professionals ready and able, in the words of Under Secretary Teets, "to create the required space doctrine; to engineer, acquire, and operate [increasingly] complex space systems; and to execute the necessary warfighting operations to meet the national security space challenges of the future."[65]

Mastering these challenges should not only ensure the Air Force a satisfactory near-term future for itself and the nation in space. It also should help enable it over time to shore up its end-strength and the intensity of its day-to-day training (both eroded since Desert Storm) to fulfill its abiding and no less important mission responsibilities in the *air* arena.

---

[65]Statement by the Honorable Peter B. Teets, p. 1.

DoD DRAFT DIRECTIVE ON SPACE EXECUTIVE AGENT

SUBJECT: Executive Agent for Space[1]

References:

(a) Secretary of Defense Memorandum, "National Security Space Management and Organization," October 18, 2002

(b) DoD Directive 5160.32, "Development of Space Systems," September 8, 1970 (hereby cancelled)

(c) DoD Instruction 4000.19, "Interservice and Intragovernmental Support," August 9, 1995

(d) Under Secretary of Defense for Acquisition, Technology, and Logistics Memorandum, "Delegation of Milestone Decision Authority for DoD Space Systems," TBD

(e) through (f), see enclosure 1

1. <u>PURPOSE</u>

   This Directive:

   1.1. Establishes policy and assigns Executive Agent responsibilities, functions, and authorities for planning, programming, and acquisition of space systems within the Department of Defense.

   1.2. Implements reference (a) and supersedes reference (b).

---

[1] *Inside the Pentagon*, March 7, 2002, pp. 15–18.

2.   APPLICABILITY

2.1. This Directive applies to the Office of the Secretary of Defense, the Military Departments (including the Coast Guard when it is operating as a Military Service in the Department of the Navy), the Office of the Chairman of the Joint Chiefs of Staff, the Combatant Commands, the Office of the Inspector General of the Department of Defense, the Defense Agencies, and the DoD field Activities (hereafter referred to collectively as "the DoD Components"). The term Military Services, as used herein, refers to the Army, the Navy, the Air Force, and the Marine Corps.

2.2. This Directive does not change the space and space-related responsibilities and functions of the Under Secretary of Defense for Acquisition, Technology, and Logistics (USD/AT&L), the Under Secretary of Defense (Comptroller) (USD/C), or the Assistant Secretary of Defense for Command, Control, Communications, and Intelligence.

3.   DEFINITIONS

Terms used in this Directive are defined in enclosure 2.

4.   POLICY

It is DoD policy that:

4.1. The Department of the Air Force shall be the Executive Agent for Space within the Department of Defense, with DoD-wide responsibility for planning, programming, and acquisition of space systems.

4.1.1. The Secretary of the Air Force shall re-delegate authority as the Executive Agent for Space, as appropriate, to the Under Secretary of the Air Force—Director of the National Reconnaissance Office (USecAF—DNRO).

4.2. The Executive Agent for Space shall carry out DoD-wide responsibility for planning, programming, and acquisition of space systems in accordance with National and Department of Defense policy and guidance.

4.2.1. The Executive Agent for Space shall carry out DoD-wide responsibility for planning, programming, and acquisition of space systems with the primary goal of providing operational space force capabilities to ensure the United States has the space power to achieve its national security objectives.

4.3. The Executive Agent for Space shall establish appropriate DoD-wide processes for the development, coordination, integration, review, and implementation of space system plans, budgets, and acquisition programs, in conjunction with the other Military Departments and Defense Agencies.

4.3.1. The Executive Agent for Space may arrange for and execute inter-Service support agreements, in accordance with DoD Instruction 4000.19 (reference c), memoranda of understanding, and other necessary arrangements, as required, to fulfill assigned responsibilities and functions

4.4. Planning

4.4.1. The Executive Agent for Space shall develop, coordinate, integrate, review, and implement a National Security Space Program, in conjunction with the Director, National Reconnaissance Office (DNRO), the other DoD Components, the Deputy Director of Central Intelligence for Community Management (DDCI/CM), and, as appropriate, other U.S. government departments and agencies. The Executive Agent for Space, with assistance from the National Security Space Architect (NSSA), shall provide the Office of the Secretary of Defense and the DDCI/CM:

4.4.1.1. A National Security Space Program Plan.

4.4.1.2. National security space architectures across the range of DoD and Intelligence Community mission areas.

4.4.2. Each of the Military Departments and Defense Agencies shall be responsible for developing Service- or Agency-unique:

4.4.2.1. Requirements and system characteristics for space systems for its employment.

4.4.2.2. Space doctrine, education, and training requirements and standards.

4.4.2.3. Space research, development, testing, evaluation, and acquisition.

4.4.2.4. Related military construction efforts.

4.5. Programming and Budgeting

4.5.1. The Executive Agent for Space, with the assistance of the NSSA, and in conjunction with the DNRO, the other DoD components, the DDCI/CM, and, as appropriate, other U.S. Government departments and agencies, shall submit an annual National Security Space Program Assessment to the DoD Senior Executive Committee comprised of the Secretary of Defense, the USD/AT&L, and the Secretaries of the Military Departments; and, in coordination with the DDCI/CM, to the Executive Committee comprised of the Secretary of Defense and Director of Central Intelligence. The Assessment shall report on the consistency of the implementation of the defense and intelligence space programs with policy, planning guidance, and architectural decisions, based upon the Program Objective Memoranda and Intelligence Program Objective Memoranda Future Years Defense.

4.5.2. Each of the Military Departments and Defense Agencies shall provide Service or Agency-unique space programs to the Executive Agent for review, coordination, and integration into the National Security Space Plan and National Security Space Program Assessment. Provision of such program information normally shall be accomplished through a Program Objective Memoranda submission.

5. RESPONSIBILITIES

5.1. The Secretary of the Air Force shall:

5.1.1. Ensure all Executive Agent for Space responsibilities and functions are assigned and executed, in accordance with this Directive and reference a.

5.1.2. Ensure that the requirements and equities of the other DoD Components for space systems and capabilities are met.

5.1.3. Strongly represent DoD-wide space interests in the planning, programming, and budgeting process and in the defense acquisition process.

5.1.4. Harmonize requirements for space programs generated by the DoD Components through the Joint Requirements Oversight Council (JROC) process with plans, programs, and budgets before submission to the JROC.

5.1.5. Develop an annual National Security Space Program Plan, with the assistance of the NSSA, in conjunction with the DNRO, the other DoD Components, and the DDCI/CM.

5.1.6. Recommend proposed space and space-related planning and programming guidance to the USD/P and the USD/C for consideration in their formulation of planning, programming, and budgeting guidance documents.

5.1.7. Support the USD/P and USD/C, as appropriate, with program analysis and evaluation of space policy, plans, and programs.

5.1.8. Support the USD/C, as appropriate, with the development, integration, and maintenance of space program financial strategic plans as well as reengineering of associated business practices.

5.1.9. Support the USD/C, as appropriate, to ensure preparation and validation of economic analyses in support of space program financial systems.

5.1.10. Develop, coordinate, and integrate DoD and Intelligence Community space architectures, with the assistance of the NSSA, and in coordination with the DoD Components and the Intelligence Community. Such architectures shall integrate space architectures and systems, eliminate unnecessary vertical stove-piping of programs, achieve efficiencies in acquisition and future operations through program integration, and thereby improve space support to military and intelligence operations.

5.1.11. Develop an annual National Security Space Program Assessment, with the assistance of the NSSA, and in conjunction with the DNRO, the other DoD Components, the DDCI/CM, and, as appropriate, other U.S. Government departments and agencies.

> 5.1.11.1. Submit the National Security Space Program Assessment to: (1) the Senior Executive Committee comprised of the Secretary of Defense, the Deputy Secretary of Defense, the USD/AT&L, and the Secretaries of the Military Departments; and (2) the Executive Committee comprised of the Secretary of Defense and Director of Central Intelligence, in coordination with the DDCI/CM.

5.1.12. Serve as the Milestone Decision Authority for Major Defense Acquisition Programs and other designated space programs, upon delegation by USD/AT&L, in accordance with reference d.

> 5.1.12.1. Supervise the performance of space Major Defense Acquisition Programs and other designated space programs, upon delegation by USD/AT&L, in accordance with reference e and f.

> 5.1.12.2. Enforce the policies and practices in references e and f during space program acquisition.

> 5.1.12.3. Consult the USD/AT&L, in coordination with ASD/C3I, on Program Objectives Memoranda and budget estimates submissions for space that reflect a significant change to any program subject to review by the DAB, before their submission to OSD/AT&L.

> 5.1.12.4. Provide recommendations to the USD/AT&L regarding the issuance of DoD Instructions, DoD

Publications, and one-time directive type memoranda, consistent with DoD 5025.1-M that implement space acquisition policies and procedures for functions assigned to the SecAF.

5.1.12.5. Provide recommendations to the USD/AT&L regarding making certifications, providing reports, and approving waivers for space Major Defense Acquisition Programs required by Title X, U.S. Code.

5.1.13. Coordinate DoD Component space program research, development, and production programs to eliminate duplication of effort and ensure that available resources are used to maximum advantage.

5.1.14. Develop and recommend to the USD/AT&L policies and programs that improve, streamline, and strengthen DoD Component space and space-related technology access and development programs, encourage space-related open market competition and technology driven prototype efforts that offer increased military capabilities at lower ownership costs and faster fielding times, and exploit the cost-reduction potential of accessing innovative or commercially developed technologies.

5.1.15. Develop assessments and recommend the establishment of policies to the USD/AT&L to maintain the capability of the U.S. space industry to meet DoD needs.

5.1.16. Develop space acquisition plans, strategies, guidance, and assessments to ensure that acquisition milestone review and the Planning, Programming, and Budgeting System processes are timely and effectively implemented.

5.1.17. Realign Air Force headquarters and field commands to support the adoption of a "cradle-to-grave" approach for space activities to more closely integrate space acquisition and operations functions.

5.1.17.1. Take appropriate actions to ensure, to the maximum extent practicable, that DoD Component space development and acquisition programs are carried out through joint program offices.

5.1.17.2. Develop and implement a process to align Air Force and NRO programs and permit both organizations to use each other's "best practices" for space research, development, acquisition, and operations, in coordination with the USD/AT&L, the USD/P, the Chairman of the Joint Chiefs of Staff, and the DDCI/CM.

5.1.18. Oversee development testing and evaluation strategies, conduct test and evaluation planning, and oversee Operational Test and Evaluation in coordination with the Director, Operational Test and Evaluation (DOT&E) for DoD space Major Defense Acquisition Programs and other programs on the OSD Test and Evaluation Oversight List.

5.2. The Under Secretary of the Air Force-Director of the National Reconnaissance Office (USecAF-DNRO) shall:

5.2.1. Serve as the Executive Agent for Space upon delegation by the Secretary of the Air Force.

5.2.2. Establish an Executive Secretariat for Executive Agent for Space functions. The Executive Secretariat shall maintain appropriate liaison with OSD Principal Staff Assistants responsible for space and space-related matters.

5.2.3. Periodically review the space program, budget, and accounting mechanism (referred to as a "virtual" Major Force Program (MFP) for Space) established by the USD/C, in coordination with the other DoD Components, and recommend to the USD/C changes in the content of the "virtual" MFP for Space.

5.2.4. Serve as the Air Force Acquisition Executive for Space.

5.2.5. Serve as the Senior Procurement Executive (SPE) for Air Force space programs, upon delegation by the Secretary of the Air Force, with authority to:

5.2.5.1. Approve Sole Source Awards (Justification and Approval Documents) over $50 million.

5.2.5.2. Approve Procurement Integrity supplements and changes (Federal Acquisition Regulation (FAR) Parts 3-104).

5.2.5.3. Approve Commercial Acquisition supplements and changes (FAR Part 12).

5.2.5.4. Execute and enter into contracts.

5.2.6. Serve as the Head of the Contracting Activity (HCA) for Space with authority to:

5.2.6.1. Approve continued performance or award in the face of Government Accounting Office Protest.

5.2.6.2. Waive requirements of the Truth in Negotiation Act (TINA).

5.2.6.3. Approve award of a contract to a Government employee.

5.2.6.4. Approve Contractor Performance Assessment Reports (CPARs).

5.2.6.5. Review and comment on space Defense Acquisition Executive Summaries.

5.2.6.6. Submit selected acquisition reports to the USD/AT&L and the Secretary of Defense.

5.2.6.7. Approve reprogramming of funds in the "virtual" MFP for Space in the year of execution.

5.2.6.8. Approve acquisition strategies, acquisition program baselines, and system acquisition management plans (SAMPs).

5.2.6.9. Review Program Management Directives.

5.2.6.10. Review program documentation provided to OSD and other DoD Components.

5.3. The Heads of DoD Components shall:

5.3.1. Develop requirements through the JROC process and provide space and space-related requirements information to the Executive Agent for Space for harmonization with space plans, programs, and budgets before submission to the JROC.

5.3.2. Develop space and space-related doctrine, strategy, education, training, and operations, in coordination with the Executive Agent for Space.

5.3.3. Recommend proposed space and space-related planning and programming guidance for Service- and Agency-unique programs to the USD/P and the USD/C for consideration in their formulation of planning, programming, and budgeting guidance documents.

5.3.4. Continue to develop and fund space research, development, and acquisition programs that meet their unique requirements and submit such programs to the Executive Agent for Space for inclusion in the National Security Space Program Plan.

5.3.5. Consult with the Executive Agent for Space on Program Objective Memoranda and budget estimate submissions that reflect a significant change to any program subject to review during the program assessment for space, before submission to the Office of the Secretary of Defense.

5.3.6. Provide applicable information and assistance to support the Executive Agent for Space's Department-wide responsibility for planning, programming, and acquisition of space systems.

5.3.6.1. This includes information regarding:

5.3.6.1.1. Space science and technology priorities, programs, and funding.

5.3.6.1.2. Operational requirements for space and space-related systems.

5.3.6.1.3. Plans for space systems, force structure, capabilities, measures of performance, and schedules.

5.3.6.1.4. Programmatic and budget data on space programs.

5.3.6.1.5. Space acquisition program data.

5.3.6.1.6. Key indicators on their cadre of space professionals.

5.3.6.1.7. Recommendations on priorities for space support to DoD Components.

5.3.7. Acquire Service- and Agency-unique space programs and submit program information to the Executive Agent for Space, in accordance with this Directive.

5.3.7.1. Participate in Executive Agent for Space planning, programming, and acquisition activities.

5.3.7.2. Maintain a sufficient cadre of space-qualified personnel to represent their Component in space requirements, planning, acquisition, and operations.

5.3.7.3. Support the Executive Agent for Space's planning, programming, and acquisition activities with appropriate resources to represent their Component.

6.   EFFECTIVE DATE

This Directive is effective immediately.

Enclosures—2

1. References

2. Definitions

E1. ENCLOSURE 1

REFERENCES

(e) DoD directive 5000.1, "The Defense Acquisition System," October 23, 2000

(f) OMB Circular No. A-109, "Major Systems Acquisitions," April 5, 1976

E2. ENCLOSURE 2

DEFINITIONS

E2.1. Space Forces. The space and terrestrial systems, equipment, facilities, organizations, and personnel necessary to access, use, and, if directed, control space for national security.

E2.2. Space Power. The total strength of a nation's capabilities to conduct and influence activities to, in, through, and from the space medium to achieve its objectives.

E2.3. Space Superiority. The degree of dominance in space of one force over another which permits the conduct of operations by the former and its related land, sea, air, and space forces at a given time and place without prohibitive interference by the opposing force.

E2.4. Space Systems. All of the devices and organizations forming the space network. These consist of: Spacecraft; mission package(s); ground stations; data links among spacecraft, ground stations, mission or user terminals, which may include initial reception, processing, and exploitation; launch systems; and directly related supporting infrastructure, including space surveillance and battle management/command, control, communications, and computers.

BIBLIOGRAPHY

OFFICIAL DOCUMENTS AND PUBLICATIONS

AFDD 2-2, *Space Operations*, Maxwell AFB, Alabama: Air Force Doctrine Center, 1998.

"Air Force Position Paper on Space Commission Issues," Washington, D.C.: Headquarters USAF, August 14, 2000.

Aldridge, the Honorable E. C., Jr., "Memorandum on Delegation of Milestone Decision Authority for DoD Space Systems," Washington, D.C.: Office of the Under Secretary of Defense, February 14, 2002.

Berkowitz, Marc J., Director, Space Policy, "Action Memorandum on the DoD Directive 'Executive Agent for Space,'" Washington, D.C.: Office of the Under Secretary of Defense for Policy, February 26, 2002.

"Commission to Assess United States National Security Space Management and Organization (Space Commission) Implementation," Washington, D.C.: Department of Defense, interim report to the Committees on Armed Services of the U.S. Senate and House of Representatives, May 2002.

Defense Science Board, *Joint Operations Superiority in the 21st Century: Integrating Capabilities Underwriting Joint Vision 2010 and Beyond*, Washington, D.C.: Office of the Under Secretary of Defense for Acquisition and Technology, October 1998.

"Department of Defense Directive 'Executive Agent for Space,'" Washington, D.C.: Department of Defense, February 25, 2002.

Fogleman, General Ronald R., USAF, and the Honorable Sheila E. Widnall, *Global Engagement: A Vision for the 21st Century Air Force*, Washington, D.C.: Department of the Air Force, November 1996.

Long-Range Plan: Implementing USSPACECOM Vision for 2020, Peterson AFB, Colorado: U.S. Space Command, March 1998.

New World Vistas: Air and Space Power for the 21st Century, Space Applications Volume, Washington, D.C.: USAF Scientific Advisory Board, 1995.

Report of the Commission to Assess United States National Security Space Management and Organization, Washington, D.C., January 11, 2001.

Rumsfeld, Secretary of Defense Donald H., letter to the Honorable John Warner, chairman, Senate Armed Services Committee, May 8, 2001.

_____, "Memorandum on National Security Space Management and Organization," Washington, D.C.: Office of the Secretary of Defense, October 18, 2001.

_____, *Quadrennial Defense Review Report*, Washington, D.C.: Office of the Secretary of Defense, 2001.

Ryan, General Michael E., USAF, and the Honorable F. Whitten Peters, *Global Vigilance, Reach and Power: America's Air Force Vision 2020*, Washington, D.C.: Department of the Air Force, June 2000.

_____, and the Honorable F. Whitten Peters, *The Aerospace Force: Defending America in the 21st Century*, Washington, D.C.: Department of the Air Force, May 2000.

CONGRESSIONAL TESTIMONY

Estes, General Howell M. III, USAF, "Posture Statement for Senate Armed Services Committee Hearings," Washington, D.C., March 11–12, 1997.

House of Representatives, *Missile Development and Space Sciences: Hearings Before the Committee on Science and Astronautics*, 86th Congress, 1st Session, February –March 1959.

BOOKS

Beard, Edmund, *Developing the ICBM: A Study in Bureaucratic Politics*, New York: Columbia University Press, 1976.

Boyne, Walter J., *Beyond the Wild Blue: A History of the U.S. Air Force, 1947–1997*, New York: St. Martin's Press, 1997.

Daso, Dik Alan, *Hap Arnold and the Evolution of American Air Power*, Washington, D.C.: Smithsonian Institution Press, 2000.

DeBlois, Major Bruce M., "Ascendent Realms: Characteristics of Air Power and Space Power," in Colonel Phillip S. Meilinger, ed., *The Paths of Heaven: The Evolution of Air Power Theory*, Maxwell AFB, Alabama: Air University Press, 1997.

DeKok, Lieutenant General Roger G., USAF, and Bob Preston, "Acquisition of Space Power for a New Millennium," in Peter L. Hays et al., eds., *Spacepower for a New Millennium: Space and U.S. National Security*, New York: McGraw Hill, 2000.

Estes, General Howell M. III, USAF (Ret.), "The Aerospace Force of Today and Tomorrow," in Peter L. Hays et al. eds., *Spacepower for a New Millennium: Space and U.S. National Security*, New York: McGraw Hill, 2000.

Futrell, Robert Frank, *Ideas, Concepts, Doctrine: Basic Thinking in the United States Air Force, 1907–1960*, Vol. 1, Maxwell AFB, Alabama: Air University Press, 1989.

Gray, Colin S., *Explorations in Strategy*, Westport, Connecticut: Praeger Publishers, 1996.

_____, and John B. Sheldon, "Spacepower and the Revolution in Military Affairs: A Glass Half-Full," in Peter L. Hays et al., eds., *Spacepower for a New Millennium: Space and U.S. National Security*, New York: McGraw Hill, 2000.

Hays, Peter L., James M. Smith, Alan R. Van Tassel, and Guy M. Walsh, "Spacepower for a New Millennium: Examining Current U.S. Capabilities and Policies, in Peter L. Hays et al., eds., *Spacepower for a New Millennium: Space and U.S. National Security*, New York: McGraw Hill, 2000.

Lambakis, Steven, *On the Edge of Earth: The Future of American Space Power*, Lexington, Kentucky: University of Kentucky Press, 2001.

Lambeth, Benjamin S., *The Transformation of American Air Power*, Ithaca, New York: Cornell University Press, 2000.

McDougall, Walter A., *The Heavens and the Earth: A Political History of the Space Age*, Baltimore, Maryland: The Johns Hopkins University Press, 1997.

Nadel, Joel, and J. R. Wright, *Special Men and Special Missions: Inside American Special Operations Forces, 1945 to the Present*, London: Greenhill, 1994.

The New Lexicon Webster's Dictionary of the English Language, New York: Lexicon Publications, Inc., 1991.

Schoettle, Enid Curtis Bok, "The Establishment of NASA," in Sanford Lakoff, ed., *Knowledge and Power: Essays on Science and Government*, New York: Free Press, 1966.

Spires, David N., *Beyond Horizons: A Half-Century of Air Force Space Leadership*, Washington, D.C.: U.S. Government Printing Office, 1997.

Stares, Paul B., *The Militarization of Space: U.S. Policy, 1945-1984*, Ithaca, New York: Cornell University Press, 1985.

Van Inwegen, Brigadier General Earl S., USAF (Ret.), "The Air Force Develops an Operational Organization for Space," in Cargill Hall and Jacob Neufeld, eds., *The U.S. Air Force in Space: 1945 to the 21st Century*, Washington, D.C.: USAF History and Museums Program, 1995.

Worden, Brigadier General Simon Peter, USAF, "Space Control for the 21st Century: A Space 'Navy' Protecting the Commercial Basis of America's Wealth," in Peter L. Hays et al., eds., *Spacepower for a New Millennium: Space and U.S. National Security,* New York: McGraw Hill, 2000.

MONOGRAPHS AND REPORTS

Augenstein, Bruno W., *Evolution of the U.S. Military Space Program, 1945-1960: Some Key Events in Study, Planning, and Program Management,* Santa Monica, Calif.: RAND, P-6814, September 1982.

Federici, G. A., B. Wald, et al., *Commission on Roles and Missions of the Armed Forces: Space Activities,* Alexandria, Virginia: Center for Naval Analyses, May 1995.

Mantz, Lieutenant Colonel Michael R., *The New Sword: A Theory of Space Combat Power,* Maxwell AFB, Alabama: Air University Press, May 1995.

Moorman, General Thomas S., Jr., "The Challenges of Space Beyond 2000," in Alan Stephens, ed., *New Era Security: The RAAF in the Next 25 Years,* proceedings of a conference held by the Royal Australian Air Force, Air Force Studies Center, RAAF Fairbairn, Canberra, Australia, June 1996.

Perry, Robert L., *Origins of the USAF Space Program, 1945–1956,* Vol. 4, History of DCAS 1961, Air Force Systems Command Historical Publications Series 62-24-10, Los Angeles: Space Systems Division, AFSC, 1961.

Preston, Bob, and John Baker, "Space Challenges," in Zalmay Khalilzad and Jeremy Shapiro, eds., *Strategic Appraisal: United States Air and Space Power in the 21st Century,* Santa Monica, California: RAND, MR-1314-AF, 2002.

Preston, Bob, Dana J. Johnson, Sean J. A. Edwards, Michael Miller, and Calvin Shipbaugh, *Space Weapons, Earth Wars,* Santa Monica, California: RAND, MR-1209-AF, 2002.

Rothstein, Major Stephen M., USAF, *Dead on Arrival? The Development of the Aerospace Concept, 1944–58,* Maxwell AFB, Alabama: Air University Press, November 2000.

Vick, Alan, et al., *Aerospace Operations in Urban Environments: Exploring New Concepts*, Santa Monica, California: RAND, MR-1187-AF, 2000.

Watts, Barry D., *The Military Use of Space: A Diagnostic Assessment*, Washington, D.C.: Center for Strategic and Budgetary Assessments, February 2001.

JOURNAL AND PERIODICAL ARTICLES

"Air Force Space System Control Questioned," *Space News*, September 8, 1997.

Barry, Major General John L. and Colonel Daniel L. Herriges, USAF, "Aerospace Integration, Not Separation," *Aerospace Power Journal*, Summer 2000.

Boyne, Walter J., "A Great Tradition in the Making: The United States Air Force," *Aviation Week and Space Technology*, April 16, 1997.

Bruger, Lieutenant Colonel Steven J., USAF, "Not Ready for the First Space War: What About the Second?" *Naval War College Review*, Winter 1995.

Butler, Amy, "Pentagon Closely Studying Ramifications of Space Panel Suggestions," *Inside the Air Force*, April 13, 2001.

_____, "Air and Space Ops Chief Refutes Accusations of Political Subversion," *Inside the Air Force*, May 18, 2001.

_____, "Departing from Ryan's Rhetoric, Jumper Notes Unique Space Needs," *Inside the Air Force*, October 19, 2001.

_____, "Rumsfeld Issues Long-Awaited Guidance on DoD Space Realignment," *Inside the Air Force*, October 26, 2001.

_____, "Rumsfeld Tells Roche to Pick New Four-Star for Air Force SPACECOM," *Inside the Air Force*, October 26, 2001.

_____, "Air Force's Notional Plan for Space Budgeting Process Draws Fire," *Inside the Air Force*, November 16, 2001.

_____, "USAF Identifies Key Space Activities DoD Has Not Yet Fully Funded," *Inside the Air Force*, November 16, 2001.

_____, "DoD Space Program Could Get Additional $4.8 Billion Through FY07," *Inside the Air Force*, December 21, 2001.

"Command Plan Revision Will Not Declare Space a CINC's Regional Area," *Inside the Pentagon*, November 27, 1997.

Correll, John T., "Destiny in Space," *Air Force Magazine*, August 1998.

De France, Linda, "Myers: Future of Military Space Requires Use of Civilian Capabilities," *Aerospace Daily*, May 8, 2001.

"Defense Department Should Consider Developing Space-Based Weapons, Teets Says," *Aerospace Daily*, March 7, 2002.

Donnelly, John, "Laser of 30 Watts Blinded Satellite 300 Miles High," *Defense Week*, December 8, 1997.

_____, "Commander: Clinton's Vetoes Won't Halt Space Weapons," *Defense Week*, December 15, 1997.

_____, "Cohen: Attack on U.S. Satellite Is Attack on United States," *Defense Week*, July 26, 1999.

"Estes Sees Need for Continued ASAT Planning," *Aerospace Daily*, December 4, 1997.

Evans, Michael, "Fabrizio's Choice: Organizational Change and the Revolution in Military Affairs Debate," *National Security Studies Quarterly*, Winter 2001.

Friedenstein, Lieutenant Colonel Charles D., USAF, "The Uniqueness of Space Doctrine," *Air University Review*, November–December 1985.

Grier, Peter, "The Force and Space," *Air Force Magazine*, February 2001.

_____, "The Winning Combination of Air and Space," *Air Force Magazine*, January 2002.

_____, "The Combination That Worked," *Air Force Magazine*, April 2002.

Hays, Lieutenant Colonel Peter, USAF, and Karl Mueller, "Going Boldly—Where? Aerospace Integration, the Space Commission, and the Air Force's Vision for Space," *Aerospace Power Journal*, Spring 2001.

Holzer, Robert, "IT, Space Top U.S. Military Priorities," *Defense News*, February 26, 2001.

Horner, General Charles A., USAF (Ret.), "Air Power: Growing Beyond Desert Storm," *Aviation Week and Space Technology*, April 16, 1997.

Hughes, David, "USAF Aims to Forge C2ISR into a 'Weapon,'" *Aviation Week and Space Technology*, May 6, 2002.

Huntington, Samuel P., "National Policy and the Transoceanic Navy," *Proceedings*, U.S. Naval Institute, May 1954.

"Interview with U.S. Army Lieutenant General Edward Anderson," *Jane's Defence Weekly*, July 11, 2001.

Jaroff, Leon, "Dreadful Sorry, Clementine: Washington Brushes Off the Asteroid Threat," *Time*, October 27, 1997.

Jennings, Frank W., "Doctrinal Conflict over the Word Aerospace," *Airpower Journal*, Fall 1990.

_____, "Genesis of the Aerospace Concept," *Air Power History*, Spring 2002.

Laurenzo, Ron, "Jumper: Talking Is Key to Transforming," *Defense Week*, March 25, 2002.

Matthews, William, "To Military Planners, Space Is 'The Ultimate High Ground,'" *Air Force Times*, May 18, 1998.

McKinley, Lieutenant Colonel Cynthia A. S., "The Guardians of Space: Organizing America's Space Assets for the Twenty-First Century," *Aerospace Power Journal*, Spring 2000.

Millsap, Ralph, and D. B. Posey, "Organizational Options for the Future Aerospace Force," *Aerospace Power Journal*, Summer 2000.

Moorman, Lieutenant General Thomas S., Jr., USAF, "Space: A New Strategic Frontier," *Airpower Journal*, Spring 1992.

Myers, Colonel Kenneth A., and Lieutenant Colonel John G. Tockston, USAF, "Real Tenets of Military Space Doctrine," *Airpower Journal*, Winter 1988.

"New Space Race," *Jane's Defence Weekly*, August 26, 1998.

"Pentagon Says Rumsfeld's Space Report Response Will Be 'Complex,'" *Inside the Air Force*, April 27, 2001.

Plummer, Anne, "Draft Memo Outlines Air Force Role as Executive Agent for Space," *Inside the Pentagon*, March 7, 2002.

Rife, Major Shawn P., USAF, "On Space-Power Separatism," *Airpower Journal*, Spring 1999.

Roosevelt, Ann, "New Air Force Space Role Has Army Concerned," *Defense Week*, May 14, 2001.

"Rumsfeld Says $1 Billion Will Boost Missile Defense R&D," InsideDefense.com, March 1, 2001.

"Ryan Says Space Force Unwarranted for Next 50 Years," *Aerospace Daily*, February 9, 2001.

"SAB Releases Its Space Surveillance Recommendations," *Inside the Air Force*, December 12, 1997.

Scott, William B., "USSC Prepares for Future Combat Missions in Space," *Aviation Week and Space Technology*, August 5, 1996.

_____, "Pentagon Considers Space As New Area of Responsibility," *Aviation Week and Space Technology*, March 24, 1997.

_____, "Wargames Underscore Value of Space Assets for Military Ops," *Aviation Week and Space Technology*, April 28, 1997.

_____, "Air Force Opens New Space Center," *Aviation Week and Space Technology*, November 24, 1997.

_____, "'Space' Competing for USAF Funds," *Aviation Week and Space Technology*, December 1, 1997.

_____, "CINCSPACE Wants Attack Detectors on Satellites," *Aviation Week and Space Technology*, August 10, 1998.

_____, "U.S. Adopts 'Tactical' Space Control Policy," *Aviation Week and Space Technology*, March 29, 1999.

_____, "Commission Lays Foundation for Future Military Space Corps," *Aviation Week and Space Technology*, January 15, 2001.

_____, "Detachment Brings 'Space' to Nellis Air Operations," *Aviation Week and Space Technology*, January 15, 2001.

_____, "USAF Space Weapons Officers Find Unique Niche in Air Warfare," *Aviation Week and Space Technology*, January 15, 2001.

_____, "Wargames Zero In on Knotty Milspace Issues," *Aviation Week and Space Technology*, January 21, 2001.

_____, "USAF Warned to Bolster or Lose 'Space Force' Franchise," *Aviation Week and Space Technology*, January 29, 2001.

_____, "USAF Gives Nod to Space Report," *Aviation Week and Space Technology*, February 12, 2001.

_____, "CINCSPACE: Focus More on Space Control," *Aviation Week and Space Technology*, November 13, 2001.

_____, "Milspace Comes of Age in Fighting Terror," *Aviation Week and Space Technology*, April 8, 2002.

_____, "'New' Strategic Command Could Assume Broadened Duties," *Aviation Week and Space Technology*, October 14, 2002.

Sobie, Brendan, "Former SPACECOM Chief Advocates Creation of Separate Space Force," *Inside Missile Defense*, November 19, 1997.

Suddarth, Lieutenant Colonel Steven C., USAF, "Solving the Great Air Force Systems Irony," *Aerospace Power Journal*, Spring 2002.

"The USAF Reports to Congress," *Air University Quarterly Review*, Spring 1958.

Wagner, Gary, "Fighting the First 'Space War,'" *Space Tracks*, January 2001.

Wall, Robert, "Rumsfeld Revamps Space, Pushes 'Black' Projects," *Aviation Week and Space Technology*, May 14, 2001.

White, General Thomas D., USAF, "At the Dawn of the Space Age," *The Air Power Historian*, January 1958.

_____, "The Inevitable Climb to Space," *Air University Quarterly Review*, Winter 1958-59.

"Will the Air Force Lose Its Space Program?" *Air Force Times*, February 8, 1999.

Wilson, George C., "Air Force's Jumper Catches a Tailwind: The Revolution in Aerospace Jumps Forward with a New Air Force Chief," *National Journal*, March 16, 2002.

Worden, Brigadier General Simon Peter, "The Air Force and Future Space Directions: Are We Good Stewards?" *Aerospace Power Journal*, Spring 2001.

"World News Roundup," *Aviation Week and Space Technology*, February 25, 2002.

NEWSPAPER ARTICLES

"Air Force Space Command Developing Strategies for Satellite Protection, Warfare Advances," *Florida Today*, June 22, 2001.

Diamond, John, "Rumsfeld Hedges on Space Arms," *Chicago Tribune*, May 9, 2001.

"If Ordered, AF Ready to Arm Space," *San Antonio Express-News*, May 11, 2001.

Jaffe, Greg, "Military Feels Bandwidth Squeeze as the Satellite Industry Sputters," *Wall Street Journal*, April 10, 2002.

Pae, Peter, "Doubts Trail 'Son of Star Wars' Proposal," *Los Angeles Times*, May 23, 2001.

_____, "Missile Base Is on an Upward Trajectory," *Los Angeles Times*, May 29, 2001.

"Panel Urges U.S. to Defend Space," *New York Times*, January 12, 2001.

Pincus, Walter, "U.S. Satellites Vulnerable to Attack, Officer Warns," *Washington Post*, June 21, 2001.

Ricks, Thomas E., "Post Interview with Defense Secretary Donald H. Rumsfeld," *Washington Post*, May 20, 2001.

Stares, Paul B., "Making Enemies in Space," *New York Times*, May 15, 2001.

MISCELLANEOUS

Aldridge, E. C., Jr., "Thoughts on the Management of National Security Space Activities of the Department of Defense," unpublished paper, July 6, 2000.

Allen, General Lew, Jr., USAF (Ret.), U.S. Air Force oral history interview, Maxwell AFB, Alabama, Air Force Historical Research Agency, January 1986.

Chain, Major General John T., Jr., USAF, AF/XOO, remarks at the Air University Air Power Symposium, Maxwell AFB, Alabama, February 23, 1981.

Creech, General W. L., USAF (Ret.), presentation to the commander and senior headquarters staff, Air Force Space Command, Peterson AFB, Colorado, April 15, 1999.

Estes, General Howell M. III, USAF, address to the Air Force Association annual symposium, Los Angeles, October 18, 1996.

Fogleman, General Ronald R., USAF (Ret.), comments at a seminar on "Organizing for Future National Security Priorities in Space" jointly sponsored by DFI International and AF/QR, Washington, D.C., February 1, 2001.

Hartinger, General James V., USAF (Ret.), U.S. Air Force oral history interview, Washington, D.C.: USAF Historical Research Center, Office of History, Headquarters USAF, September 1985.

Jones, Major General William E., USAF (Ret.), former deputy chief of staff for operations, Air Force Space Command, white paper on the creation of an air and space force within the USAF prepared at the request of Major General David McIlvoy, AF/XPX, December 22, 1997.

Looney, Major General William R. III, USAF, commander, 14th Air Force, briefing at the Air Force Doctrine Symposium, Maxwell AFB, Alabama, April 6, 2001.

Mueller, Karl, "Space Weapons and U.S. Security: Why and How to Avert a Dangerous Potential Revolution," unpublished paper, School of Advanced Airpower Studies, Maxwell AFB, Alabama, September 28, 1997.

Roche, Honorable James G., Secretary of the Air Force, "Transforming Our Air and Space Capabilities," remarks to the Air Force Association National Convention luncheon, Washington, D.C., September 18, 2002.

Ryan, General Michael E., USAF, speech to the Air Force Association national symposium, Los Angeles, November 14, 1997.

Smith, Senator Bob, "The Challenge of Space Power," speech to an annual conference on air and space power held by the Fletcher School of Law and Diplomacy and the Institute for Foreign Policy Analysis, Cambridge, Massachusetts, November 18, 1998.

Smith, Major M. V., USAF, "Ten Propositions Regarding Space-power," M.A. thesis, School of Advanced Airpower Studies, Maxwell AFB, Alabama, June 2001.

Teets, the Honorable Peter B., Under Secretary of the Air Force, statement to the Commission on the Future of the U.S. Aerospace Industry, Washington, D.C., May 14, 2002.

Webb, R. C., "Implications of Low-Yield High Altitude Nuclear Detonation," Defense Special Weapons Agency (DSWA) presentation to an OSD/Net Assessment workshop on nuclear weapons and the revolution in military affairs, September 16–17, 1997.